Ray Bolger

Ray Bolger

More Than a Scarecrow

Holly Van Leuven

OXFORD
UNIVERSITY PRESS

OXFORD
UNIVERSITY PRESS

Oxford University Press is a department of the University of Oxford.
It furthers the University's objective of excellence in research, scholarship,
and education by publishing worldwide. Oxford is a registered trade mark of
Oxford University Press in the UK and certain other countries.

Published in the United States of America by Oxford University Press
198 Madison Avenue, New York, NY 10016, United States of America.

Library of Congress Cataloging-in-Publication Data

Names: Van Leuven, Holly, author.
Title: Ray Bolger : more than a scarecrow / Holly Van Leuven.
Description: New York ; Oxford : Oxford University Press, 2018. |
Includes bibliographical references and index.
Identifiers: LCCN 2018003760 (print) | LCCN 2018015442 (ebook) |
ISBN 9780190639051 (updf) | ISBN 9780190639068 (epub) |
ISBN 9780190639044 (alk. paper)
Subjects: LCSH: Bolger, Ray. | Actors—United States—Biography. |
Singers—United States—Biography. | Dancers—United States—Biography.
Classification: LCC PN2287.B4845 (ebook) |
LCC PN2287.B4845 V35 2018 (print) DDC 791.4302/8092 [B]—dc23
LC record available at https://lccn.loc.gov/2018003760

9 8 7 6 5 4 3 2 1
Printed by Sheridan Books, Inc.
United States of America

To Dan Weaver and Michael Caputo,
a small token of my esteem and affection

CONTENTS

ACKNOWLEDGMENTS

This book would never have been possible without the extreme tenacity of my parents, Jan and Bill Van Leuven, who organized their entire lives around the goal of making my sister and me first-generation college graduates. My eternal thanks to you both. And thanks, Dad, for your persistent refrain throughout my writing: *"illegitimi non carborundum."* I am grateful to all of my family members and friends who encouraged me as I embarked on something different and new.

Sylvia Lewis, Ray Bolger's dance partner and choreographer, first believed in me and gave me unfailing support as I took on this life-changing task. I am humbled and gratified to carry on the "More than a Scarecrow" mantle from her.

Ann Rickard, niece of Ray Bolger and Gwen Rickard Bolger, helped the book along extensively by connecting me to the surviving figures from her uncle's life. I could not have completed this endeavor without her kindness, generosity, and intercessions. Revitalizing visits spent with Ann and her dear husband, Richard Thompson, powered me through years of writing. They have made this book possible.

Several figures key to my work have passed away before seeing this book in print: Wells K. Wohlwend, attorney and close friend of the Bolgers, who shared his stories with me and enabled me to become the first researcher to access the Ray Bolger papers; Katherine "Kappy" Reeve Rickard, chorus girl of *Where's Charley?* and later sister-in-law to Bolger; Fritz Weaver, Bolger's co-star in *All American* and brother of my esteemed mentor, Dan Weaver; and Allyn Ann McLerie, co-star of *Where's Charley?*—all granted me interviews with graciousness and patience as I first embarked on this project.

Christianna Rickard shared many happy hours of fruitful conversation and generously provided family correspondence and photos. Her contributions have added something truly special to these pages. Reeve Rickard also shared family history and excitement for this book and championed my efforts.

Many subject experts and colleagues of Ray Bolger shared crucial insights, especially those who helped me when I was just beginning. Betsy Baytos, eccentric dance historian, opened her home, collection, and rich knowledge of dance history. Gregory Maguire, Marge Champion, Kathleen Quinlan, and Anita Gillette also granted me early and important interviews. I extend special thanks to William Stillman and Jay Scarfone, who provided me with their expertise, assistance, and big-heartedness as I traversed the Land of Oz. They helped me improve my manuscript by sharing photos from their collection and offering insights and corrections for my text.

Archivists gave crucial support, especially Julie Graham and her team at the University of California, Los Angeles (UCLA) Special Collections Library. I was able to complete the most important research for this book because of their hard work during a difficult time. Sandra Joy Lee Aguilar and Jonathon Auxier of the USC Warner Brother Archives, Jenny Romero of the Margaret Herrick Library, Mark Swartz and Sylvia Wang of the Shubert Archive, Miles Kreuger of the Institute of the American Musical, and Christina Zamon, formerly of the Emerson College Archives, also offered crucial guidance. Ned Comstock of the USC Cinematic Arts Library was the very first archivist I ever conversed with, and, with great thoughtfulness, he provided many good ideas for this project over the years.

I am deeply grateful to the Hazel Rowley Prize Committee of the Biographers International Organization for awarding me the inaugural North American Rowley Prize for First-time Biographers in 2014. I offer special thanks to Gayle Feldman, the committee chair, who has been my advocate and confidante. I hope Hazel would be pleased. I am grateful to the hosts and instructors of the 2015 CUNY Biography Clinic, including Michael Gately, Gary Giddins, and Amanda Vaill, for creating an excellent forum that deepened my knowledge of the craft of biography. Thanks to my compatriots of the Boston Biographers Group, especially Ray Shepard and Nigel Hamilton, who made this process much less isolating. Thanks also to Kathleen Di Scenna and Michael Siewart, who invited me to share some early work at the 2014 Wizard of Oz Spectacular in Syracuse that spurred on my writing of the book. I extend special and sincere thanks to the members of Dan Weaver's Book Editing classes at Emerson College in the Fall 2013, 2016, and 2017 semesters: your close reading and encouragement guided three drafts of this book.

John Taylor "Ike" Williams and Katherine Flynn of the Kneerim and Williams Agency took a chance on me as a first-time author, and I will always appreciate them as well as Norm Hirschy, my thoughtful and caring editor, for understanding the great importance of securing Bolger's place in entertainment history with this biography. Joellyn Ausanka, Senior Production Editor at Oxford University Press, helped me navigate copyediting and proofreading with great skill and kindness. I also wish to thank copy editor Patterson Lamb for her work on the book. In addition, OUP's Marketing Manager, Alyssa Russell, and Publicist Amanda Dissinger assisted me with generosity and skill to send this book out into the world. Neil Giordano served ably as my photographic rights and permissions assistant.

Megan Marshall gave me insight, guidance, straight talk, and smart feedback. The Writing, Literature and Publishing Department of Emerson College and my additional professors there, including Bill Beuttler, Brian Cronin, David Emblidge, Ethan Gilsdorf, Mike Heppner, Richard Hoffman, Robin Riley Fast, Cecily Parks, and Murray Schwartz, helped me develop my writing, reading, and researching skills. I extend special thanks to the department chair, Maria Koundoura, and former department chair Jerald Walker, for their assistance and guidance. I also thank my colleagues at the Harvard Education Publishing Group for freely sharing their knowledge and enthusiasm with me over the years we worked together. Additionally, Blake Campbell and Kristine Fuangtharnthip supported me with their abiding friendship and keen editorial guidance. Heather L. Long, Emily Legutko, Abbas Jamali, and Mindy Johnson offered help and support in the early days of this project. Nicole Clark and Farris Ajalat kept me healthy while I balanced many demands to produce this book. Chris Brown sat up with me until three in the morning, hearing multiple versions of passages and weighing in on which to use, and encouraged me through the end of a very long process.

The many Bolger enthusiasts and the memory of the Bolgers themselves have been great company lo these many years. It has been the honor of my life to help preserve this story.

Ray Bolger

"Had it been within his power, the vaudeville performer would have been a timeless wanderer, spanning the generations by using the bridge of his talents."
—Fred Allen, *Much Ado about Me*

"Writing is the obvious response to the consequences of forgetting."
—Alain de Botton and John Armstrong, *Art as Therapy*

Introduction

The Timeless Wanderer

Ray Bolger was called an amiable fellow with a chinless profile, skittish feet, and a snickering spirit. At five feet, ten and one-half inches, he weighed between 135 and 140 pounds at any given time and was said to be skinnier than even Frank Sinatra. After an evening of dancing on Broadway, he could come off the stage as much as three pounds lighter, his dark brown hair blackened with sweat. "His face and body acquire their unusually eccentric quality only when he's on a stage," wrote show business reporter Maurice Zolotow. "Otherwise he's quite nondescript." Bolger himself said, "I look like everyone's second cousin. I don't look like Ray Bolger."[1] He often let others do the talking, while he turned up the wattage of his charm. In 1953, Bolger, already a national star after his hit Broadway sensation *Where's Charley?*, visited Chicago with his brother-in-law James Rickard, who described the experience of being Bolger's dining companion in a letter home to his wife this way:

> He's really a tremendous guy when it comes to public relations—the greatest I've ever seen by far. [He] is completely relaxed in any type of company, always says the right things, and is terrifically amusing. You should see the people he attracts just like a magnet: "Will he come to dinner? Go to the races?"—a constant barrage. Every night we go downstairs to the Pump Room for dinner at 7 or 7:30. The earliest we've eaten yet is 10:30. The general manager of Staedtler Hotels comes over and sits down—a couple on the house. Next comes the orchestra leader and then God knows who all—politicians, actors, socialites... It's normal for Ray, but it wears me out, so now I just get up and leave him down there with someone.[2]

But Bolger wasn't given to very much self-reflection. As the *New York Times* noted, "His long, rubbery legs tell a story of their own." This was exactly as he intended. For more than fifty years, Bolger used his dancing to tell audiences his story, millions of steps performed over thousands of nights, all across the country. When it came to words, he used far fewer to talk about himself.

"The essential point about Ray," wrote Cy Feuer, one of the producers of Bolger's smash-hit Broadway show, *Where's Charley?*, "was that he had no life off the stage and fell automatically into antic character when in doubt." After researching Bolger for seven years—becoming the first writer to access his private papers, hunting down and watching the rare, ghostlike clips of his dancing on Broadway, and interviewing some of the last living stars who shared with him the stages of the Winter Garden and the St. James Theatres, the backlots of Desilu Productions, and the Congo Room of the Sahara Resort in Las Vegas—I have just one quibble with Mr. Feuer's comment: it's the truth turned inside out. Bolger in fact brought his whole life *to* the stage, keeping only what he could to make a great character. Since Bolger's death in 1987, we have forgotten great swathes of his life's story and the ways it intersected with the rise of popular entertainment in the twentieth century. Now with this book, they are brought again to light. Had Bolger not lived a rich, energetic, complicated, and contradictory life, he could not have been such a successful, individualistic performer. He came from a staunch Irish Republican working-class family in Boston. These aspects of his upbringing shaped both his politics and his dancing style in equal measure. He became a Broadway dancing sensation who was hailed by Brooks Atkinson of the *New York Times* as "an eminent hoofer of the bucolic breed."[3] He had learned to dance first on the streets of Boston, and he had worked in storerooms and offices as a young man. The lessons he learned in these improbable places enabled him to become a glittering and pristine star. But once he had ascended, he did not dwell on what he did to succeed. Instead, he tried to extend his professional and material prosperity as far as possible, in hopes of making life more comfortable not only for himself but for the everyday people who made up his audiences.

Ray Bolger ran away from a broken home and joined vaudeville. He made it onto Broadway thanks to the attentions of legendary impresarios like Gus Edwards and the Shubert brothers. As a young man on the road, he bunked in New York with the then little-known Harold Arlen. He served as master of ceremonies for the grand opening of Radio City Music Hall, and later for ABC's inaugural television broadcast from New York City. He introduced ballet to American popular audiences through his collaboration with George Balanchine in the choreographer's earliest Broadway musicals. While these roles cemented his star status for the duration of his life, Bolger's work playing the Scarecrow in the film billed as Metro-Goldwyn-Mayer's Technicolor triumph, *The Wizard of Oz*, ensured his legacy. The film's role in American culture, and Bolger's deft characterization of the straw man in search of a brain, has blotted out nearly all of his accomplishments before making the picture, and many of them after. His career extended over forty years beyond the release of the film, and his best successes did not come to him until after he was released from his MGM contract. Bolger tried to write an autobiography several times. He had the material. For a while, he even had the ghostwriters. But he could not—would not—commit the story to paper. It was, in the end, the way he preferred it.

I have studied American musicals of the 1930s and 1940s since childhood, and as a result, I am a second-generation researcher of this dominant medium of the twentieth-century. I was born a little more than four years after Ray Bolger died. Because of this, I have been assisted in my work by many newly available digital tools. In a similar vein, this book largely exists because of a chance discovery I made on YouTube.

I grew up using YouTube to find clips of old and rare films. I had long been delighted by Ray Bolger, whom I discovered outside of his role in *The Wizard of Oz* when I was fourteen, watching him as a guest star on *The Judy Garland Show*. His appearance on the program affected me: there was something about his energy, his tenderness toward Garland, that suggested an interesting and unusual man. I suspected his own sweet persona had been forged out of pain, the kind of sensitivity an adolescent picks up on. I searched the Internet for more information about his life and career. There wasn't very much, and a lot of it conflicted: I discovered a persistent myth that Bolger was in fact born Raymond Bulcao, and that he wasn't Irish, but Portuguese. I went looking for books about him to learn the facts, but there were none. While browsing the Web in the summer of 2009, I discovered that two dozen new videos of Ray Bolger had hit YouTube. Bolger had been dead for more than twenty-two years at that point, and with the exception of *The Wizard of Oz*, the milestones of his career had been mostly forgotten. The videos that appeared online were all segments, mostly specialty dance numbers, performed with a tall brunette woman. They came from a television show I didn't recognize. One user, who went by the screen name "oldgypsytap" had uploaded all the videos. I sent a message through YouTube thanking him or her for sharing them. I asked where they had come from. The message went unanswered.

Three months later, I moved into a single room above Boston's Colonial Theatre. One morning I woke up to find a response from oldgypsytap: "I am the dancer in the video, with Ray," she responded. Her name was

Sylvia Lewis. The clips were from their television series *Where's Raymond?*, which was renamed *The Ray Bolger Show* for its second and final season; they had worked together on the programs between 1952 and 1954. Before seeing these videos I had not known either program existed.

I was then eighteen years old, and Lewis was delighted to know that a member of my generation cared so much for the era of Hollywood in which she had lived and worked. Our correspondence continued, and I went on to meet and interview her several times. After two years of correspondence with her, I shared with her my interest in researching a biography of Bolger. She encouraged me and introduced me into the network of Bolger relatives. One of his nieces, Ann Rickard, provided the lucky stroke that allowed this project to grow. She put me in touch with Bolger's lawyer, who helped me to become the first researcher to gain access to Bolger's personal papers in the UCLA Special Collections Library. There had been no hope of the collection being processed, even fifteen years after its donation, until I proved to Bolger's lawyer my devotion to the project, and until he interceded on my behalf. His exact request to UCLA's president of Theater, Film and Television, he told me, was "You let that little girl in there!"

Researching and producing this book became the guiding priority of my life, from late 2011 through 2017. My work in scholarly publishing at Harvard gave me time to work on the book as well as access to Harvard's research facilities in my off-duty hours. I set out to write the most complete account of Bolger's entire career possible from the sources that remained. I followed every quality lead I found. I imagined that the story would require the most research in Boston, and perhaps the Midwest. In reality, I went to Hilo, Hawaii; Orleans, Massachusetts; and many places in between. I had never been to California before, but to pursue the story I spent months in libraries and archives throughout Los Angeles, particularly those at the University of California-Los Angeles (UCLA), the University of Southern California (USC), and the Academy of Motion Pictures. While I secured many more resources than I had hoped for, such as the deep-dive into Bolger's papers, access to rare footage of Bolger dancing on Broadway in the 1930s and 1940s, and an original interview with Allyn Ann McLerie, the original "Amy" of *Where's Charley?*, some sources I sought do not survive.

Bolger proved to be a very enigmatic and reticent figure, and his wife, Gwen, did much of the talking for him during their fifty-seven years of marriage. Her story is intertwined with his and appears prominently in these pages. In truth, their stories are dependent each upon the other. The richest insights we have into the Bolgers' partnership come from two extended periods of their forced separation. In the 1930s, early in the

Bolgers' marriage, Ray kept up a grueling schedule, touring movie houses across the country to save up money and earn recognition. Gwen stayed with her parents in Los Angeles for most of this time. She wrote Bolger letters once and sometimes twice a day, always knowing exactly which theater to send them to. Bolger's replies, however, are missing from the collection at UCLA. In 1941, even before the attack on Pearl Harbor, Ray participated in USO Camp Show Unit #1, part of the first-ever troupe that left the country to entertain soldiers, in the Caribbean. He also traveled after the Americans joined World War II with Camp Show Unit #89; he and his piano player became the first American entertainers to perform for soldiers in the South Pacific. The letters exchanged while Bolger was overseas provide rich insight into his married life.

Gwen gave her husband a great deal of support throughout his career. When he was the master of ceremonies for the opening night of Radio City Music Hall in 1932, she gave him the quip that he would deliver to the audience, which made him the hit of the morning papers with the next day: "Gee, isn't it wonderful what you can build with a few dimes?" She co-produced his most important Broadway musical, *Where's Charley?*, making her the first female producer of a musical comedy. She balanced his checkbooks, washed his special wool socks, and curated his legacy. After a life spent largely on the road, and later at the Waldorf Towers of the Waldorf-Astoria Hotel, the couple settled down in Beverly Hills in the 1950s. It was from this property that the Bolger papers were taken after Gwen's death in 1997. They included correspondence and contracts from Bolger's six decades in the entertainment industry, beginning with vaudeville agreements in the 1920s right through his final television guest star appearances in the 1980s.

Without Gwen there could be no Ray, but he barely identified with his own blood relatives. When Bolger cousins would try to meet him after a Broadway show, he would pose for a photo or exchange a quick word, and be gone. We do not know much of what transpired between Ray and his father, James Edward, except that once his son found success in entertainment, James tried to capitalize on it by hitting the road with him and serving as a manager of sorts. James eventually became a hotel manager in Bermuda but returned to the Los Angeles area with a new wife after his son had become a star. He died there in 1940. The Bolger family members occupied little of Bolger's life, and subsequently, they will occupy few of these pages. This book has been enriched by interviews with some of Bolger's last living co-stars and colleagues. Many of them found it important to discuss Bolger's political activities and their impact on his entertainment career. I find it equally important to stress what we can know and what we can't know about Bolger's political life: many of these sources were young men and women in the 1950s and 1960s, and they shared a liberal political viewpoint quite at odds with Bolger's conservative bent. Bolger, who was a generation older than many of his co-stars in this era, also faced difficulty connecting with the youth culture of these times. While his co-stars' accounts are truthful and their opinions are valid, they can limn only one viewpoint: that of Bolger as the stodgy old conservative. The stories told in their voices helped bring Bolger back to life in this book, and their contributions cannot be underestimated. They provided me with details and recollections that otherwise would have been lost to time. However, few accounts of his political opinions as a young man were left by Bolger himself or by his true contemporaries; they would likely have perceived him as more moderate during the 1930s and 1940s. Unfortunately, these colleagues had often passed away before I was born and long before I undertook this work.

After my years of research had come to a close, I reached the same conclusion many times from many different directions: performance had been Bolger's escape from a sad and economically dire youth, his raison d'être. He claimed that he had given 20,000 performances by 1954, and he danced for more than two decades after that. He enjoyed writing, storytelling, reading, and joking. But everything he ever needed and wanted to say about his own life was encapsulated in his footwork. He was not going to tease out and organize the details. He would not revisit a dysfunctional childhood filled with loss and wayward travels. His star had grown so bright in his lifetime that he earned the privilege of blotting out some of his darkest moments altogether. And he prevailed. "No one will ever know what I went through before I made it," Bolger once confided to a newspaper reporter. It is my hope, however, that after reading this book you will understand the many dimensions of this unique performer's career as a premiere American entertainer. For too long Bolger has been flattened into one-dimensionality by the reputation of *The Wizard of Oz*. There is much, much more to his story, which touches on the histories of most of the important popular media in America for most of the twentieth century. These pages hold all the evidence I could amass that Ray Bolger—vaudevillian, Broadway star, television pioneer, and Las Vegas favorite—was far more than a Scarecrow.

CHAPTER 1

"What Will You Be? It's Up to You!"

R ay Bolger almost never became the Scarecrow in *The Wizard of Oz*. This is a fact well documented by Oz historians. But even before that, Bolger almost never became a Broadway star recruited to Hollywood, or an itinerant vaudevillian tapped by Richard Rodgers and Lorenz Hart. During Bolger's adolescence in the early 1920s, he trained to become an insurance salesman in Boston, at New England Mutual Life Insurance Company.

Something else pulled at him: talent and energy and a need to express them both. He performed first for the other office boys in the company's Boston headquarters at 87 Milk Street. A long, tantalizing set of slate stairs connected the semi-basement to the first floor. Bolger, with a packet of mail for delivery in each hand, would improvise tap and percussion routines, slapping his thighs and ankles with the letters addressed to the insurance agents. He would jump up and down ten steps at a time, sometimes backward. On and on it went, Bolger sticking to the beat and tempting fate. When he finally reached the top landing, he would kick the top of the adjacent wall, about six feet high, and change direction, then tap back down the stairs. His routine provoked the office's janitor to fetch his wet sponge and erase the "familiar, but seemingly impossible" footmarks.[1]

Bolger's need to dance stemmed from his troubled home life. Most who fled Ireland during the Irish Potato Famine of 1849 never got to know their aunts and uncles and cousins, and the large and fragmented Bolger family was no exception. A family member recalled that Bolger's mother was "part of a large Wallace family, maybe a dozen or so [children] and not very many of her brothers and sisters ever got married. There were a lot of old maids and confirmed bachelors. Many of them died at an early age."[2]

Johannah Cecilia "Annie" Wallace was born in Bridgewater, Massachusetts, and later settled with her parents and some of their siblings in Fall River, Massachusetts. There, she met her future husband.

Ray's father, James, was a first-generation Irish-American born in Fall River. He presented himself with confidence, swagger, and authority despite living in tenements and bouncing from one low-skilled job to the next. His high forehead suggested intelligence, and his thick eyebrows framed his dark, mischievous eyes. He often kept a corncob pipe pressed between his thin lips. In 1902, he married Annie, a lithe and light-haired colleen with small, bright eyes in a careworn, birdlike face. They were both twenty-six. The bride was a frequent smiler, but she still looked older than her years. The newlyweds settled in Dorchester, Massachusetts, and James took a job driving a bakery delivery wagon. The couple lived with James's widower father, Raymond. For a time, James's father worked as a house painter. But James and Annie began to support him just before Annie became pregnant with her first child.

On January 9, 1904, Annie went into early labor. The danger of the situation sent her to St. Elizabeth's Hospital in nearby Brighton, which featured one of the most advanced obstetrics departments of the era. The son she delivered, Raymond Wallace Bolger, later described himself as "a four-pound worry for my mom and dad"[3]—a premature baby born to a poor family. The Bolgers brought their son home to the heart of Dorchester.

Ray Bolger's mother, Annie Bolger, née Wallace. Courtesy of Christianna Rickard.

Ray Bolger's father, James Edward. Courtesy of Christianna Rickard.

In the first months of Bolger's life, the musical adaptation of the author L. Frank Baum's novel, *The Wonderful Wizard of Oz*, was playing on Broadway. Less than a year after Bolger's birth, the first issue of the weekly paper *Variety* spun off the press. For the next twenty-eight years it chronicled the happenings of vaudeville, the country's dominant form of entertainment. All the elements of this story were now in place: the first truly American entertainment narrative to capture the public's imagination (variety arts), the media to chronicle the nascent American show business industry and heighten its importance, and a small Irish-American boy who would find in music and dance an escape from an otherwise grim life, and who would literally and figuratively become the transition between stage entertainment and motion pictures. Several years would pass before they converged.

In the meantime, life passed quietly for the Bolgers. Ray Bolger's only sibling, his sister, Regina, arrived in 1909. James bounced around among the painting companies of Boston and the surrounding suburbs. At times he took to the road and worked as a salesman. The family never had much, and James took a keen interest in trying to make it big and lifting them into a higher social class. Growing up, Bolger most enjoyed the company of his mother and sister. Annie endowed her son with two lifelong passions: Catholicism and reading. Bolger's first exposure to the power of theater came through his participation in Catholic life. The priest chanted and sang the Mass in Latin, a language in which Bolger—like most of the parishioners—could not claim fluency. However, he understood the importance of the words through the priest's expressions, gestures, and tone. The Mass offered a lesson in the observance of the fourth wall. In a Catholic mass, the division between "star" and "audience" was always maintained: the priest performed most of the Mass with his back turned to the congregation. Comedians have long been drawn to Catholicism. For four hundred years, the Vatican engaged in a love-hate relationship with clowns and fools who wandered into the celebrations of Catholic holy days in Rome.[4] The Irish Catholics of Bolger's day were preoccupied with a fear of death. Church was the first place that encouraged him to seek immortality.

Annie incorporated her Catholic faith into the lessons she taught her children at home. Bolger said:

> I was brought up on those books of *The Wizard of Oz*. My mother gave them to me when I was yea-high. She said "Raymond, those books have a marvelous philosophy. They teach that everyone has a brain, everyone has a heart, and

everyone has courage. And if you use the gifts God gave you on this earth, you find the pot of gold at the end of the rainbow. And that pot of gold is at home—not in a house or an abode, but with people who you love, and who love you."[5]

In 1918, when he was fourteen, Bolger bought a ticket to his first full-length musical with his mother's blessing. *Jack O'Lantern* starred Fred Stone, a premiere eccentric dancer who had achieved fame while originating the role of the Scarecrow in L. Frank Baum's stage rendition of *The Wizard of Oz* when it opened in Chicago in 1902 and when it came to Broadway in 1903. The role of Scarecrow made Stone a nationwide celebrity with whom Annie Bolger would have been familiar. Stone was old enough to be Bolger's father, and yet he was one of the most nimble, athletic performers on the American stage.

Stone began his career as a physical comic and performed acrobatics-influenced dance with a partner, David Montgomery, through the 1890s. When Baum adapted *The Wonderful Wizard of Oz* for live performance, he wanted Montgomery & Stone, as they were known professionally, to have parts. The pair were the most popular celebrities in Chicago. Stone was always Baum's choice for the Scarecrow, but at first Baum offered Montgomery only a bit part. Stone withheld his participation in the show unless Montgomery also received a leading role. Baum assigned Montgomery to the Tin Woodsman role, and the show went into rehearsals.

Stone felt the part of the Scarecrow could be the perfect vehicle for his style of dance, which featured contortionism, acrobatics, and comedy. After reading Baum's book, he remained haunted by the sparse W. W. Denslow illustrations. Stone likewise envisioned the straw man as "grotesque" and wanted to replicate the drawings in his costume choices. He used a thick grease paint that obliterated all the lines of his face, eyebrows, eyelashes, and then used kohl to draw a straight mouth and nose. He set one eyebrow low and the other high, and he drew a small circle around his left eye and a large one around his right. Those who saw *The Wizard of Oz* first in Chicago and later on Broadway felt transported by the wobbly, bumbling strawman, who in photos exudes the otherworldliness of a ghost. The role of the Scarecrow so endeared Stone to audiences that for the rest of his career he was called on to reprise the part.

In 1917, David Montgomery died. As Stone embarked on his solo career, he performed a familiar and comfortable role while adjusting to professional life without his partner. He brought back his Scarecrow for the musical *Jack O'Lantern*. Produced by Charles Dillingham, the show revolved around an evil old man who decides to kill off his pretty young ward, who resembled the character of Dorothy Gale from *The Wonderful Wizard of Oz*. The villain mistakes Stone's scarecrow character, named Jack O'Lantern, for his hired cutthroat. Stone's acrobatics and circus tricks made audiences forgive the tepid plot. To rescue the young girl and evade the villain, Stone spent most of the show gliding around an onstage skating rink. For the climax of the show—the rescue of the helpless little girl from the villain—Stone jumped up and down on a trampoline (disguised as a haystack) to evade police, ran up a tree, back-flipped over the heads of police, leaped on a bicycle, and somersaulted with it through the window of a house where the little girl was held captive. Following a respectable Broadway run, the show toured the country, stopping in Boston.

After seeing the show, Bolger considered the loose-limbed Stone his idol, not only for his dexterity but also because of the way he transported Bolger to another world with his performance, "a world that I never knew really, actually existed," he said.[6] But Bolger's day-to-day reality had little room for imagination and creativity. Life at home was still hard.

Government records suggest that Bolger's parents separated around the time that Ray took refuge in theater. Both Annie and James were staunch Catholics and would not have divorced, but the nuclear family nonetheless dissolved. James secured a job painting ships with Hamburg America in 1918 that kept him away from home a great deal. While on the job, he contracted pleurisy and double pneumonia. As a result, Ray worked odd jobs after school. He ran errands for neighborhood grocery stores and swept floors for the Kelly Peanut Company. By this time, he was truly an adult. He resembled his father in the most obvious features: strong brows, a prominent forehead, and thin lips. But his face also suggested his mother's refinement, the same way that constant running water refines even craggy stone. His father's receded chin, for example, was softer and more becoming on his own face. And although he inherited his father's beak-like nose, it was tempered by his mother's radiant smile. Ray also had Annie's narrow shoulders and lissome build. But on the whole, he was thin and unremarkable. As Bolger recalled of this time, "Two things worked to my advantage: I was the smallest kid in the neighborhood, so I had to think my way out of a fight, and I had to excel in school."[7]

In 1919, at the age of fifteen, Bolger segued from child to adult without much of a pause for adolescence. His mother died of a cerebral hemorrhage that July in Fall River—her girlhood home. On her death certificate, her marital status was listed as "Single," but the signatory witness to her death was James E. Bolger. While Bolger's parents were clearly involved in each other's lives to some degree, raising the children had not been a cohesive

Bolger as a teenager. UCLA Library Special Collections, Charles E. Young Research Library.

venture. Now, Ray had just his father for support, but from this point in time, the son became the greater supporter of his father than otherwise.

With his father's poor health and unsteady work habits, Bolger would need to supply an income for the shattered family. He was a junior in high school, though, and his father felt he should stay on to graduate with the class of 1920. For his final year of school, Bolger rearranged his class schedule so that he attended Dorchester High School in the mornings but went to work in the afternoons for the First National Bank in Boston. As a clerk, Bolger earned about $18 a week, which he gave to his father at the end of each week. But Bolger worked just steps away from Boston's theater district. He was surrounded by intrigue, entertainment, and rabble rousing, and not all of it passed him by.

Just beyond the bank on Winter Street, Scollay Square overflowed with actors and hopefuls. A tattoo parlor, a saloon, a casino, and a subway station cordoned it off from the rest of Boston and gave approaching pedestrians a good idea of the morality inside. Within its borders, Scollay Square housed Austin and Stone's Dime Museum, a freak collection curated by P. T. Barnum. The Old Howard Theatre hosted shows by small-time actors who considered Boston their territory for life. These sorts of showfolk— who would rather conquer one less important territory than try to make a break in New York City—were nicknamed "coast defenders." Every week, the Old Howard presented a new burlesque show in two acts. Between the acts of burlesque were three acts of vaudeville. Ten cents granted a spectator all-day admission to the gallery. But for boys like Bolger, interested in dance, the place to congregate was in front of the Rexford Hotel where both "challenge" dances and fights broke out on the Rexford's pavement. The steps of dancers who appeared at the Howard in the afternoon would be mimicked, replicated, and perfected outside the hotel afterward. This in turn drew school boys eager to enter show business. The most effective way of learning tap dance came from imitation.

In addition to this informal sparring, organized contests occurred throughout Boston's neighborhoods. In the years before and after World War I, ballrooms grew in popularity. The large spaces allowed crowds to enjoy the new music of the times, as the Jazz Age and later the Big Bands required many instruments. Often, ballrooms hosted dance contests in tribute to vaudevillians touring the area.

After leaving work and before heading home, Bolger traipsed over to Scollay Square. Here he could get the trolley back to Dorchester or take in some of these events. In those days in Boston, dance did not belong only in the academy or in the theater. An important part of socializing, especially for Irish and African American men, was engaging in challenge dances on the streets. The profession with the most lucrative possibilities and the lowest barrier to entry was entertainment. While not every dancer on Boston's street corners had aspirations of stardom, no one discarded stardom as a possibility.

The tap-dancing education Bolger picked up here came down through three hundred years of tradition from Irish and African Americans. In the early twentieth century they shared a history of subservience: in their not-so-distant past, African Americans suffered slavery, and the Irish experienced indentured servitude. As tap scholar Constance Valis Hill points out, "The Irish indentured servants and the West African slaves worked and lived together" in the days of the English sugar plantation owners.[8] She explained:

> Similarly, the African American style of dance that angled and relaxed the torso, centered movement in the hips, and favored flat-footed gliding, dragging, and shuffling steps, melded with the Irish American style of step dancing, with upright torso, minimized hip motion, and dexterous footwork that favored bounding, hopping, and shuffling.[9]

The Irish Potato Famine sent nearly two million emigrants fleeing their homeland. Many arrived in the port cities of Boston and New York.

Bringing with them Catholicism and cholera, they took up residence in the slums and were regarded with mistrust and suspicion by their Protestant neighbors. The deep segregation they experienced led the Irish to create their own amusements, social codes, and public spaces. In the face of the grimness that America offered them, the Irish found relief in the love and proliferation of dance from home. From traditional Irish step-dancing, two major styles grew and gained popularity in the late nineteenth century: the jig-and-clog step dancing of George M. Cohan, and the lofty soft-shoe of a less-remembered popular dancer, George Primrose.

Primrose performed in minstrel shows through the early twentieth century. He became a patron saint for both the Irish and the black dance communities. Harland Dixon, a black tap dancer who achieved success on the Broadway stage and who worked for the Primrose Minstrels early in his career said, "He was of medium height, weighed a little over a hundred and ten, and could wear clothes like Fred Astaire; he smoked cigars but he didn't drink; I never heard him raise his voice or swear . . . just the way he walked was poetry."[10]

Primrose was an important role model for the first generation of Irish American popular dancers. He was the original "Irish prince" of tap dancing: his personality and character, not just his fine dancing, won the favor of his fellow dancers and his audience.

Dancers of the Primrose school minimized the motion of their hips. The movement was centered below the knee. Aural clarity, body control, and a sense of timing were of chief importance in their tapping, which covered the entire stage. One of the most important dancers of the twentieth century to practice the Primrose style and develop it further was Jack Donahue. Born just eight years before Bolger, Donahue grew up in Charlestown, Massachusetts. Around the time Bolger was learning to dance on the streets, Donahue was already a star on Broadway. He was the boy who "made it" out of Boston, and the kids in Scollay Square mimicked much of his work.

Boys of Boston interested in dance swapped steps with each other. They found dancers they could learn from by prowling other parts of the city. In the Back Bay, Bolger found Dinny Healy, a night watchman at Boston's Horticultural Hall. Healy was an ex-vaudevillian who taught him "eccentric steps among the rhododendrons."[11]

Bolger was referring to "eccentric dance," a tradition of stylized physical comedy that exploded in America in the late nineteenth and early twentieth centuries. Its origins could be traced all the way back to pantomime performed in Ancient Greece. Eccentric dance depended upon loose-limbed, rubber-legged parody. The term "eccentric dance" comprised three main styles. The most popular was "legmania," which required the performer to execute high kicks and grotesque leg extensions. "Snake hips" evolved with African influence and required loose torso, hips, and pelvis. "Traditional" eccentric reflected Celtic styles; particularly, it demanded a great deal of leg flailing below the knee. Ballet required all dancers to master traditional positions, and tap dancing was built on the time step and break, but eccentric dance style varied widely from individual to individual. The dancer relied on unique physical attributes and flexibility to create a style, which could be a blend of all three eccentric types. To be successful, the eccentric dancer needed to develop a physicality and steps unique to a character and storyline. An eccentric routine needed raison d'être and a beginning, a middle, and an end.

Bolger's shins were unusually long, and the combination of his long legs and short torso were well suited to a comic style of dance. He was also extremely flexible through the hips and hamstrings, and so he became a natural student of legmania as well as the Celtic-influenced style of eccentric.

Although Bolger mostly learned from his peers, he began to save a little money out of his take-home pay to spend on admission to live musical performances. He looked for other outlets to practice the kind of dance that captured his imagination. Enough practice and inspiration could elevate the local boys with real promise to the level of the amateur performer. A whole circuit of Amateur Nights around the city, hosted by dance halls and neighborhood theaters, egged on dancers and other kinds of performers to compete with each other. The promise of cash prizes and local fame encouraged neighborhood kids to develop their own acts. Audiences chose the winners with their applause and the losers with their condemnation. The recipient of the top prize usually took home around $25: one winning night earned a performer more than a well-paid employee like Bolger earned for a whole week of office work. In Bolger's time and place, entertaining was not a lofty, artistic ambition. It was a good way to survive and, in his realm of experience and opportunities, the only way to thrive.

Victory often enough eluded even the most talented performers. "Sympathy acts" infiltrated the bills at theaters. Crackly voiced hunchbacks, shriveled old women, and down-at-the-heels children took to the stage to warble sorrowful songs and encourage the audience to vote out of pity.

Emotion and adrenaline fueled the audience through these evenings. Acts judged to be below par got taunted, booed, pelted with avocados, and removed from the stage with "The Hook"—a long pole with an iron hook wielded by the master of ceremonies, who stood behind the curtain. Under these conditions, the best performers needed to make immediate connections with their audiences. The best way to appeal to their emotions was to develop charisma. Bolger crafted the persona of a bumbling country bumpkin who could not control his own motion. He used falling, tripping, and splitting to charm the crowds. It's not clear how many amateur contests Bolger participated in, but he acknowledged that he won his first contest, for being the best impersonator of the vaudevillian Joe Frisco, in 1922 at the State Ball Room.[12] That means he practiced for two solid years without earning recognition.

By this time, Bolger's father was working as a traveling vacuum-cleaner salesman. His sister was staying with relatives of their mother. And Bolger, while living in Somerville, took on work as a clerk and office boy for the New England Mutual Life Insurance Company. This is where Bolger took to dancing up and down the stairs as he went to deliver inter-office mail, his after-hours world blending into, and threatening, the stability of his paying job. While loitering around the Back Bay, he discovered O'Brien's School for Social and Formal Dancing, which was part of a commercial complex on Huntington Avenue. Dancing schools of this era offered not only formal lessons, but also the opportunity for boys and girls to find each other and practice. Bolger wasn't popular with potential partners because of his highly individualized style, and so he often danced alone. At O'Brien's he noticed a Dutch door at the back of the studio that allowed air to circulate through from an adjacent hallway in the days before air conditioning. The class was visible from this hallway and the class pianist was audible. For a time the cash-poor Bolger observed classes from beyond the half door, imitating what he saw in the studio. Later, he enrolled under the proprietor William H. O'Brien. O'Brien's daughter, Alyce, described young Ray haunting the studio:

> Dad said that Ray always seemed to be bubbling over with nervous energy—
> "He can do better than buck and wing," was one of his comments. Ray never said
> much about wanting to get into show business.... [H]e would say, "I like the
> banking business, but I can't make up my mind whether to be a teller, a book-
> keeper, or a president."[13]

Bolger bumped into another dance instructor, whose studio was in the same building as O'Brien's school. Senia Rusakoff was a Russian ballet master and character dancer. Rusakoff and his wife, Regina, were Russian Jews from Saint Petersburg who settled in Boston after a few years of touring vaudeville. They frequently told clients they lived on "the Hill"—referring to Boston's elite Beacon Hill neighborhood. They really slept on cots in Senia's office. Despite their small and shabby studio, the Rusakoffs had a reputation for generosity.

Rusakoff watched Bolger dancing one night at O'Brien's. "You're not too bad, my boy," Rusakoff called out. "And what do you do?"

Bolger stopped dead. "I work downtown and I'm the world's greatest bookkeeper," Bolger said.

"A bookkeeper is just what I need," Rusakoff responded.[14] Rusakoff possessed a genuine sense of compassion and picked up all sorts of misfits at his studio.[15] When not at work at New England Mutual, Bolger began trading bookkeeping for dancing lessons. He later recalled that the instruction was never very fancy; he more or less lingered at the Rusakoff studio to pick up whatever knowledge he could, whenever he had the chance. At night Bolger mopped the dance floor. It gave Bolger a greater sense of belonging and home than his own family was able to provide.

Bolger, *upper right*, at the company picnic for New England Mutual Life in Swampscott, Massachusetts. UCLA Library Special Collections, Charles E. Young Research Library.

Hanging around Rusakoff's studio gave Bolger his first exposure to ballet. He achieved proficiency in the genre by wandering into classes uninvited. In time, he was able to teach the beginner's section. All of this would help him cultivate his own unique style. "That was really, actually, the beginning of what later became a career," Bolger said.[16] Many of the steps that Rusakoff taught him, including the *pas de chat* and the *prisyadki*, a Russian character step requiring the dancer to squat and alternately kick out his legs, became staples of his routine.

But it was also the beginning of a career in dance because Bolger was forced out of his career as a life insurance clerk. One of Bolger's colleagues at this time later wrote to him, "I remember very distinctly the episode at our old building at 87 Milk Street, when you were five or ten minutes late one morning and that efficiency expert, Lowell Baker, terminated your association with the New England Mutual. He didn't realize what a special favor he was doing you."[17]

Bolger was now focused solely on becoming a professional entertainer. He wanted to be a comic before he considered becoming a dancer, but dance provided him with social outlets and a mentor. The best way an aspiring entertainer could ensure his success starting out was to diversify his talents. Rusakoff put Bolger onstage for a recital at the Grand Opera House in the South End of Boston. By the end of the recital, Bolger had earned the title of "the new-style jazz Nijinsky" for his unintentionally haphazard take on Russian ballet: "I did everything in that recital from a mazurka to an interpretive dance—my interpretation of a Chinese dope fiend," he recalled.[18] He had found a taste for stage work and the talent for dance. In addition to working and dancing for Rusakoff, Bolger took up employment as a dishwasher in a cafeteria on Huntington Avenue. He was renting a room of his own in Boston, but when even that became too expensive, he pitched a cot in Rusakoff's office.

When badly down on his luck, Bolger used his sweet charm to borrow money from Mabel Harris, the cute blond piano player on Rusakoff's staff. "'Say, Mabel, d'ya have a quarter you could spare me?' was his favorite opening for a touch," she said. "You couldn't help liking Ray—he was always such a nice fellow."[19] His image as a nice fellow would also compensate for whatever formal training he lacked in dance.

One night in 1923, Bob Ott, proprietor of the Bob Ott Musical Repertory Company, visited the O'Brien dance studio. He was looking to hire ballerinas for his act. He walked out with Ray Bolger and signed him to his first professional theatrical job. Ott said, "I didn't hire him as much for his dancing as I did for his funny-looking face."[20] Now a paid performer for the first time, which was an unprecedented accomplishment for a member of his family, Bolger packed his possessions into cardboard suitcases and left Boston behind. The unlikelihood of Bolger's succeeding was captured well by Marge Champion, the celebrated American dancer and choreographer who would later see Bolger dance on Broadway, and whose own father was the first to leave his family profession of butchery: "I think in those days it was not considered at all OK [to pursue the arts]. If you were in a tradesmen family, you were supposed to follow. It took a very strong person who was really touched by the arts very deeply, so that they really couldn't do anything else."[21]

By signing on to Bob Ott's company, Bolger found more than a gig: the company was an all-in-the-family business. Bob was the boss, the entrepreneur. His wife, Carol, served alternately as the leading lady and assistant character actress. Bob's niece, Ann Ott, was the skinny ingénue. With 21-21-21 measurements, she was said to be a "carbon copy" of her mother, Flo, pianist and musical director, and the widow of Bob's brother Joe. The company was rounded out with Mildred and Fred Wright, the romantic leads and dancers, a character actor, four chorus girls for the musicals, and Ray Bolger, the second comic and "general gofer."[22] Bolger's father also joined the company as publicist and advance man. To James, show business was just another business, although far more glamorous and lucrative than any he had known before. He thought he could jump in and figure it out. The industry was young enough that this was not a totally naïve proposition. He made his son split his salary of $75 per week with him. The quality of the Bolgers' relationship is difficult to gauge, although it seems that, at least until he began seeking female companionship, Ray was dominated by the presence of his father in his life. They would attend Mass together wherever they traveled for bookings. No correspondence between them survives. Bolger seldom spoke of his father in public and only when he explained why he had to work at jobs other than dancing as a young man. He practiced and preached the filial piety endemic to his generation, and so it is no surprise that Bolger would not speak ill of his father. Bolger's preference for his mother's company, however, suggests he would have been at least somewhat displeased by how James's difficulties added to Annie's discomforts, and perhaps even expedited her death. The little that Bolger did say, and the great amount that he did not, suggests that the son helped his father more than the father helped his son.

The pair was guaranteed forty weeks of work. Ott paid the Bolgers' transportation for them—a rare luxury for stock performers. Bolger paid for his own costumes.[23] In addition to appearing in eight performances a day, he sold souvenir programs between the shows and counted the number of balcony seats in each theater where the show performed. It was a common practice for a stage manager to skip a row on his theater chart and pocket all the money for those tickets, hence the need for the visiting company to do their own tallying.

The Ott show was different from the other repertory shows touring the country. Instead of the standard gamut of well-known plays, Bob Ott's brother Matthew wrote "original" plays and musicals influenced by the current hits in New York. At the time that George M. Cohan was starring in *Forty-Five Minutes from Broadway*, Ott put on a show called *One Hour from New York*. Bolger wrote, "Whatever popular show an audience could name, Matthew Ott would rename it, the company would play it, and the crowds would devour it."[24] Whereas a vaudeville show was a variety performance of unrelated acts sharing the same bill, the Ott company filled the theater for the entire day, with eight performances, each of a different show. In his two years of touring, Bolger played a wide variety of parts, most of them tropes—"butler, lover, farm boy, second comic, and dancing dude"—and had to figure out what bits of business made audience members laugh before reworking them and perfecting them for repeat effect.[25] The more frustrating lesson to learn, though, was that the same material delivered in the same manner could be received very differently as the troupe traveled to new locations. Bolger and the Ott company traveled the country as far west as Peoria, Illinois, and as far south as Baltimore.

The humble town of Mount Carmel, Pennsylvania, in the heart of anthracite country, inspired Bolger's affection. He spent Christmas of 1923 with a local family while the Ott company played the Grand Army of the Republic Opera House there. Opera houses of the time in the places where Bolger toured were nothing more than a hall on the second floor of an uninspired concrete or wood building. The locals came as much for access to a working baseboard heater as for the entertainment. The stage was just a platform, a few feet high, with steps leading up to it from the audience. The accommodations were simple, but the need to act was real. The immediacy of these small settings helped Bolger learn how to feed off crowds. He could look out and see his audience roaring or nodding off. He could quip, he could wiggle, he could smirk, and instantly he felt their response. At Mount Carmel, a great wood rafter system ran from wall to wall, supporting an A-shaped roof. The miners would sit on the rafters, dangling their legs in the air. When Bolger walked onstage on opening night, he heard the miners screaming from the rafters, "You better be good!" He looked up at them. The line "dog dirty and loaded for bear," from Robert W. Service's poem "The Shooting of Dan McGrew" sprang to his mind.[26] Perhaps he recited it to himself in his head to steady his nerves. The miners' eyes seemed to glow in the dark as he performed his high kicks, leaps, and bounds. The yelling changed to "Do it again, kid!"[27] So he did. It did not take long for him to learn the vaudevillian's motto: the right kind of work, approached with the right kind of mindset, could be good fun. But fun—the sort that could amuse audiences—is very hard work.

No matter how rowdy their audiences, performers were expected to adhere to a strict code of conduct on and off the stage, and theater managers would keep records on actors' behavior. Reports of the way actors dressed and how they conducted themselves in their free time would go straight back to the booking offices. When an actor arrived in a theater office to pick up the mail waiting for him, he was greeted with a sign, which featured a finger pointing down to blank forms pinned to the wall. These forms were the manager's reports. The sign declared, "What will you be? It's up to you!" In the Ott company, one actor's behavioral episode proved to be Bolger's boon.

The company played Cambridge, Maryland, a town that seemed as small and insignificant as all the others. Bolger called the theater "dark, dirty, and totally impractical," but it didn't matter to him. He was still brimming with enthusiasm for landing his first paid, touring theatrical work. The optimistic newcomer shared the tiny space between the coal bins and the furnace that heated the Opera House with a curmudgeonly veteran of the stage who had seen better days and better theaters. The cast had spent enough time on the road by that point that the warm family atmosphere in the beginning had dissolved by the time they prepared for their first show in the new venue. The washed-up thespian that Bolger shared his space with reeked of alcohol as he sat before the cracked, speckled mirror. He slapped his makeup on "like a one-armed house painter with the St. Vitas dance, all the while cursing his fate that he was in Cambridge, Maryland, not Cambridge, England where he 'definitely belonged.'" Bolger said:

> The best performance that night was not in the "Opry House," but the center of the town square. Dwarfed by the statue of Robert E. Lee, [my] dressing room companion stood, declaring in no uncertain terms, his stentorian tones being heard throughout the whole town that "the slings and arrows of outrageous fortune" had placed him in the miserable spit of earth that passed for civilization. It only got worse from there. He attracted a large but sleepy audience with

his ranting. They did not appreciate this encore performance. It was not long before the local constabulary had him securely locked in jail. His sentence the next day was to remove his presence from the town. Ray Bolger, very young, very inexperienced, and very nervous had to become the new character actor, and the show had to go on.[28]

And on it went until a suitable replacement could be found. It didn't take long for the Otts to come up with Ralph Sanford, and Bolger was stripped of "first comic" status. Both Sanford and Bolger were Massachusetts natives—Sanford hailed from Springfield—of non-theatrical families. Where Bolger was skinny and affable, Sanford was a rough-and-tough bruiser. Sanford was also an established comedian on the Columbia Wheel Burlesque circuit. Sanford was given the role as "top banana" with Ott, and Bolger was demoted because Sanford was all charisma and machismo, while Bolger was a spaghetti noodle with a prominent Adam's apple. Bolger was enchanted by the urbane and conniving Sanford, who had a routine for seemingly everything. Even off stage, Sanford could reply to a simple question like "How do you do?" with an extemporized, five-minute act.

Ott allowed Sanford and Bolger to devise a double act for use in the company, called "Sanford and Bolger." They formed a sloppier version of the slapstick variety duo Joe Weber and Lew Fields. A representative joke from the Sanford and Bolger routine went like this:

SANFORD: Are you a connoisseur? (Pronounced like, "corner-sewer")
BOLGER: No, I live in the middle of the block.

Despite the corniness of the material, the pair had good chemistry, and they became a hit around Boston and New England. At the conclusion of the 1924–25 touring season, they decided to leave the Ott company and make a break for New York. Bolger received some advice for how to get the act into New York from a fellow vaudevillian, Joe Roth. However, in a time before television and radio broadcasts were able to standardize national tastes, there was no guarantee that what sold out in Massachusetts would be well received in New York, as young Bolger learned the hard way. Sanford and Bolger stopped in Brooklyn's Greenpoint Theater thanks to some of Sanford's connections. The theaters in Brooklyn served as test kitchens of sorts. The audiences for these shows were made up primarily of theatrical bookers, talent scouts who set the salaries for shows they liked. They hated Sanford and Bolger. No offers came their way.

The distraught duo decided to revamp their act and paid $500 (all of their savings) for the successful but brash vaudevillian Jimmy Duffy, one-half of the last great Irish knockabout-comedy team of Duffy and Sweeney, to smarten them up. Duffy and Sweeney succeeded partly because they combined great politeness with the use of violent force in their act: they would call each other "sir" and feign manners only to devolve into fisti-cuffs onstage. Duffy likewise tried to balance Sanford and Bolger's stale humor with fresh fashion. They became "Sanford and Bolger: A Pair of Nifties." Sanford was naturally nifty, but Duffy thought that Bolger needed some help. They went to Louis Gutenberg's Second Avenue Second Hand Shop, which catered to down-on-their luck members of the theatrical trade, and picked up gray striped trousers, a morning jacket, and pearl gray spats. Following his polish-up, Bolger proceeded with Sanford to Cohen's Theater in Newburgh, New York. The proprietor was George Cohen—a Poughkeepsie entrepreneur, not the dancer George M. Cohan.

Portrait of the artist as a young vaudevillian. Bolger appears at the Strand in 1924. UCLA Library Special Collections, Charles E. Young Research Library.

Sanford and Bolger were booked for three days to play between film showings, and they were to be paid $62.50 collectively. They planned to work out the act in upstate New York before trying to break into the city again. As Bolger said, "We opened with confidence and closed after the first performance." Cohen stormed back stage after their act and cried, "'Sanford and Bolger: A Pair of Nifties'? Ha! Cancelled!"[29]

CHAPTER 2

Entering Show Business

Despite his initial failure in New York City, Bolger marveled at the possibilities around him. He wrote,

> The First World War had ended. The Volstead Act had created a new breed—bootleggers, speak-easies, and it seemed everybody you knew had a flask filled to the top with the real stuff right off the boat....The bright lights of Broadway dazzled this young novice.[1]

In the early to mid-1920s, New York entertainers were as off-the-wall as ever. One night Bolger's friends Jimmy Duffy and Freddy Sweeney, who would perform their act while drunk, were having a hard time winning over their audience. Duffy stopped the act and said, "Ladies and gentleman, my partner will tell one more joke and if you don't laugh, he will go amongst you with a baseball bat and beat the beejesus out of you!"[2] There was no muting the color of vaudevillians, but the management system controlling them had become systematized and rigid. At the turn of the twentieth century, the moguls of vaudeville, B. F. Keith and Martin Beck, sought to put the business in "show business." The success of efficient mass-marketing systems like Sears Roebuck, A&P grocery stores, and variety stores like S. S. Kresge and Woolworth showed them what their own industry could become. They wanted to "perfect a standardized vaudeville show that met the average taste of the new urban consumer audience, and like the manufacturing chains, market their product successfully."[3] That meant that originals like Bolger ran the risk of being squeezed out of lineups. Surviving in show business now truly required knowing a thing or two about serious business, and Bolger's father, who had been his only manager, was way out of his depths trying to navigate these new, deep channels.

There were two tiers of vaudeville: the big time and the small time, also known as family time. Most of the theaters in the country offered small-time vaudeville: they booked cheaper acts and often offered a film as part of the show. They played on a "continuous" policy: the moment one show ended, the next began. The acts in small-time vaudeville did three or four shows daily. Any act that had to perform four or more shows a day was said to be working the "grind." The first act of a family-time vaudeville show was a lecturer or some other dry presentation. Because the vaudeville shows played continuously, the audience knew it was time to leave when they realized they had already heard the droning first act. The curtain did not even have to fall.

Big-time vaudeville, by contrast, booked true stars who could draw crowds and who received higher salaries. They performed just two shows a day, at 2:15 in the afternoon and 8:15 in the evening. Audiences for these performances were considered more sophisticated. The biggest big-time theater in the country, which every performer dreamed of playing, was the Palace in New York City, where the entertainment was fast and witty. Theaters on the big time or small time that hosted only vaudeville and did not show motion pictures were known as "straight vaudeville" houses. Those that screened films were known as "combination" houses. Performers could be booked for one-day, half-week (called "split week"), or full-week appearances. Most performers had to make all travel arrangements for themselves. In the East, split weeks were divided so that the first half encompassed Monday, Tuesday, and Wednesday and the second half started on Thursday and played through Sunday night. In the West, the first half ended after the matinee on Wednesday, and the second half began with the evening performance.

Vaudeville was composed of empire-like circuits, each fronted with a powerful impresario (or two). B. F. Keith and Edward Albee managed the Keith-Albee circuit in the East. Martin Beck and Morris Meyerfeld Jr. controlled the Orpheum circuit in the West. Jacob J. "J. J." and Lee Shubert, and Marcus Loew also owned systems of theaters and promoted vaudeville. Many of these leaders took a business interest in producing the shows that filled their theaters.

A vaudeville house, for instance, offered a show with as many as a dozen acts up to three times a day. The owners of the major chains fought each other for the best talent to send across the country under their brand and to ensure a consistent stream of quality and revenue. To inspire loyalty in their players, they often banned for life those who left their enterprise to appear on other circuits.

The small-time actor striking out on his own still had an opportunity to make his living, though. Theater managers ran the risk of boring their paying audiences by bringing in the same acts too frequently, and so thousands of performers were needed just to keep the machine fed. Not every act needed to be of artistic merit to succeed; many got by with personality or a pet monkey. Likewise, vaudeville offered endless opportunities for reinvention. An actor could be out of work for months, but by changing his partner or adding new material to his act, he could become a sensation somewhere.[4]

The 1920s were a transitional decade for American entertainers and entertainment. It was the last decade in which performers could "come up the hard way" alone and make themselves into celebrities with hard work, good sense, and plenty of endurance. While there will always be "up-by-your-bootstraps" performers, after this decade it became incredibly difficult to succeed without a talent agent, publicity firm, or other manager honing the performer's image and schedule.

Bolger struggled to find success for the "Pair of Nifties" act, especially as Sanford's interest in their partnership began to wane. The onus was on Bolger to make the act a success because Sanford had Bolger under contract. It had been a risk for Sanford to break out of the Ott troupe with a young and inexperienced actor, and he demanded loyalty via legalities. Sanford also had a desire to perform on Broadway. He looked for roles for himself and intended to void Bolger's contract if anything came his way.

Although Sanford offered Bolger little professional help, the two became close friends. Sanford took Bolger to all the nightclubs. Both of the Lindy's— the one occupied by actors, the other where Damon Runyon hung out with gangsters and bookies—dazzled him. In Times Square, he was exposed to low culture, as well as to high, which mingled as closely in the city as the haves did with the have-nots. In particular, the mix of high and low culture was influencing the evolution of motion picture presentations, which had become the most elaborate entertainment to be found in Manhattan. Motion picture "palaces" sprang up. Rather than shutting out the poor, these ornate structures welcomed them in—as long as they could pay the price of admission. As George Rapp, one of the most important movie theater architects of the time, said, "The picture-palace is a shrine to democracy where the wealthy rub elbows with the poor."[5] In the heart of the square, a cascade of light proclaimed "Rialto." Just beyond it, the block-wide Rivoli Theater bulged onto the sidewalk, forcing pedestrians to walk under marquees proclaiming Paramount Pictures could be viewed inside. A little farther up Broadway at Forty-Ninth Street, a massive French Renaissance-styled chateau made out of Indiana limestone—the Criterion—completed the trifecta. Worthy of its name, the ornate theater showed some of the most important early films, like Cecil B. DeMille's first version of *The Ten Commandments*. Bolger passed it frequently on his way to St. Malachy's Chapel, the Roman Catholic church on Forty-Ninth Street between Broadway and Eighth Avenue that catered to show people.

These great theaters all had ties to the powerful Samuel Lionel "Roxy" Rothafel, a movie palace magnate. Throughout the 1920s, Rothafel was one of the most influential tastemakers in popular entertainment. He famously quipped to the press, "Don't give the people what they want—give 'em something better than they expect."[6] Rothafel worked ceaselessly for two decades to provide average Americans the best and classiest entertainment he could envision. To that end he went on tour with his vaudeville troupe, "Roxy and His Gang," along with creating and managing deluxe movie houses all over the country. He revolutionized the Strand, Rialto, and Rivoli theaters in New York City with technical and artistic innovations. "If imitation is really the sincerest form of flattery," journalist Golda Goldman wrote, "it is impossible to question the public appreciation of the Rothafel type of entertainment.... Everything about it has been copied—the stage settings, orchestra, lighting effects, interpolation of ballet and concert numbers—all are to be found in two-hour program form in every up-to-date picture house in the country."[7]

Symphony conductors Charles Previn, Erno Rapee, and Eugene Ormandy scored his pictures. Rothafel is credited with pioneering the motion picture "presentation": combining silent movies not only with orchestral music but also with pageants, tab shows (shortened versions of popular shows), and variety acts on stage, organized around a theme suggested by the featured motion picture.

When Bolger arrived in Manhattan, the Rialto, the Rivoli, and the Criterion were under the directorship of one of Rothafel's protégés—Hugo Riesenfeld. He continued to use Rothafel's formula for motion picture presentation. Riesenfeld was a gifted Austrian American composer, but he was no snob. Whether he conducted Wagner's Overture to *Tannhäuser* or the accompaniment of an animated feature did not matter. He was most interested in understanding each of his audiences, knowing what they wanted and selling them what his talents could offer. He conducted a thirty-six-piece orchestra at the Rialto, and he also helped to book the other necessary talent into the theater.

Bolger, on behalf of himself and Sanford in 1926, auditioned for Riesenfeld at the Rialto. Unable to perform his comedy routine without his partner, Bolger performed a desperate ad lib dance. The concertmaster hired him for $125 per week. When Bolger explained that he had a partner, Riesenfeld allowed Sanford to join in, but they would have to split the $125 between them.

Bolger became best friends with one of the other Rialto actors—Ruth Fleischer, daughter of the animation pioneer Max Fleischer. Her act began with an animation on a projection screen. The picture transitioned to live action footage of her dancing. She would appear to jump off the screen, at which point Fleischer in the flesh began dancing on stage. She was trained in eccentric, ballet, and tap dancing. She and Bolger dated for a short time. The cause for their breakup is unknown, although it is possible that Bolger's father disproved of the match.[8]

During Bolger's engagement at the Rialto, Riesenfeld gave him another job, this time in motion pictures. Riesenfeld was a business partner of Ruth's father, Max, and her uncle, Dave Fleischer, who was also a cartoonist. The Fleischers had begun producing a series of sound cartoons using orchestral music. They brought in Riesenfeld and a couple of other investors[9] and created Red Seal Pictures. In addition to distributing American and foreign pictures, Red Seal also allowed the Fleischers to create their own films. They produced a series of live-action, two-reel comedy shorts called "Carrie of the Chorus," which followed the eponymous vaudeville trouper and her ragtag co-stars through the plights of working the small-time circuit. The role of Carrie was played by Peggy Shaw, a chorine most famous for her work in Florenz Ziegfeld Jr.'s first *Midnight Frolic*, an annual summer show held on the Ziegfeld roof after the performance of the *Follies*. Ruth Fleischer played Carrie's best friend.

Riesenfeld offered Bolger the opportunity to play opposite Shaw in the short called "The Berth Mark," a story of performers traveling by train (hence "berth"), in which Carrie and her vaudevillians get stuck in a backward small town and meet a banker played by Bolger who pays their fare to the next town on the stipulation that he can travel with them.[10] When they arrive, they are met by a moral reform society, which tries to break up the act. It's the vaudevillians, though, who break up the convention of moral reformists. The poor banker finds himself in trouble when he realizes his wife is among the moralists.

Shortly after the completion of "The Berth Mark," Red Seal Pictures collapsed, like many small movie studios in the twenties. The experience left Bolger uncertain of the value of pursuing a career in film. It literally left a bad taste in his mouth: he later wrote that his work at the Pathé Studios gave him bad teeth from having a white paste rubbed on them to make them glisten, but that infected his gums and roots.[11]

Roxy Rothafel saw one of Ray Bolger's performances at the Rialto and booked him into the Mark Strand Theater at Forty-Seventh Street and

Broadway, a combination house, for four more weeks. From there, he was recruited out of Manhattan to dance and clown at Shea's Hippodrome Theater in Buffalo, New York. Bolger became friends with another young man who worked there, Harold Arlen, who composed pieces for the Opus Wurlitzer, the theater's pipe organ. Bolger was held over at Shea's for an amazing seventeen weeks. Working through the Loew's commitment, Bolger then returned to Boston, where he appeared at the State Theater. Bolger was now being billed as a dancer, even though he still felt like a comedian. That would soon change. While in Boston, he caught the attention of J. J. Shubert.

Shubert and his surviving brother, Lee, were two of the most important businessmen working with both Broadway and vaudeville entertainments.[12] J. J. Shubert was known for producing shows under the umbrella of "summer fare"—musical revues that were a balance between pretty and witty. They featured big stars to entice New York clientele into the hot theaters in the summertime. When ticket sales started to fall off, usually between July and October, Shubert would remove the show from one of his costly Broadway houses and launch a "second edition" of the revue to send out on the road. This involved removing the most expensive stars, whittling down the scenery and props, and bringing in cheaper performers. The Shuberts wanted to increase their revue-earning output to compete with George White's *Scandals* and Florenz Ziegfeld's *Follies*, and feed their theaters across the country with roadshows. It behooved them to snatch up promising artists before they became aligned with another circuit or before they got too expensive. Bolger was interested in jumping to the Shubert company, as he had performed with bands for more than a year and he felt he was not progressing.

Shubert signed Bolger, giving him $175 a week—$50 a week more than he had been making at the Rialto. The contract began on June 6, 1926, the opening night of the first revue in which he would appear: *The Merry World*. The show fed the popular appetite for "international" revues, those that featured English sketches, French accents, women decked out in bathing suits, and "amusing nonresident entertainments."[13]

Bolger spent May of 1926 rehearsing the show in Newark with no pay, as performers at that time did. The prestige of working with the Shuberts, and the prospect of making his Broadway debut at the Imperial Theatre, buoyed the twenty-two-year-old through rehearsals. J. J. Shubert cut down his optimism. He came from Manhattan to visit rehearsals just ahead of opening night and decided that the revue did not have enough popular stars with which to cross the Hudson. Bolger said, "He broke our hearts and [all but] took us out of the show—this other fellow and myself doing the comedy. And all I had to do, . . . was one dance."[14]

Though Bolger's role in *The Merry World* was diminished, it is notable because his limited responsibilities forced him to recognize himself as a dancer rather than as a comedian. Bolger said of his skill at the time, "Once in a while maybe [I did] a dance, but not many dances because I didn't have the ability to, I didn't have that variety. Everything I had to do in dancing was not anything that had any form.... They were just natural movements I created with my body and with my feet, and with my taps."[15] Bolger was using the elements of dance he had picked up in his youth to develop his own style of physical comedy.

In *The Merry World*, Bolger played a popular stock character of the day: the collegian with baggy pinstripe pants, a beanie, and an urge to chant fight songs. His work in *The Merry World* earned him his first recognition as a dancer by a major New York critic. John Anderson of the *New York Post* wrote:

> A young suit of clothes came out and blew about the stage in the oddest and most uninhabited [*sic*] manner. It was listed in the program as Ray Bolger, but it was impossible to believe that it was occupied and propelled by the usual machinery. Either there is no Mr. Bolger or people have been getting up a lot of hokum about bones being fragile.[16]

Despite the notice, Bolger's standing with the Shuberts did not change, and he disliked dancing "behind the chorus girls." He felt that he should have more prominent placing if his career were to advance.[17] In September 1926, Bolger knew he was due for a raise according to the terms of his Shubert contract, which would increase his salary to $200 per week on October 2. He suspected that they would terminate his contract rather than put him in more prominent roles or give him more money to do the same low-status work. Bolger was ready to move on, and so at the end of September, he went to the Shuberts to request his leave, and they agreed.

In the meantime, vaudeville mogul Gus Edwards picked up Bolger. Working closely with his wife, Lillian, Edwards turned his companies into family affairs. In this warm environment Edwards incubated Walter Winchell, George Jessel, Eddie Cantor, the Marx Brothers, and Eleanor Powell.

On October 11, 1926, at the Piccadilly Hotel, only a block away from the stage where Bolger had made his Broadway debut in *The Merry World*, he and Edwards signed a contract. The terms were similar to the Shubert agreement: Bolger was guaranteed $175 per week for ten consecutive weeks out of twelve. After the ten-week option expired, Bolger would receive a raise to $200 per week.

While the terms of the contract may have been similar to that of the Shuberts, the experience of being part of the Gus Edwards company was completely different. The master traveled with his troupe. He remained close to his talent and offered them coaching and affection. Instead of being a background dancer for a Broadway show, Bolger shared top billing in *Ritz Carlton Nights* with the Lane Sisters, Leota and Lola, harmony singers from Des Moines, as they toured theaters across the country. Because he produced his shows on a more economical scale than Shubert, Edwards did not gut his productions and re-fill them with cheaper talent. He specialized in recruiting youngsters of promise and promoting them with pride. He dubbed the *Ritz Carlton Nights* Company "the Gus Edwards Class of 1926."

Whereas the Shuberts earned the reputation as being hard men of business, most theater owners felt great warmth for Edwards, who had built his brand on courtesy and fairness. The company enjoyed the cordiality of managers and bookers for most of the major circuits: the show transferred among theaters that were part of the Loew's, Keith-Albee, and Orpheum circuits.

Bolger found in Edwards a father figure, although his real father was also traveling with him: James wanted to get in on the action, too. Once again, he stepped in as his son's press and advance man. Edwards did not have the senior Bolger under a contract or agreement, which suggests that the father's travel and boarding expenses came from his son's pay. In return for his keep during the Edwards tour, James kept a fat scrapbook full of his son's reviews, candid snapshots, and letters. The clippings, though disorganized, trace the *Ritz Carlton Nights* route for the duration of the tour. The earliest entries date to November 1926, when the company was in St. Louis, playing a week and a half on Loew's time.[18] They headed back east, via Pittsburgh. For the week of Christmas, the troupe appeared at the Palace in Washington, DC. The reviewer of Bolger's debut in the nation's capital noted that Edwards's gang had lost their luggage somewhere on the way down south, but, in the true spirit of vaudeville, they played the first matinee in their street clothes. Bolger received kudos for being "a 'nut' comedian with the emphasis on 'nut.' He's an animated cubist—or futurist—model."[19]

The show stopped in forty different cities over the course of two years and made many repeat engagements. The working arrangements Bolger enjoyed on the *Ritz Carlton Nights* were some of the plushest of the time. Many vaudevillians scrambled to fill their weeks with the longest gigs possible. They often settled for one-day appearances (acts could be booked to perform three shows on Sunday), and then needed to move on to a new theater for Monday. Half-weeks were a welcomed convenience. Even when they secured bookings, performers still worried over travel. Making complicated jumps between cities ate away at time and money, but often they were necessary.

The cast of Gus Edwards's *Ritz Carlton Nights* in St. Louis, 1926. Bolger, *upper right* with guitar, played a cheeky waiter. UCLA Library Special Collections, Charles E. Young Research Library.

By contrast, *Ritz Carlton Nights* was booked for a minimum of one week in almost every city visited. Often, it was held over an extra week due to demand. The company made reasonable journeys (the most difficult jump was between Cleveland and Tulsa). The core cast stayed with the show for its entire two-year run, a testament to the prestige and pleasure an Edwards show gave its participants. *Ritz Carlton Nights* featured a wide variety of vaudeville acts—everything from blackbottom dancers to "rag artists," who formed intricate images on stage out of strips of cloth. In an attempt at cohesion, the acts were set in the famous Ritz Carlton night-club, and Edwards oversaw the proceedings playing himself. He opened the show singing his hit, "I'm the Knight of the Night Club Now," which reminded the audience of the stars he had already made, and then introduced his Class of 1926. Bolger acted as his sidekick, a quick-witted waiter whose legs were as limber as his tongue. The reviewer in New Haven said, "Bolger's comedy art is not so much his dancing as it is his cleverly humorous clowning. He gets to one's risibles long before he dances a step."[20] Reviewers all across the country singled out Bolger for praise. The differences of tastes in different states and regions gave him the opportunity to experiment with jokes and timing. What went over well in a Saturday performance in Chicago would not be the same as what the Monday crowd in

Gary, Indiana, cared about. By the time the tour reached California, Bolger was a seasoned performer. But in 1926, being a seasoned vaudevillian was as promising as being a horse-and-buggy driver. *Variety* proclaimed that

> 1926 has been the toboggan for Vaudeville. Its slide has been swift and almost clean....East or west, wherever vaudeville encountered pictures, vaudeville has been rerouted...."The world is mine," said the Count of Monte Cristo, probably with his eyes shut. It's the same [thing] the monopolistic, big time vaudeville managers said as they gazed upon their office staff, neglecting to look out of the windows.[21]

And beyond the windows of the theaters where *Ritz Carlton Nights* played stood the movie theaters.

Edwards did not seem to notice them. He was called the "Star Maker" after all, not the "Trend Setter." He kept his eyes on the development of his talented protégé, the emerging star of the revue. In an interview when the company arrived at San Francisco's Golden Theater in June 1927, Edwards said of Bolger, "He is developing splendidly; adds something new all the time to the act and grows as a dancer."[22] When *Ritz Carlton Nights* moved down to Martin Beck's Los Angeles Orpheum Theater, Bolger also earned the praise of a smitten young lady.

In the heart of downtown near Pershing Square, the Los Angeles Orpheum beckoned full-fledged Hollywood stars to see each other and the new vaudeville show every Sunday night. The average Angelinos came as much to see the audience as to see the performers. The star-struck patrons had another reason to visit the Orpheum: Edwards tried to recruit new, undiscovered talent, by advertising in local newspapers, inviting hopefuls to interview backstage before and after performances. A pert teenager, Gwendolyn Rickard, brought along a friend to catch Edwards's show one afternoon. She also wanted to peddle songs she had written for piano and voice to Edwards. Her stylish bob haircut, skinny figure, and big, almond eyes made her a dead ringer for Adele Astaire, Fred Astaire's older sister and dance partner who had been voted by *Dance* magazine as the nation's favorite female eccentric dancer of 1924; the Astaires' smash hit on Broadway that year, *Lady, Be Good!*, began their apotheosis as American icons. Gwen felt she could become a star if only she were to be discovered. That afternoon, it was she who made an important discovery: she saw the lanky hoofer billed as Ray Bolger for the first time. After his number, she turned to her friend to express her attraction to him. She then went backstage to look for Edwards but discovered that he had left the theater; instead she found Bolger lingering. Rickard never sold a tune to Edwards, but she asked the dancer out. He accepted.

During the week they shared in Los Angeles, Bolger learned a lot about Rickard. Like Ruth Fleischer, Bolger's only other known girlfriend, Rickard had a reputation for being a free spirit. She came from a well-off family, but she had dreams and ideas and ambitions and she tormented her aggrieved parents with them. She loved learning to read and play music and singing, and she wanted to break into Hollywood. Rickard was drawn to Bolger's horse-like features, which could be both funny and touching. Perhaps what impressed her most was the realization that Bolger had come so far on so few resources.

Their separation when the Edwards show left Los Angeles was bitter-sweet: bitter because Bolger and Rickard made no definitive plans to stay in touch and sweet because Martin Beck liked the *Ritz Carlton Nights* and wanted to give it prominent bookings. Rickard still wanted to try to develop a career of her own, and she was not prepared to give up that chance to follow Bolger's growing career. At that moment, a big opportunity tantalized Bolger. *Ritz Carlton Nights* would continue to play Orpheum theaters on its way back East, including the second-most important vaudeville theater in the second-most important vaudeville city: the Chicago Palace. If all went well, the show would arrive back in Manhattan and be received at the most important vaudeville theater of them all: the New York Palace.

New York City's Palace Theatre stood at Broadway and Forty-Seventh Street. Of the approximately fifty thousand troupers roaming the country in any given year between 1914 and the early 1930s, the Palace booked only 438 performers. No one who wasn't appearing at the Palace dared to set spat or peep-toe heel on the stretch of sidewalk that ran from the Palace's entrance on Broadway to the corner of 47th Street, nicknamed "The Beach." With their lapels and noses turned up as they strutted back and forth, the Palace players were the proudest people in the world, and rightly so. They could be heard congratulating themselves and drumming up publicity for their acts. These vaudevillians had risen to the top, not by chance but by force, and the crazy stunts and personae that earned them so much acclaim onstage were not far removed from the people they were after the curtain fell.

Of the Palace, Bolger said, "The theater itself had charisma. Whether seated in the audience or appearing on the stage, one could sense that there was about to be a 'happening' and more than likely it would happen."[23] Though *Ritz Carlton Nights* was his first time at the Palace as a performer, he was well acquainted with the theater from the other side of the footlights. Theater professionals in New York made up most of the audience for Monday afternoon vaudeville shows because most of them had that day off. They were anxious to see the city's most popular performers, and their top competitors, at work.

The autographed portrait Bolger gave his future wife in the 1920s. He wrote, "Gwen, I am looking down in scorn and pity on those who do not know you. And someday I hope to know you better than I do." UCLA Library Special Collections, Charles E. Young Research Library.

After dancing on tabletops on Sunday night, Bolger went to the Palace on Mondays. It was here he saw comics like Lewis and Dody, famous for drawling, "Hello, hello, *hello!*" for their entrance and cracking corny jokes such as, "You can't swim in a pool room." His favorite comedians, though, were Duffy and Sweeney. They were "so inside, so Palace," he said, "that they died almost everywhere else and were in constant trouble with the Booking Office."[24] Bolger's favorite comic dancer was Joe Frisco. Despite winning a contest at the State Ballroom in Boston in 1922 for impersonating Frisco, Bolger did not see him perform until 1927, at the Palace. Such was the power of mimicry that Bolger learned the routine not from the star but from other amateurs who imitated him. Frisco closed his comedy act with a dance number to the "Darktown Strutters' Ball." He wore a dark suit with a white carnation on his lapel and a derby hat. While he danced, he puffed a cigar. He would take a white handkerchief from his pocket, wrap it around his hand, pull two ends up between his fingers and thumb and moving them, give the illusion of a rabbit, nibbling away at the carnation. His exit was a shuffle: with his hands in his trouser pockets, he made a train-like sound with his feet, and exhaled smoke like a locomotive. Bolger's other favorites, and influences, included the Two Black Crows, Herb Williams, Dr. Rockwell, and Willie and Eugene Howard. In 1929, after two years of touring the country in a first-rate show, Bolger and the rest of the *Ritz Carlton Nights* company were booked into the New York Palace.

Ritz Carlton Nights encountered difficulties at the Palace, though. The show had been performed as a full-length revue across the country. Now it had to be condensed to fit onto the Palace vaudeville bill, which boasted plenty of other competition. *Ritz Carlton Nights* at least had received the best slot on the bill: the sixth of seven acts. Gus Edwards's troupe beat out such known names as Fred Allen and his wife, Portland Hoffa, who performed as the "Disappointments of 1927" in the fourth slot. The couple received kudos for offering "20 minutes of...honest laughs without hokum." Fanny Brice followed Allen and Hoffa, with thirty minutes of singing, including her signature torch song, "My Man." The audience members were in their seats and well warmed up by these renowned stars before Edwards brought his kiddies onstage.

Bolger outperformed himself on the Palace boards. Again he foiled Edwards as a waiter, giving him lip, dangling a checkered tablecloth in front of him and crooning a spoof of the "Toreador Song" from *Carmen*. But *Variety* scolded the act for running too long: *Ritz Carlton Nights* took the stage at 3:45 for the afternoon show and 9:45 for the evening show, and did not get off until 5:00 and 11:00, respectively, taking up most of the time allotted for the final act.

The *Variety* reviewer noted that the show would be "a whale" if it tightened up its schedule. He added that two performers in particular, the dancing comic Ray "Rubberlegs" Bolger and the Spanish soubrette known as Signorita Armida, already earned that qualification: "These two young people added to the prestige of Edwards himself in person, working with easy smoothness, a bright production, and a talented group, make the revue one of the best in the Edwards series."[25]

This blessing was enough to ensure the company as many more weeks of work as they wanted, in any cities that they chose. Once an act had appeared at the Palace, managers booked it into their theaters sight unseen. The company spent the remainder of December 1927 and the first half of spring 1928 making an easy tour around the East. By now they were bona fide vaudeville stars, but they were starting to feel the impact that movies were making on vaudeville. Under increased pressure from movie competition, the two major vaudeville circuits—Keith-Albee in the East and the Orpheum in the West—merged to create the Keith-Albee-Orpheum

(K-A-O) Corporation in December 1927. The merger would increase the efficiency of vaudeville tours, ensuring continuous work for actors and a stream of revenue for the theaters.

In the last six months of the two-year *Ritz Carlton Nights* tour, Bolger's future and that of straight vaudeville were determined. They were not traveling on the same trajectory. *Ritz Carlton Nights* appeared not just in straight vaudeville houses but also in combination houses: an abridged version of the show played in rotation with motion picture screenings. In December 1927, Edwards brought the show to the Moss Franklin Theater in the Bronx. The entertainment reviewer for the local paper printed in large, emphatic type, "Hey Gus! Tie that fellow Bolger up tight. They'll steal him for sure. He's a STAR, Gus."[26]

As vaudeville started to disintegrate, Edwards and Bolger's relationship strengthened. In January 1928, the town of New Rochelle also got the sense of Bolger's worth to Edwards, this time on a more personal level. The reviewer who visited the show at Proctor's Theater said, "One might write a column about Ray Bolger and yet fail to say all that should be said about him. Edwards should be, and is for that matter, proud of him."[27] This was more than an attempt for publicity. The two socialized extensively outside of the theater, often joined by Edwards's wife, Lillian. In the summer of 1928, Edwards performed a kind favor for Bolger. Perhaps knowing that Bolger needed more support in his career than just his father acting as a "press and advance man," Edwards helped Bolger secure his first agent, Abe Lastfogel of the William Morris Agency. Edwards would have known that theatrical syndicates were threatening to take over all aspects of star-making and that performers increasingly needed a good agent to ensure a steady stream of work and to navigate the tricky politics of booking offices. Theater operators now had to genuflect to rich and powerful moguls when choosing acts to book into their properties; an owner's or manager's preferences and sensibilities were no longer the prime considerations in these matters. The prestige of the William Morris Agency would help get Bolger through many doors that his father could not.

Lastfogel, the son of a poor immigrant, had begun his career in the William Morris agency in 1912, when he was fourteen. He had been interested in obtaining one of two job openings: one at a tailor's shop and one at the William Morris Agency. The Morris offer was closer to home, so he decided to apply there. He got the job and spent the next couple of years placing newspaper ads and putting press releases into envelopes. Over time, he earned agent status when he received permission to bring one Ray Bolger, movie palace dancer, under contract. Bolger's agreement with the agency guaranteed him at least $495 a week for at least thirty-five weeks, more than doubling his salary.

Edwards had another reason beyond his fondness for being generous to Bolger: he announced to the press that *Ritz Carlton Nights* would be the last show he staged and toured. *Ritz Carlton Nights* would resume only for August. Lastfogel's contract with Bolger officially began on September 1.

Following the final engagements of *Ritz Carlton Nights*, Bolger appeared almost exclusively in combination houses, dancing between film showings. While "flat actors" (screen actors) and "round actors" (stage actors) shared the public's attention, the vaudeville and picture corporations were also strengthening their ties to each other.

Marcus Loew, creator of the Loew's theater circuit, had been the first to realize that the popular entertainment medium was shifting: motion pictures had to be incorporated into vaudeville. Eventually, film would supplant live action in the theaters. Since 1905, he had shown one-reelers at the theaters in his People's Vaudeville Company circuit, but by 1920 this was no longer enough. First, he purchased the Metro Pictures Corporation. Then, in 1924, he bought controlling interest in Goldwyn Pictures, taking the helm from Lee Shubert. Loew was more interested in managing his theaters in New York than in heading the film operations in Hollywood. For his master stroke, Loew chose a film producer of promise, Louis B. Mayer, and Mayer's chief of production, Irving Thalberg, to manage the newly formed Metro-Goldwyn-Mayer pictures in 1924. Loew now had a continuous flow of first-run motion pictures to screen in his theaters.[28]

Bolger wrote of his time working in the movie houses, "The defections to the new media were wholesale, who could refuse. [I] was offered three times the money I earned in vaudeville to play there. So [I] defected along with a great number of others who went over to the Paramounts, the Capitols, the Roxys, the picture houses."[29] The pay was excellent—"My salary jumped from 250 to 750 to 900 to 1100 before I could remember my middle name," he said—but gone were the comforts of tours that Gus Edwards put on.[30] Bolger frequently played two to three cities a week, making seven appearances per day. He sped around the country in a blur and made a great deal of money while doing so. Bolger also worked his way back to Los Angeles. He reunited with Gwen Rickard and took the time to get to know her. Gwen was the oldest child of intellectually gifted parents—a federal government official and a devoted theosophist—which, gave her insights that Bolger lacked into how the world worked. Her contributions and accomplishments are still extraordinary when one considers that she was born into a world where

American women could not even vote. She bravely forged for herself a life and a tenacious philosophy of success uncommon in her social class.

Rickard was born on October 7, 1909, in Nickwall, Montana, to Harold Edward Rickard, a commissioner for the Bureau of Indian Affairs, and his wife, the former Edna Nelson. They had four children: Gwen, the eldest and only daughter, and three sons—James, William, and Robert. Despite their wealth, the Rickards lived humbly in Poplar, partly because of a keen sense of frugality exercised by Harold and also because the untamed Montana of the early twentieth century afforded few luxuries; Gwen slept in the family's living room for most of her young life. She helped her mother, who felt overwhelmed by the isolation of Montana, raise the other children. Life in the Montana wilderness eroded her mother's composure, although it seemed to suit Harold. He was elected to the Montana House of Representatives in 1921. They remained in the state, but when Gwen was fourteen, the family packed up and moved to Los Angeles. Gwen enrolled in the junior class of Fairfax High School. She began exploring the new kind of wilderness that Los Angeles offered: show business. "I was a crazy kid in those days. And like all crazy kids in Hollywood, my Big Idea was to go in pictures," Gwen wrote in her journal. "The best formula for discovery was to get around and meet a lot of people, important people."[31] Cracking into adult social circles was very easy for Gwen, with her confidence and her interest in intellectual subjects. It also helped that she was an accomplished singer and piano player: the ability to perform well earned a girl many invitations to parties. But even though Gwen was a sought-after party guest, her parents were wary of her companions. As Gwen explained it:

> I had a heck of a time convincing my parents that these [parties] were important to my career. My father was particularly difficult. He could not see why a fifteen-year-old schoolgirl should be permitted to go out with a lot of Hollywood people who drank liquor and carried on. But every time my tearful pleading and the burden of blighting my life got to be too much for him and he gave in and out I would go to seize my golden opportunity.[32]

Even as a fifteen-year-old, Gwen assimilated well into a circle of writers, artists, and intellectuals. Men flocked to her. She kept a scrapbook full of calling cards, postcards, and letters they showered her with as tangible reminders of her progress in building her own career: pages of well-wishes from gentlemen precede newspaper clippings for Gwen's appearances on Warner Brothers' Motion Picture Radio Station KFWB, launched in March 1925; she appeared frequently to sing the blues. Gwen hoped that her involvement in the Warner Brothers' radio shows would eventually get her in front of a camera. In the meantime, she was enjoying the life of a smart, vivacious young woman in a period when ideas about femininity were rapidly changing. Embodying the true flapper ideals, she pushed back on her parents' rules and considered herself the intellectual equal of men.

After graduating from Fairfax she enrolled for a time in the University of Southern California, then located on a twenty-five-acre campus on Vermont Avenue. She found the Hollywood nightlife surrounding her more enticing than her journalism courses. She and her friends would gather for literary discussions, and, once her "intellectual poise wore thin," they would pick a friend's home to nestle in dimly lit rooms, perform dramatic readings, and listen to records like those of Italian tenor Tito Schipa. At such a gathering in 1926 she met Gladys Dubois, a stylish blonde with green eyes, who was reciting Kipling's "The Bastard King of England." Gladys, like Gwen, came from a good family, but unlike Gwen she was as vulnerable as she was beautiful. The two forged a friendship, but Gladys's alcoholism and anorexia forced Gwen to look at the people around her and to consider the impact this scene had on her own life. She decided to focus on her already burgeoning career as a musician rather than pursue movie stardom, which seemed like a hollow dream too easily filled with degeneracy. From this time forward, Gwen found talent and discipline more appealing than Hollywood flimflam.

Once Ray mentioned the idea of their marrying, though, they had a frank conversation about their ambitions. Once a vaudevillian got married, the tradition was to make room for his wife in the act, but Gwen did not think this was the right path for them; their talents were too different. Since they first met, she had reconsidered her ambitions: she was willing to give up her hopes of becoming a star in her own right, however, to support Bolger. And so, when the Irish Catholic eccentric dancer headed back East, the blue-blooded Episcopalian heiress went to Manhattan with him.

On July 3, Bolger and Rickard boarded a train for Saranac Lake, New York. The agent William Morris annually brought his talent to the village, called the Capital of the Adirondacks, to perform a variety show for the benefit of the Saranac Lake Day Nursery, his wife's pet philanthropic project. On board were lyricist and screenwriter Irving Caesar, eccentric tap dancer Harland Dixon, and the comedians Pat Rooney and Pat Rooney Jr.

Back at the William Morris Agency office at 1550 Broadway, a telegram arrived for Bolger and Rickard. Mr. and Mrs. Harold Rickard offered the following message to the couple: "Hope our approval will give to both of you exquisite happiness and much success throughout the years ahead of you. Bon voyage and heaps of love to Gwen from her dad and mother."[33] After their performance at the Pontiac Theater on the Fourth of July, Gwen and Ray went to the shores of Saranac Lake. There is no record that

A sweetheart photo of the young couple. UCLA Library Special Collections, Charles E. Young Research Library.

James Bolger approved of the marriage or attended the ceremony. Gwen was not Catholic and had no plans of converting. But she married Ray on July 9, 1929, in a civil ceremony in Port Chester, New York, on the way back to Manhattan; he slipped on her size-four finger a simple gold band adorned with a tiny diamond. Abe Lastfogel was one of the witnesses.

The Bolgers went off to Europe for a working honeymoon. Thanks to Lastfogel's connections, Bolger was invited to appear in London. The newlyweds had little time to make domestic arrangements before leaving, but the current events of the day concerned Gwen. She recalled decades later:

> I timidly ventured to my young spouse that something was wrong with the stock market—that stocks couldn't continue to go up 10 points every day, that someday they would reach a peak and start down—so, please, sell yours before we go to Europe—he laughed and patted me condescendingly on the head and said, "My darling, if you were a man of the world and had to choose between the advice of your new young bride, and that of Charles Schwab, what would you do?" I wasn't a man of the world but I got the idea.[34]

The newlyweds departed on the SS *Paris*, the grandest Art Nouveau liner of its time. Gwen at least sensed that the America they would return to would be far different from the one they had left behind, that the note of "rampant optimism"[35] on which they had married would soon die.

CHAPTER 3
Steppin' in Society

U nlike his wife, Bolger could not bring himself to worry about much. A *lune de miel* shimmered not only over his marriage but also, seemingly, over his career and future prospects.

Once the SS *Paris* pulled out of port on July 19, 1929, the trade papers announced Bolger's performance schedule abroad and his attachment to a new, legitimate musical back in the United States that would go into rehearsal in the fall. With the decline of vaudeville, the aspiration of every ambitious musical comedy performer now was to perform in a "show with a book." Even Broadway revues were a step below book musicals. Because so much of Bolger's comic dancing—and, indeed, all eccentric dancing—was character-based, he could survive in the theatrical realm if he found opportunities to prove he could develop and perform rich characters in a full-length musical production.

Abe Lastfogel and the William Morris Agency secured for Bolger the second-comic role in the first Alex A. Aarons and Vinton Freedley musical of the 1929–30 season, *Me for You*. Aarons and Freedley, as they were known, had made their mark as Broadway producers through a string of very successful musicals starring Fred Astaire and his sister, Adele. The Bolgers hoped the role would likewise establish Ray as a true Broadway dancer. Aarons in particular also understood music. He helped George Gershwin and Vincent Youmans establish themselves with his productions. As a pianist and songwriter herself, Gwen must have appreciated the caliber of Aarons and Freedley productions and anticipated the opportunity to be associated with them.

But the couple was also happy to immerse themselves in their travels. On board the SS *Paris*, the Bolgers became close with fellow passenger Leon

The Bolgers on board the SS. *Paris* for their honeymoon. UCLA Library Special Collections, Charles E. Young Research Library.

Leonidoff, a prominent choreographer and producer of Roxy Rothafel's lavish stage pageants. Bolger had been acquainted with his work at the Rialto. Leonidoff and his wife, Maddy, were taking a working tour of Europe. Rothafel's production assistant wanted to meet with European entertainment producers to exchange notes on popular trends and get new ideas. The Bolgers debarked at Le Havre and continued on to Paris, arriving at the Hotel Stevens on July 24. After a couple of weeks of relaxation, they proceeded to London. Although alcoholic drinks had to be off their tables by midnight, London nightclubs offered a rich society life that could not be replicated in the United States during Prohibition. The Brits welcomed an influx of their thirsty American cousins in the summer months, and they enjoyed the entertainers who followed them. Bolger's act was new to them, but his style resonated with the British, who were no strangers to pantomime or dry humor. His routine by this point combined great physicality—athleticism and flexibility—with intellectual humor by way of satire. He often began routines with his lyrical soft-shoe, covering the floor with beautiful and precise taps, establishing himself as a very talented dancer. The taps that Bolger used on his shoes at this time were not metal; instead, he had a thin piece of maple wood hand-sewn to the shoe's upper. He believed that he could use the wooden taps to make distinct sounds with his toe, heel, half-sole, ball of foot, and whole foot, and that "a tap dancer who is any good eventually learns to orchestrate these sounds as his feet twitch."[1] Bolger, of course, considered himself a good dancer.

Once he had won the audience's respect, he went for their hearts. He introduced comedy into the routine. He would tap in circles, and after three or four laps around the stage, intimate with his sad eyes, long face, and a shrug that he could not get his feet to stop moving. The comedic aspect of the dance was the climax. He incorporated eccentric, aerial steps into the routine for excitement. He kicked his heels over his head. He mimed a stock character or a current celebrity. Imitating the Wright Brothers in flight, he touched the soles of his feet together while jumping five feet in the air and pretending to steer his aircraft. Other characters in his repertoire included a cowboy riding his pretend horse, a boxer being pummeled by an invisible sparring mate, and an adagio dancer who performed, either whimsically or poignantly, with an imaginary partner.

A number of his steps also brought him low. In his daily rehearsals, Bolger performed a corrective exercise for his hamstrings in which he sank into a full split and, by degrees, pulled himself back up using just his gluteal muscles. He found the comic potential in this sight gag and made it a staple of his routine, an extension of the hapless sadsack without control of his motor skills. He swept gracefully into the split and, with a jubilant glow, attempt to charge back up to standing, only to fall nearly to the floor again. After going through several more rising-and-falling cycles, wearing an expression that conveyed, "I think I can, I think I can!" Bolger at last returned to his feet, and skittered back into his routine.

His finale was often a variation of the *pas de chat*, a catlike leap the ballet dancer uses to travel from one foot to the other. He had been practicing this move since he was a teenager in Boston dancing with Senia Rusakoff. Bolger floated across the stage and behind the curtain. After a full twenty-minute routine, he would not be out of breath for more than thirty seconds.[2]

Looked at individually, the elements of a Bolger dance do not appear remarkable. Like so many performers who came out of vaudeville, Bolger's success depended on the cocktail he alone could shake up and serve. He offered up just the right amounts of a very deep, but not broad, technical talent (his Irish tap dancing); topical material (his impersonations); an electrifying personality; a unique and impressive physicality (his flexibility, his endurance); and a self-deprecating persona that his audiences found endearing, rather than threatening. While other eccentric dancers could also jump high and perform funny splits, they were not as successful as Bolger at creating a character for themselves that audiences would remember and love. Offstage at the clubs, people passing the Bolgers on the streets would stop and curtsy. The couple didn't understand why. Confused, they would reciprocate and chock it up to formal pleasantries. Perhaps, they thought, those genuflecters had caught his act. In reality, Bolger was being mistaken for Albert, Duke of York. Through the work, the newlyweds met and befriended several Brits, including Evelyn Waugh, before returning to New York in August for the rehearsals of *Me for You.*

A hot and glittering confluence, Manhattan absorbed America's great talents on their way in and out to new enterprises. Bolger was not the only dancer returning to the city from London that summer. On August 15, Fred and Adele Astaire arrived after completing the West End run of their Broadway hit, *Funny Face.* Like all goodbyes bade on Broadway in those days, theirs had only been temporary. The West End and Hollywood offered Broadway's stars loads of money and glamorous vacations, but even these riches could not compensate for the creative and collaborative possibilities that magnetized New York.

Great music, and the musicians who created it, energized talent in all of the performing arts. The adjoining penthouses of George and Ira Gershwin on Riverside Drive hosted dozens of people each weekend. Moss Hart, Oscar Levant, and Harpo Marx riffed off each other's talents in the living room. There seemed no better place on Earth to get exposure for young musical talent. In August 1929, Midtown lacked its modern skyline—the first major skyscraper there, the Chrysler building, was still under wraps. It was the theaters, and the bright new lyricists, composers, producers, and performers who cycled through them, leaving a lilting memory of themselves on the stage and in the atmosphere, that brought the swarms to Broadway.

Established institutions dominated the legitimate stage: men like George White, Florenz Ziegfeld Jr., the Shubert Brothers, and Max Gordon; and songwriters including Buddy DeSylva, Ray Henderson, Lew Brown, Arthur Schwartz, and Howard Dietz. But New York talent in the summer of 1929, like illicit champagne and loose cash, was in abundance. Throughout the ornate theaters and under the banners of these men of the establishment, new talent emerged, converged, and dispersed, always with the goal of creating the next big sensation, always experimenting with new ideas and talents, and always unsure of just what combination would work. The right moment, the right music, the right cast, and the right storyline aligned could make a hit, like Aarons and Freedley's *Hold Everything.* The show ran for 404 performances between October 1928 and October 1929, with a cast including a very popular and handsome romantic lead, Jack Whiting, and a new Broadway comedian who had come up through the Burlesque circuits, Bert Lahr, who earned star status with his role.

With *Me for You*, Aarons and Freedley recruited newcomers who, like Lahr, had the potential to become stars. In addition to Bolger, they brought in an up-and-coming music-and-lyrics team: Richard Rodgers and Lorenz Hart. To anchor the cast, Aarons and Freedley brought in Victor Moore. He had won acclaim in their 1927 musical, *Oh, Kay!*, playing opposite Gertrude Lawrence. In *Me for You*, the doughy and lovable Moore was to play a well-to-do cad who smuggled booze. Betty Starbuck played his daughter, who was dating a district attorney, to the dismay of her father. He wanted her to fall for his boozy buddy, played by Aarons and Freedley's choice romantic lead, Whiting. With this snoozer of a storyline, the show opened on September 10, 1929, at the Detroit Opera House, a Shubert theater.

As Rodgers recalled, the book was not strong enough to excite an audience.[3] The show died in Detroit. Aarons and Freedley, however, were not ready to give up on having a show to put in the Alvin Theatre on Broadway that season, as they had already booked the Alvin for *Me for You*. They agreed that the score and the cast were solid enough. Everyone returned to New York and went on hiatus while two hit script writers, Paul Gerard Smith and Jack McGowan, rewrote the book. During the first week of October, while the show was being reworked, Bolger returned to the Capitol Theater. He received top billing for his live performance but was dwarfed by the film, *His Glorious Night*, which shared the bill. This was the first sound picture for John Gilbert; it also featured Hedda Hopper. Increasingly, films were being used to draw audiences to live performances, instead of the other way around. The public was growing tired of seeing vaudeville acts at the movie theaters. A review of a Bolger appearance later that year summed it up by saying, "Bolger, 'in one' for a scene change, tells a few gags and goes into a gag dance."[4]

By October 12, Aarons and Freedley called back the *Me for You* company to resume rehearsals on the rewritten show: *Heads Up!* Most of the *Me for You* cast was retained. The story now took place on a yacht which, unbeknownst to its upper-crust owners, is being used to smuggle booze. Moore played the unassuming chef onboard. Jack Whiting, whose character was refashioned into a Coast Guard officer, was still the male romantic lead. The role of his love interest, though, switched from Betty Starbuck to Barbara Newberry. Bolger kept the minor role of Georgie. For Bolger, being in a lackluster Aarons and Freedley show was more prestigious than being part of a good performance at a movie house. *Heads Up!* offered him little chance to establish himself on the legitimate stage, though. Because Moore levied his star power, Bolger's minor role became more so in rehearsal. Moore, who had a reputation for being a show-stealer, grew suspicious of the laughs that the skinny new comedian got. He pressured the scriptwriters and producers into whittling away Bolger's part. In the end, Bolger felt he was only feeding the star. On the final day before the opening of Philadelphia tryouts, October 24, 1929, the situation worsened. As Rodgers recalled, "Alex Aarons came charging down the aisle of the Shubert Theater with staggering news: 'Boys, you can forget about the show. You can forget about everything. The bottom's just dropped out of the market!'"[5]

On October 30, 1929, *Variety* ran its most famous headline ever: "Wall Street Lays an Egg." The trade paper reported that twenty-two million people owned stock in the market at the time of the crash. The devastation hit the marginal traders the worst, and there were many in Manhattan. Some of these men had invested their entire life's savings only to realize they had been tempted to destruction by ever-growing dividends. Rodgers recalled that before the crash, even the elevator operators talked about making a grand in the market overnight.[6] Broadway suffered right along with its financial angels. *Variety* insisted that stories of show business investors losing upward of $300,000 (more than $4 million in 2018 dollars) was "not hearsay."[7] Most New Yorkers had no idea what really happened to their money; even bankers could not explain it well. The dropping of the market to "unthinkable depths" was a story that "probably never will be told."[8] The only explanation was that $30 million had simply vanished. It was clear enough that the rampant borrowing and speculation of the twenties had reached its end.

The frenzied mergers and acquisitions characterizing the entertainment industry of the late twenties deserved some of the blame for what happened. As theater chains reorganized and media companies turned into conglomerates, investors rushed to acquire stock in the new, glamorous enterprises. Two weeks before the market crashed, several show people bought five-thousand-share lots of Radio-Keith-Orpheum (RKO) stock and paid between $34 and $36 per share. After the crash, it was valued at $20 per share. Insiders had similarly bought up stock in Paramount in anticipation of a merger with Warner Brothers. They, too, were devastated.[9] Powerful financiers and even the Federal Reserve Bank were blamed for the pooling going on in all industries, but there were no reparations.

The corporatization of show business perhaps contributed to the crash, but even after 1929, there would be no return to the way things were before. Vaudeville imploded. With the onset of the Depression, the theater chains were forced to streamline. People felt the ramifications instantly.

No one had any cash. Luxuries large and small were returned or forsaken. No one in the *Heads Up!* company thought opening on Broadway would be viable now that the public had gone broke. Some of the production members, like Rodgers and Hart, survived Black Tuesday with minimal damage. They had not been investors. Aarons and Freedley were affected, but they said little about their losses. Casualties were sporadic; this was as true of the people as of particular shows on the boards at the time. As Gwen remembered it, "We returned from London just in time to see speculators falling from windows like ticker-tape in a parade."[10]

Heads Up! moved forward: Philadelphia attendance was good enough to warrant opening in New York on November 11, 1929. *Variety* called the show "a pleasing musical amusement. Perhaps it will not rate with the actual leaders in its field, but it is tastefully and colorfully presented."[11] Of the all-but-forgotten second comic, *Variety* said, "It's Ray Bolger whose eccentric stepping had him back for several bows. Did the same thing later.... Bolger certainly tickled the first nighters."[12] Apparently, the reporter for the *New York Times* was not so impressed, as he never mentioned Bolger beyond the cast list in his review.[13]

Although not feted, Bolger was at least employed, earning several thousand dollars per week at a time when even dimes had gone scarce. How long the show would last remained an unanswered question. Even with rewriting, the book for *Heads Up!* was flimsy. Charles Moran, reviewing the show for the *Billboard*, wrote, "Generally, this pretty good show manages to hold the interest, but this is not due to the music or the book."[14] While the storyline, the performances, and many of the actors of the show have been forgotten, it remains in memory today for introducing "A Ship without a Sail" to New York audiences. The *Times*'s Broadway gossip column for November 17, a week after opening, noted that "the most promising entertainment of the preceding week, according to the ticket men, is 'Heads Up!' Nothing sensational, you understand, but pretty good."[15] *Heads Up!* ran for 144 performances and closed on March 15, 1930. When the cast and crew disbanded, no one except for Moore seemed to benefit much from the show. But behind the scenes, Bolger earned "his first champion," Lorenz Hart, who promised that some day, he and Rodgers would write a musical show just for Bolger.[16]

In the meantime, the young hoofer returned to the movie house grind. In 1925, the vaudeville circuits operated fifteen hundred theaters. By the time *Heads Up!* closed, about three hundred remained. The only theater in Times Square that played vaudeville was the Palace. The rest had converted into movie theaters equipped with sound.

Although Gwen's recollections of their married life before the crash confirm that at least some of Bolger's money was tied up in the stock market, it remains unclear how much he, or the wealthy Rickard family, lost. The Rickards favored investing in industry and manufacturing, as well as food production. These areas survived October 1929 and would have provided security to the family. It is also unclear if James Bolger was impacted by the stock market crash, but he did relocate to Florida at this time. However, the Bolgers seemed to be on their own financially, adding to the difficulties of their first years of married life. Gwen traveled with Ray, finding inexpensive furnished rooms with kitchen privileges that they could rent. She would cook their meals to allow them to save some money, which became difficult for overworked performers on the road without the help of a supportive spouse. Every cent mattered to them as they tried to make their way through the tough economic times. There was less work for live performers, and the Bolgers tried to squeeze the most out of the opportunities still available to them.

Across the country, vaudeville houses were disappearing. The Orpheum Theatre in Los Angeles, where Gwen and Ray had met, had changed locations since their union. On Christmas Day 1929, this final home of straight vaudeville in Los Angeles became a movie theater.[17] The more films a house screened, the less overhead it contended with. Popular audiences were willing to substitute the new novelty, sound pictures, for the old tradition, live entertainment. Movies were cheaper than vaudeville. The legitimate stage on Broadway also suffered, but to a lesser extent. Broadway's top entertainers, like Bert Lahr, never felt the impact of the Depression: the best comedians could still command $5,000 a week during the nation's bleakest period.[18] The public found some solace in escapism, and audiences still had an appetite for humor and glitz.

Bolger found steady work exhibiting his comic dance in the "Blue Mill" and "Romantic Knights," unit shows designed to be performed in conjunction with film screenings, that toured the Paramount-Publix movie houses in the Northeast and the Midwest. A representative example of Bolger's style of joking in these performances was for Bolger to ask the actress he appeared with, "Darling, why do you always dress in half-mourning?" to which the actress responded, "Because you always complain of being half-dead at night."[19] When the travel got to be too strenuous, Gwen returned to the Rickard homestead in Los Angeles, joining Bolger for select engagements on the road. The Rickards, however, never criticized their dancing son-in-law for his profession, and Gwen managed to set aside loneliness and yearning in order to work toward making a better future. She gained admission into important clubs and hotel restaurants throughout Los

Angeles and met as many influential people in show business as she could. While she remained logically cool in her day-to-day affairs, her despondence at being separated from her husband colored the letters she sent to him as he traveled.

Gwen's creative spirit was not totally satisfied by shaping her husband's career; she held on to a few artistic ambitions of her own. She reported to Ray that the historian William "Mort" Thompson had given her writing lessons. He insisted she could produce a novel in six months, but she dismissed the project. Gwen even performed onstage with her husband once, singing as part of his vaudeville act in New York. But ultimately, they stuck to their decision that the best chance a Bolger had for success was for one to be a star and one to be a supporter: Ray would perform, and Gwen would continue to do everything she could offstage and behind the stage to prepare him for success. Despite her occasional restlessness, Gwen truly believed Bolger could become a legitimate star. She wanted to elevate him out of the movie chain circuit. She believed that his stage persona and mannerisms, particularly his style of dress, were holding him back. To exaggerate his comic movement in front of the movie house audiences, he depended on his clothing: a "disreputable" brown felt hat, a tight vest, and baggy pants. Gwen recalled, "He argued that he had to dress as he did in order to get laughs, but one night in the second year of our marriage, at a theater in New Haven, Connecticut, he agreed to try out my idea."[20] Bolger went on, instead, in dress clothes: a white suit with pleated pants and a double-breasted jacket. He slicked his hair close to his scalp. And Gwen was entirely correct: his new image earned him the attention of Broadway producers.

The importance of Gwen's entering Ray's life cannot be overstated. She was a surprising choice for his bride, but their union was the prime reason that Bolger became a star. He had talent, dedication, and an astonishing work ethic, and these alone would have earned him a decade or so of touring around movie houses. Gwen, however, provided him with strategy and savvy. She persuaded him that his talents alone would not take him to the top: he also had to acquire business sensibilities or allow her to steer his career. She wanted to reinvent Bolger's act altogether. With few exceptions, she would always watch from the wings and her husband would remain in the spotlight on his own. But she felt he could transcend the boundary from vaudeville into musical comedy permanently. They both sensed the final decline of vaudeville. The options were Hollywood or Broadway, and Broadway seemed the better bet for a very spontaneous dancer.

Between Gwen's efforts and Lastfogel's connections, and Ray's own good reviews on the Paramount tour, the comic dancer earned an audition for the impresario George White, who produced an annual revue under the banner *George White's Scandals* every fall in Atlantic City before transplanting it to Broadway. The popularity of the musical revue had hit its climax in the 1910s and 1920s and had begun its decline. In the early thirties, the revues of repute remained Florenz Ziegfeld Jr.'s annual *Ziegfeld Follies* and George White's *Scandals*. They appealed to two different sets of people through two different operating methods. Ziegfeld's shows were classified by their extravagance—ornate costumes worth thousands of dollars, plush sets, lots of peachy skin, and plenty of sparkle. Bolger noted that George White could not—and did not—try to compete with Ziegfeld on aesthetics (although he had his own gaggle of beautiful girls). As Bolger reminisced, "The difference between Ziegfeld and White, I should think, was about a couple of hundred thousand dollars."[21] Nonetheless, Bolger accepted a role in *George White's Scandals of 1931* as a ticket back to Broadway via Atlantic City.

White assembled a bouquet of celebrities, including popular crooner Rudy Vallee, who had never appeared on Broadway before; Everett Marshall, a baritone vocalist with the Metropolitan Opera, was also making his debut; and Ethel Barrymore Colt, the ninth-generation representative of the Barrymore dynasty, who had not appeared in a musical before. Another greenhorn, Barbara Blair, was brought on for a comedy sketch with Bolger. Three late imports from Aarons and Freedley's 1930 hit *Girl Crazy* were acquired after the show finished 272 performances at the Alvin. This trio gave the bill the gravitas it needed: Willie and Eugene Howard, the celebrated comedians, and a rising starlet, Ethel Merman.

To tie together the personalities and talents in his shows, White had long employed the musical services of Buddy DeSylva, Lew Brown, and Ray Henderson. But just before the *Scandals* went into production, the celebrated triumvirate splintered. Over the course of six years and a dozen Broadway shows, they had created such hit songs as "Button Up Your Overcoat," "Black Bottom," and "Birth of the Blues." Brown, the librettist and lyric writer, and Henderson, the composer, wanted to continue writing for Broadway. DeSylva, also a librettist and a lyricist, wished to travel to Europe, and then work in Hollywood.[22] The three had been friends with White, as well as business partners. Their contracts with White had always been matters of speech. So great was their trust in him that they selected him as the messenger to announce their dissolution to the press. Although White reported that his three friends had come to their decision amicably, tension crept into his continued partnership with Brown and Henderson, who were providing the songs for the *Scandals of 1931* without DeSylva.

Rehearsals began in Atlantic City in August, and bad feelings among the cast and crew soured the preparations. On their first day together, White wanted to impress the rest of his cast with the beauties he had secured for the chorus. He lined up all the girls across the stage and placed the then-unknown Alice Faye in the center. "She was a milk-white beauty," Bolger said, "Blond hair; décolletage; silk bathing suit very low and clinging; long, lithe limbs reaching right down to the ground it seemed. And I stopped and did a double take. But the funniest [incident] was when Rudy Vallee walked in, walked across the stage, staggered for two or three seconds, and looked at this magnificent, gorgeous girl and just gulped and went on."[23]

The women in the cast fought among themselves. The prospect of becoming a musical star had enticed Colt to sign with White, and Henderson and Brown had prepared several songs for her. Once she tried to sing them, however, it became clear that she could never perform "Life Is Just a Bowl of Cherries" or "Ladies and Gentleman, That's Love" on Broadway and be taken seriously. She had no singing voice. White, Brown, and Henderson reassigned the songs to Merman, and Colt felt the newcomer was upstaging her. Barbara Blair grew frustrated with unspecified cast members and wanted to negotiate an exit from the show. There was talk of replacing her, but this fell through.

Worst of all, bitterness between Brown and White threatened to derail the entire production. The two quarreled about the score but mostly about how much money Henderson and Brown should be paid for their services. In the past, they had received 6 percent of the gross from White's shows in their spoken agreements, but now the producer was offering only 4 percent. The score was the show's strongest asset; everyone knew it. For that reason, Henderson and White did not back down. The quarrel continued. White went so far as to ban Brown from rehearsals, and they were not on speaking terms when the show transferred to Broadway at the Apollo Theatre.

The Broadway season was technically six weeks old by the time *George White's Scandals of 1931* opened. Three shows had already folded, and only the annual edition of *Earl Caroll's Vanities* was playing to capacity. Emotions, hopes, and ticket prices were high for opening night, September 15, 1931. Seats sold for as much as $100 per pair—the equivalent of about $1,700 in 2018. Hours before the curtain rose, Brown and Henderson sought an injunction against White to prevent him from using their songs in the show. The injunction was denied.[24] Brown and Henderson were barred from the theater, but Brown found his way to the lobby. White met him there and a fistfight began. Theater guards separated them and ejected Brown. The audience took their seats, and the actors on stage managed to win their attention.

White had transformed the Atlantic City chaos into two acts and twenty-five scenes. The curtain opened on a backdrop of the façade of the just-finished Empire State Building. Bolger strutted out to imitate ex-governor Al Smith with a comic song, "The Marvelous Empire State." Everett Marshall sang the racial protest song "That's Why Darkies Were Born," which, by suggesting with irony that African Americans were born to endure a long list of hardships, challenged audiences to confront inequality. Hits of the evening included Vallee's rendition of "This Is the Missus," Vallee and Merman's renditions of "Life Is Just a Bowl of Cherries," and the Howard brothers and Colt's satire of Ethel Barrymore and two of her interviewers.

The next morning, in the *New York Times*, Brooks Atkinson declared the *Scandals* "a first-rate show."[25] He likened Bolger to Jack Donahue, the Irish prince of Boston and a hero of Bolger's who had recently passed away after a brief illness. Ed Sullivan, astonished at the transformation he saw between the Atlantic City trials and opening night, wrote, "It is the lift and pulse of this score that distinguished the eleventh edition of the 'Scandals.' In other years, the White show has been conspicuous for its great dances. This time, lacking novelties in dancing, the 'Scandals' scores on lyrical pace and beauty."[26]

Although he was no vocalist, Bolger's comic delivery made up for his technical deficiencies. White challenged Bolger to use both song and dance only as extensions of his comedy. This suited Bolger well—his first chance of being a comedian on Broadway in *Heads Up!* had not amounted to much. Ben Washer of the *New York World-Telegram* summed up Bolger's predicament well: "Deep down in the Bolger heart is the determination to be a comedian. Non-vaudeville Broadway will not listen. He had a hard time making it recognize him as a stellar dancer.... George White is first letting him nibble at speaking funny lines."[27]

White was rewarded for taking the risk. Bolger received the best reviews for his various impersonations. David Carb, writing for *Vogue*, said, "Ray Bolger and Willie Howard are the brightest stars of a bright entertainment. The former caricatures ex-governor Al Smith, Adam of apple fame, Graham McNamee, the radio announcer, Walter Winchell, a columnist, a janitor—and in every one of those mad impersonations he is delightful. He is even more delightful when he is just himself. He resembles the late Jack Donahue in many ways—the same sense of comedy, the same elasticity of body and limb."[28] The New York papers made a hit out of the *Scandals* on opening, and of Bolger, too.

Despite the tough economic times, some shows prospered. Thanks to the strength of its score, the *Scandals* was one of them. But White's dependence on Brown and Henderson's score, and his unwillingness to pay them what he owed, only spurred on the unraveling of their relationship. In an attempt to stifle the songwriters, White opened up a lawsuit of his own after the songs of the *Scandals* became radio hits in New York.

Though the concept of a cast album did not become standardized for Broadway shows until the 1950s, the songs of the 1931 edition of the *Scandals* proved so popular that the close harmony trio the Boswell Sisters, joined by Bing Crosby and other notable voices, made a recording of an abridged version of the show. Songs from Broadway frequently, and legally, ended up on the radio; the American Society of Composers, Authors and Publishers licensed the songs to radio stations and provided royalties to the songwriters. DeSylva, Brown & Henderson Inc., music publishers, observed this practice. White did not own the songs and was not entitled to any royalties from them, nor did he have the right to ban them from the airwaves. Nonetheless, in October 1931 he took the stand for two-and-a-half hours, whining and contradicting himself as he tried to assert his right to one-half the copyright equity of the songs. It was the first lawsuit of its kind, and White lost. [29]

Despite (or perhaps because of) all the publicity White's various lawsuits stirred up, the show continued in the face of plenty of competition. Just across the street from the Apollo Theatre, at the New Amsterdam, the Astaires and comedian Frank Morgan were four months into their roles headlining *The Band Wagon*, a Max Gordon revue with music by Arthur Schwartz and Howard Dietz. The press called the *Scandals* "the first deserving success since 'The Band Wagon'" when George White's 1931 edition debuted.[30] *The Band Wagon* closed after 260 performances on January 16, 1932. Adele Astaire was retiring from the stage to marry Lord Charles Cavendish. This sent Fred Astaire to Hollywood.

Bolger also received offers from film studios but demurred. He said, "You know yourself that he [Fred Astaire] held out a long time before listening to the overtures of the movie moguls. Well, I plan to do the same. The longer I hold out, the more they will want me, so I might as well let them wait awhile."[31] Bolger had just attained Broadway stardom, and he wanted to enjoy it for a while. He also began what would be a lifelong practice of giving back to the public who had given so much to him. He served as master of ceremonies for the 1931 New York American Christmas and Relief Fund variety show at the Lyric Theatre. He performed with the cast of the *Scandals* and the performers from other hit shows on Broadway. The proceeds benefited the unemployed. As the public began looking at Bolger, they liked what they saw: a man, not unlike Astaire, with a long, thin body, who cut a beautiful silhouette in his sharp clothes. He deviated from Astaire, though, in the sense that his personal style reflected the eccentricities of his nature and not just the popular British fashions that Astaire wore so well. Thanks to Gwen's grooming, Bolger started to receive sartorial accolades from smart society.

A few weeks into the *Scandals*' run, A. T. Gallico, a fashion columnist for the *Times*, profiled the "swank dancer's duds." He tipped his hat— figuratively—not only to Bolger's fashion choices but also to his skills as a performer. He explained, "As is the case with other well dressed men I have known, the hat is no criterion of Mr. Bolger's wardrobe, for he is one of the best dressed men on the stage. The lapse from sartorial rectitude in regard to hats may be put down to one of the eccentricities which clever and talented people may be permitted. And so, unless you are as grand a comedian as Ray Bolger, you'd better get that new hat you were thinking of."[32]

Bolger was no longer invisible to New York. His rotations through various nightclubs were reported, especially his favorite, Dinty Moore's, a high-priced Irish saloon and steakhouse on West Forty-Sixth Street where warm brass gleamed under low lights. The restaurant was named after a similar establishment featured in the popular comic strip "Bringing Up Father," which featured a stereotypical Irish American who won a sweepstakes and married a society woman. That Bolger's life to that point ran along a similar narrative thread to the comic strip did not seem to influence his dining choices.

Unlike Jiggs, the hero of the cartoon strip, Bolger had not won his place in New York high society: he had earned it. And at the same time, he seemed to be replacing the generation of performers that he had loved. Jack Donahue had passed away. And Joe Frisco, the comic dancer Bolger imitated and thought far beyond his ken, was sitting near him one night in November 1931 at Dinty Moore's, all alone, while friends surrounded Bolger. Frisco had descended considerably in popular estimation by 1930, in part because of his struggles with alcoholism. Even his professional friends no longer thought his bumbling drunk antics were funny. Frisco sat cramped at a tiny table near the entrance, wearing "an orb-destroying orange tie, endeavoring to look the part of a celebrity."[33]

Now twenty-eight years old, Bolger had surpassed an early idol. In January 1932, as the run of the *Scandals* was winding down, Gwen hosted a birthday party for her husband at Dinty Moore's. Barbara Blair sang, Nicky Kempner played the piano, and a small group including Harold Arlen toasted him. Gwen was happy to be settling into a comfortable, successful life with her husband in New York. The Bolgers took a lease on an apartment at 25 West Fifty-Fourth Street, six blocks from Central Park. A quarter of a mile away, in the opposite direction, was the only active construction site of the Great Depression: Rockefeller Center. While Bolger had toiled to make a name for himself on the legitimate stage, Roxy Rothafel had united with the richest man in America in the hopes of reviving vaudeville.

CHAPTER 4

Depression Days

The Great Depression hit the movie business so hard that dusting off the old vaudevillians and inserting them back into live shows seemed like a good way to make money. In 1931, RKO reported a $5.6 million deficit and stockholders were worried. The board decided to hire an old pro, Martin Beck, to enhance the vaudeville attractions at the New York Palace. At the time, the Palace stood as the country's only two-a-day vaudeville theater. Beck complied, but the high cost of his stars meant the Palace went $4,000 to $5,000 in the red each week. To offset costs, the theater converted to a combination house in the summer of 1932, offering six acts of vaudeville and a feature film.[1] Beck had tried and failed to revive vaudeville. But Roxy Rothafel thought he had a deeper understanding of the entertainment landscape than Beck did. Rothafel felt certain that the entertainment he had spent his career cultivating was about to diverge, despite the amount of merging the entertainment industry had undergone since 1920. In June 1930 he had predicted, "The day of merging the so-called presentation idea with the picture is past. . . . [Y]ou are going to have a purely motion picture entertainment without any other form of entertainment that may go with it. . . . I think, on the other hand, that entertainment is coming back, and very strongly in another form. I think that variety, that is vaudeville, in a much finer way will have a tremendous field in the next five years."[2]

While most of the investors Rothafel had relied on to build theaters in the past were broke, there was one man who had money to spare to help Rothafel create his vision of a high-class straight vaudeville palace: John D. Rockefeller Jr., known in his milieu as "Junior." A mutual acquaintance, Ivy Ledbetter Lee, had introduced Junior to the Metropolitan Opera Real

Estate Company in May 1928. The finest families in New York—from the nouveaux riches like the Astors to the Dutch "first families" like the Beekmans—used the Metropolitan Opera House on Broadway between Thirty-Ninth and Fortieth Streets as a place to see and be seen on Monday nights, but they did not care for the hideous "yellow-brick pile," as they called the Opera House.

The interior inspired more scorn, as 25 percent of the house's seats had obstructed views. The structure had been built in 1883 in service to the "Diamond Horseshoe" of boxes used by the best families, and even these patrons were now eager for new environs.[3] Lee, the founder of modern public relations, claimed both Junior and Otto Kahn, chairman of the board of directors of the Metropolitan Opera Company, as friends. The Opera Company was in a position to finance a new building, but they needed support to secure the land. They were eyeing eleven acres in Midtown that belonged to Columbia University, bordered by Forty-Eighth and Fiftieth Streets, and Fifth and Sixth Avenues. Extracting it from the university would be no small task: Columbia's board was not enthusiastic about putting an opera house in Midtown, where it would dominate valuable rental properties. Lee thought the project would be profitable for Rockefeller. It would also give him a chance to claim ownership of a grand project; the shy and timid Junior had none of the celebrity recognition of his father, nor even of his own son, Nelson, who was already beginning his ascension as the most prominent and powerful Rockefeller.

Junior agreed, and in so doing undertook the greatest challenge of his life. Daniel Okrent, historian of Rockefeller Center, compressed the painstaking difficulty of developing the site into a sentence:

> The Rockefeller organization or its designees would have to purchase leases on 203 different lots in the tract or wait out their expiration; pay several score subtenants to give up their dwellings; tear down 228 buildings; cart away massive piles of rubble; and build something on the site that would yield at least $3.6 million net rent, plus enough additional revenue to profitably amortize the cost of building.[4]

The day before Junior signed the lease with Columbia, the Metropolitan Opera Real Estate Company let him know that they "would probably not be able to finance a new house after all."[5] As Junior recalled, "It was clear that there were only two courses open to me. One was to abandon the entire development. The other to go forward with it in the definitive knowledge that I myself would have to build it and finance it alone.... I chose the latter course."[6]

From this chaos grew Rockefeller Center, a fifteen-building campus enshrining media, big business, and modern architecture in the heart of Manhattan. These three interests overlapped a great deal in the planning process. Once the Metropolitan Opera Company backed out of the deal with Junior, the Radio Corporation of America (RCA) emerged as the replacement tenant. David Sarnoff, the brand-new president of RCA, had been instrumental in linking the company to the Keith-Albee-Orpheum vaudeville theater chain to create RKO Pictures.[7] He wanted to find an impressive home for RCA's broadcasting operations and offices. True to the original intent of his deal, Junior would also bring high-class entertainment to the new campus. He and Sarnoff recruited Roxy Rothafel to oversee the construction of two theaters: the RKO Roxy, to become New York's most prestigious home for sound motion pictures, and Radio City Music Hall, which would resurrect vaudeville by hosting two eight-act shows daily. Entertainment would become even bigger business when the entertainment at Radio City was broadcast and distributed through RCA's network. The *Christian Science Monitor* reported, "The overhead of the theater proper would be met by its paid admissions, and the returns from the sale of the radiocasts to advertisers would be enormous."[8]

The public was torn on what to think of these developments. Those who supported the endeavor, including the Bolgers, looked forward to the ways the vast project could help the local economy. From the time planning began in 1928 to the completion of the main campus in 1932, the Rockefeller Center project provided employment for forty thousand New Yorkers—architects, designers, laborers, artists, and contractors. Once finished, it comprised more than 120,000 cubic feet of enclosed, heated, wired, plumbed, and elevator-equipped space—a feat no one anywhere on Earth had ever dared to attempt before.

Despite the optimism generated by the Rockefeller press offices, critics pointed out that the only other place where construction was under way in New York was in the Hooverville shanties huddled together in Central Park. Grand dreams seemed out of place amidst so much abject poverty. New Yorkers were resentful that John D. Rockefeller Jr. had led the project. The public had not forgotten his miserly father who, while sitting on great riches, deigned to hand out only dimes to children on the street. This is precisely why Rothafel, one of the most popular radio broadcasters between the war years and a curator of popular taste, had been brought in. The boosterism and grand declarations that churned out hourly from his own publicity operations drowned out the city's gripes.

By summer 1932, Bolger was a friend of several important show people who claimed friendship with Rothafel. After *George White's Scandals of 1931* closed at the Apollo Theater on March 5, 1932, an abridged version of the show toured the RKO movie houses for the remainder of the year. The tour returned to New York in November, just as Rothafel was making his final selections for the opening bill of Radio City. Bolger had worked with conductor Hugo Riesenfeld at the Rivoli. Now, like most conductors after the silent film had been displaced, Riesenfeld conducted for movie studios in Hollywood. Bolger had befriended Leon Leonidoff, Rothafel's most trusted production director, who had been given great responsibility in launching Radio City. Bolger's associates, his star status minted by the *Scandals*, his good work for the RKO theaters, and his ability to inspire great affection from his audiences all contributed to his receiving the role of master of ceremonies for Radio City's opening program.

The week of Christmas 1932, a few days ahead of the December 27 opening, Rothafel held a private tour of the new Radio City Music Hall for Max Gordon. It began in the Grand Foyer, which measured one city block long by six stories high. After a few moments to admire the pendulous chandeliers made of Lalique glass (in reality there were two, but carefully placed full-length mirrors made it seem as if there were eight), they traveled up a copper staircase rendered in the sleek Art Deco style. They explored each of the three mezzanines, which Rothafel had insisted should cantilever from the back wall. He disliked the notion of patrons being crowded by a balcony that would divide the house in half, nor did he think those on the floor should be hemmed in by box holders above them who would spend more time looking at each other than the show on the stage. Rothafel had earlier defended his choice to the architect Walter H. Kilham, insisting that unless the audience could "laugh and cry together," you couldn't have a theater.[9] No man surpassed Rothafel's gifts for self-promotion and publicity, and so three hours passed before the tour of the stage hydraulics, the lounges, powder rooms, artwork, and even Rothafel's permanent apartment hidden on the fifth floor, concluded. In the lobby once again, Gordon exclaimed to his tour guide, "It's a marvelous layout—but tell me, have you got any jokes?"[10]

On December 27, 1932, exactly 6,200 American luminaries would rush in for the new theater's official opening night, and as it turned out, the joke would be Radio City Music Hall itself. Rothafel had assembled such a strange cast for his opening night that everyone was dying to see how it unfolded. Whatever talents Hollywood hadn't siphoned out of the city found their place on the bill, in addition to some imports. Martha Graham and her dance troupe would be making an appearance in the first act. The press had gone wild over stories told by the other actors in the cast of how Graham and her troupe traveled in a pack, spoke to no one, and wore only black. Everyone backstage at Radio City was convinced they could only speak Greek. There was to be a ballet of more than eighty dancers led by Patricia Bowman, as well as ninety-six highly trained precision dancers who picked up the nickname "the Roxyettes" long before they became the Rockettes. Bolger would dance as well as emcee.

A steady rain fell on opening night at Radio City, sparkling in camera flashbulbs and sullying the red velvet carpet that had been laid down before the entrance. The celebrity crowd took their seats. Al Jolson, suffering from a one-hundred-degree fever, brought Ruby Keeler. Bernard Gimbel, department store mogul, escorted Amelia Earhart.

The show dragged. The audience fidgeted. In addition to Graham, three other interpretive dances took the stage, as did a lyric soprano from Berlin, the Tuskegee choir of one hundred voices, and radio-nut comic Dr. Rockwell. Veteran actor DeWolf Hopper recited "Casey at the Bat" around one in the morning. The show was not yet half over. By this time, most of the newspaper columns had sent assistants running up the aisles with their stories for that morning's papers, which would miss the best quip of the evening. For days, Bolger had worried obsessively about what to say to the crowd. While extemporized dance came easily to him, impromptu speech was another matter. He left Gwen in the Grand Foyer before the show began, though not before she gave him a quick kiss and a whispered suggestion. He should say something to bring people together and break the ice, as the thousands of guests were still bowled over by the size of the Music Hall. After Hopper left the enormous stage Bolger emerged, peered out over the footlights, tugged at his collar and offered, "Gee, isn't it wonderful what a few dimes can build?"

The next day, the press had just as much fun with the opening of Radio City as Bolger did. Ed Sullivan in his "Voice of Broadway" column quipped, "Yesterday morning was a red-letter day on theatrical calendars. It was the first time in history that John D. Rockefeller, Jr., over the morning coffee, turned eagerly to the drama reviews. . . . For once in his life, John D. Jr. breathed the same air as the Bradys, the Shuberts, the Dillinghams, and the Max Gordons." He concluded, as did many in the press, "If you'd rate the show, it would read like this: (1), (2) and (3) The Theatre. (4) Ray Bolger."[11]

Bolger survived the first round of cuts made to the opening program at Radio City after the public made it clear that quantity was no replacement for quality. Despite the good publicity for his appearance, though, the money at the Music Hall was not enough to keep Bolger interested, and so by January he was signed on to RKO theaters to dance. He started in Kansas City, progressed east through Chicago and Rochester, and ended up at the New York Palace again on January 23, 1933. Once again, he was cited as the act "who pulls the bill out of its many doldrums," this time by the critic Robert Garland.[12]

The RKO tour did not earn Bolger much praise, but it paid him well: $1,250 per week. Additionally, Bolger's agent advised that he stick out the tour "to prove to Mr. Roxy we do not need his engagement" at Radio City. Lastfogel had moved to Hollywood that year to break into the motion picture casting business, and he hoped to secure screen tests that would enable Bolger to settle on the coast. Gwen returned to Los Angeles to spend time with her parents while her husband toured the RKO movie houses, allowing her to visit Lastfogel and, with him, outline her vision for her husband's career. She thought the agent could do better than allow Bolger to revert to the baggy pants act. She hoped he would start employing sharper comedy that would attract juicier roles. Lastfogel respected her ideas and her enthusiasm, and the two formed an alliance. For different reasons, they both wanted to see Bolger become a true star: Lastfogel wanted to make good with his very first client, and Gwen wanted to live vicariously through a celebrity husband.

Despite her work, Gwen was lonely and sick. She had an appendectomy. While recovering, she resumed her daily writing to her husband. Addressing her letters to "Dearest Daddy Darling," Gwen wrote every night, often after filling her days with Hollywood people. In addition to meeting with Lastfogel, she lunched with Irving Caesar, the lyricist for "Swanee" and "Tea for Two." As a once-aspiring songwriter herself, Gwen had admired the acclaimed lyricist with big round glasses. She had hoped that Caesar, who had co-written the book for the *Scandals of 1931*, could help Bolger advance his career after seeing his potential. Instead, he wanted only to get the latest news of George White from New York, and to try to seduce Gwen.

With Bolger out of town, Gwen endured plenty of unwanted male attention. With particular delight she wrote to her husband, "Georgie Raft stared a hole through me in his best gigolo manner. Wait 'til he finds out I'm your wife." She grew stir-crazy in the plush white living room of the Rickard home, tired of having only Bolger's letters and the "hair tonic" (smuggled alcohol) he sent from the road. She longed for intimacy and for a child.

"I know a secret," Gwen once signed off, "(now when you come out you won't have to be so gentle with me—get it?)" In another she said, "Position in life is everything— Perhaps we ought to take up double contortion work if we want to keep the human race from dying out. Goodnight, my precious. I'll make you a parent yet."[13] Gwen never did have a child, though the reason remains unclear. Before her death, she confided to a niece that as a young wife, she had privately visited her gynecologist to see whether or not she had fertility problems. To this day, female fertility tests are inconclusive, and they were much less reliable in the early thirties, when Gwen would have been tested. Regardless, Gwen always contended that she had passed the screening just fine, and that she believed there must have been some problem with Bolger. Ideas of masculinity at that time, coupled with her enduring love for him, prevented her from ever discussing the matter with him. Whether the problem was physically Bolger's, or whether the story was invented to keep intimate details from a young niece as to why the pair did not conceive, cannot be known. It seems that Gwen had good reasons for attributing the difficulty to Bolger. She often told her nieces that, looking back, it would have been impossible to lead the demanding and peripatetic lives of an entertainer and his keeper if the two were to become parents. Wanderlust suited them both, and they considered themselves lucky for the lifestyle they were able to maintain. However, with the resources available to the Bolgers, this rationale seems flimsy. If they had children, they could have afforded nannies and fine schools that would have minimized the strains of child-rearing while they pursued their professional work. But the Bolgers never revealed any other reasons that kept them childless.

A couple of times during 1932, Gwen could stand the loneliness no longer. In June, she boarded the Santa Fe Chief to meet Bolger in Chicago. She endured the hot leather of her seat and the white glare of the sun beating on flat land by entertaining a stranger's baby, treating herself to a couple of highballs in the Ladies' Lounge, and sleeping. She was amazed at the swarms of children that appeared at each little depot. They knew the train originated in Los Angeles, and they hoped to meet celebrities. Several times on the journey, Gwen was asked if she were a movie star. Chagrined, she told the girls and boys—not much younger than she was when she had arrived in Los Angeles with the hopes of being discovered—that she was not. It was during these quick trips that Gwen developed a ritual she observed for the rest of her married life. Bolger, too, was often taking long train rides between performance stops, and Gwen found him to be so keyed up on an opening night, due to the stress of the show as well as the traveling, that she made a point to arrive for the second night, when he was calmer.

Between 1932 and 1933, Ray traveled and worked for fifty-two consecutive weeks without taking a vacation. He was determined to earn and save money, and he had the good fortune to be a client of Abe Lastfogel, who was securing him lucrative deals. In July 1932, for example, Gwen wrote from her parents' home in Los Angeles to Ray, who was then appearing in Boston, to commend him for his ability to send home money for her to put away. She wrote that they should be grateful to Lastfogel for "having raised your salary considerably, during the Depression—when most people are happy to take a 25% cut if they can work."[14] Gwen reported to Bolger that of the money he had sent back for her safekeeping in California, she had $2,375 at the ready after she had paid her expenses—the equivalent of almost $42,000 in 2018.

After a vacation in St. Petersburg, Florida, with Gwen, Bolger accepted a part to be in another revue, *Earl Carroll's Vanities*, in early 1934. Bolger's association with the production earned him an invitation to perform at President Franklin Delano Roosevelt's Birthday Ball. Gwen said of the occasion that her husband "lunched and dined with the Roosevelts at the White House. Although he comes from a long line of staunch Republicans, he found the President and his First Lady the number one charm-merchants of his experience."[15] But otherwise, he disliked working for Earl Carroll, as the two disagreed over wages. Bolger left the company, and he would not appear in an Earl Carroll production again.

Meanwhile, the William Morris Agency realized they had a stable of young talents. *Billboard* reported, "In an attempt to develop future stars, the William Morris Agency, thru Johnny Hyde, is concentrating on a select group of young and likely talent. Hyde is giving them considerable attention, picking their dates with care and otherwise giving them the benefit of a slow buildup for prominence.... The list has two prospects for early stardom, Miss [Eleanor] Powell and Ray Bolger. To Hyde the thought along the lines of developing talent is that the performers have the ability, but guidance is what they need."[16] That spring, the William Morris Agency had sent Bolger to Chicago. The agency's strategy to catapult their young talent to stardom included "buildups...in the night club and theater fields, extending to radio, picture and production in the climb up the success ladder."[17] Bolger appeared as a headliner in the night club Chez Paree in April, and then as a cast member in a revue at the Civic Opera House, given for the benefit of the relief fund of the stagehands' union with Milton Berle and Paul Ash, among others.[18]

Bolger returned to New York to complete more charity appearances. He joined his old friend Gus Edwards and a number of their associates when he performed at the annual Friars Club Frolic. Hundreds of high-voltage stars helped to raise funds for the actors' club, which was hoping to move its quarters with the help of the donations. The charitable appearances gave Bolger a way to connect with the down-and-out public, because his reputation as a swell guy brought relief and happiness to many. People, particularly the people of power in show business who also patronized these events, would remember him down the road.

By 1934, the initial shock of the Depression had reverberated through its survivors. To cope, some Americans lost themselves in fantasy. *Gold Diggers of 1933*, an opulent film musical produced by Warner Brothers, told the story of a millionaire composer who rescued unemployed Broadway actors and put them in a lavish production dripping diamonds and feathers. The numbers created by Busby Berkeley sold the film attendees a respite from their daily privations. The famous "We're in the Money" routine featured dozens of beautiful chorines sashaying around in little more than heavy eyeliner and strategically placed coins. Ginger Rogers sang one verse in Pig Latin as a verbal affront to the seriousness of the Depression. *Gold Diggers* tried to tell audiences that everything would come out okay. It also tried to sell Broadway dancers on the notion that Hollywood would rescue them from hardship with big money. But many members of the smart young set of New York talent were not buying it. They were ready to laugh at the Depression, but they weren't ready to delude themselves or their audiences. They wanted to use musical patter and ravishing beauty to confront the truth, not bury it. And so they went to work on *Life Begins at 8:40*.

In 1934, Lee Shubert wanted to establish himself as a musical producer in his own right. Up until that point, his brother J. J. had been the mastermind. In January, with the uncredited assistance of Florenz Ziegfeld Jr.'s widow, Billie Burke, he produced the *Ziegfeld Follies of 1934*. In keeping with the Shubert mode, he launched a revue, since the Depression aroused a nostalgic interest in the format. Revues were particularly welcomed in the grueling New York summertime, when light and cool entertainment led by top comics helped people forget the perspiring city. Fred Allen, W. C. Fields, Jack Benny, and others had often come to the rescue of languishing New Yorkers, but no savior emerged for the summer of 1934. Word reached the press in June that Lee had recruited David Freedman, Eddie Cantor's comedy writer, to create the sketches for an intimate revue that the media was calling—incorrectly—*Life Begins at 8:30*.

Lee brought in E. Y. "Yip" Harburg as a lyricist and gave him four months to write all the lyrics for the show. Harburg had just completed work on the *Ziegfeld Follies* with Lee and was exhausted, but he saw in Freedman's writing "an unusual opportunity—a show that mixed the wit and critical spirit of the smaller revues with the budget and spectacle of the larger ones." Rather than pass up the job, he recruited a co-lyricist: Ira Gershwin.[19] "We started off by kidding the theater," Harburg said. "The fact that we called the show *Life Begins at 8:40* [curtain time was then 8:30

for Broadway theaters] already tells you that we had tongue-in-cheek." The title of the revue played on the title of the most popular self-help book of the day, *Life Begins at 40*, by Walter B. Pitkin. While the press speculated that the show would arrive on Broadway in late June, in time to be a summer amusement, in reality it did not even reach tryouts by then. A great deal of work lay ahead to innovate the format.

Harold Arlen, whom Bolger had known from vaudeville, was brought in to provide the music. Up until that point, Arlen's domain had been the Cotton Club rather than Broadway. Instead of the usual torch songs and ballads, he and his lyricists peppered *Life Begins at 8:40* with parody numbers, mock marches, and opera setups. He relished the opportunity to collaborate with Gershwin and Harburg. In Harburg particularly, Arlen found a compatible partner. Not only was Harburg talented, but he also brought his personal sensibilities to his work. As a humanist and a fervent leftist, Harburg could not separate the current political and social climate from his work on the show. Although Bolger did not care for President Roosevelt's politics, he understood the need to keep his head down. "I have to be with the party that's in when I'm on stage," he said.[20] That party was definitely the Democrats. *Life Begins at 8:40* became a forum for praising Fiorello LaGuardia and President Rooseevelet, lampooning disgraced New York City mayor Jimmy Walker, and questioning monogamy and standards of beauty.

H. I. Phillips, Alan Baxter, Henry Clapp Smith, Frank Gabrielson, and Harburg wrote additional sketches to fill the revue and complement the actors who had been recruited. Bolger came to Lee's attention by virtue of his success with George White, and also because of his growing roster of public appearances. He was offered the lead in *Life Begins at 8:40*. Bolger wanted to leap right in, but Gwen had reservations. Bolger said,

> We sat down and discussed it and decided that I would not be accepted as a total star in the show at that time, that I'd not been in enough things... although I got great kudos for the *George White's Scandals*...they were not the kind that would make an instant star out of a person, that I should have been better known. I took billing below Bert Lahr. We went out and got ahold [sic] of Bert Lahr.[21]

On June 17, 1934, the *Boston Globe* announced that Bolger and Luella Gear had been signed for "Life Begins at 8:30 [sic]." [22] Bert Lahr was engaged about a week later. [23] The show went to Boston for tryouts.

Time spent out of town with her husband's musical enabled Gwen to learn about where he came from. Bolger showed her Scollay Square and Washington Street, and the theaters that he had called home as a young

Bert Lahr (*left*), Luella Gear (*center*), and Ray Bolger (*right*), in a publicity still for their 1934 musical, *Life Begins at 8:40*. White Studios. Photo courtesy of The Shubert Archives.

man, like the B. F. Keith Memorial Theater, now the Boston Opera House. Gwen also learned how to put a musical together from the theatrical legends she watched working with her husband. As she wrote, "This apprenticeship of mine, where had I served it? Why in Boston, of course. Boston was my seat of learning."[24]

The show arrived in New York at the Winter Garden Theatre on August 27. Harburg recalled how the show began:

> We had this big Munich clock on stage, and out of that clock come all of the characters that would appear in the revue: the husband, the lover, the wife, the blues singer, and comedians, and dancers, and so on. And in the words of the opening, we said: "At exactly eight-forty, or thereabouts / This little play world / Not of the day world / Comes to life."[25]

The scenery and costumes convinced the audience they were in a fantasy world. But unlike the usual ostrich plumes and gossamer that lush revues offered, in this show precious metals, velvet, and silk set the tone for a sleek and sophisticated evening of entertainment, rooted in the tastes of the day. Seven costumers received billing.

Sixteen dances choreographed by Robert Alton and Charles Weldman opened the show with motion and color. When Bolger emerged for his first number, to sing the patter song "You're a Builder Upper" to Dixie Dunbar, there was no trace of buffoonery about him. He was as sleek and elegant in white when he emerged with Dunbar in his arms.

The substance of the show, as much as the costumes, reflected the world the actors lived in offstage. In the song "My Paramount-Publix-Roxy Rose," matronly Gear satirized the exhausted chorines who circulated through the combination movie houses, pretending to be "a pansy for Pantages and a cactus for Balaban-Katz." In the raciest number of the evening, "Quartet Erotica," Bert Lahr as Balzac wore a period-perfect, double-breasted coat, postilion cape, and picture hat and sang about decidedly un-period themes.

Bolger played Boccaccio, James McColl played Rabelais, and Brian Donlevy played de Maupassant. Together, the authors lament that the world favors *Ulysses* and *Lady Chatterley's Lover*, and no one finds them shocking any longer. This number and several others like it offered Bolger a departure from the puerile material that had defined his career in vaudeville, where the policy of maintaining "theatrical cleanliness" prohibited risqué material. "Quartet Erotica" exemplified the writers' skill at bending mores as well as setting. The costume team insisted on getting historical details right for every number, which only made the modern words and music fresher. "What Can You Say in a Love Song That Hasn't Been Said Before?," another period piece just before the intermission, utilized a revolving panel to present lovers from 1780, 1880, and 1934 as Bartlett Simmons and Josephine Houston sang a duet about how the protocols of love change little even as time progresses.

After the intermission, Bolger returned to perform what has been called the most enduring comic-romantic song from *8:40*.[26] Titled "Let's Take a Walk around the Block," the wistful love duet between Bolger and Dunbar acknowledged the grimness of the Depression without snuffing out the hope that someday their luck would change.

The comedy ramped up again with Bert Lahr's number, "Things." Like Bolger, Lahr had built his career around a character, which brought what Harburg called "a manic energy to a kind of free-floating buffoonery."[27] He had become famous for his antics on stage. His catch phrase was a primitive, "Gong, gong, gong," which expressed excitement. The opening night audience gasped when Lahr came on stage wearing a tuxedo and a hair piece. An accompanist sat at the piano and Lahr announced, "Ladies and gentleman, the first number of my second group was written in a little garret on the left bank of Gowanus Canal and is entitled, 'Things,' simply,

'Things.'" With plenty of trilling, pinky raising, and wig readjusting, Lahr rejects a list of fineries—Mandalay, Trees, Mothers, and Bees, to name a few—and insists he instead will sing only of "things."[28]

Then Bolger returned, serenading Dunbar with "The Elks and the Masons," another of Harburg and Arlen's sly commentaries. Bolger tries to woo Dunbar with the promise that if she joins up with him, she will also be getting the support of fifty thousand brother Elks and Masons. Bolger returned to the manic eccentric and pseudo-ballet moves that made him famous in "I'm Not Myself," the eleven o' clock number. He danced his solo and was then joined by the chorus girls, who donned replicas of his checkered sport coat and tuxedo pants for a high-energy precision tap number. He led the girls through a difficult series of *pas de chat* for the finale.

The final number of the evening, "Life Begins at City Hall," reprised scenes from the show in new contexts. "Fun to Be Fooled," a wistful ballad sung by Frances Williams in the first act, was reprised by the Taxpayers Association. Bolger, as deposed Mayor Jimmy Walker, explains his return from exile with "Let's Take a Walk around the Block." "You're a Builder Upper," reimagined as a congratulatory song for Mayor LaGuardia, ends the show.

The show became a hit. Brooks Atkinson of the *Times* noted, "When 'Life Begins at 8:40,' it is the artists who have the gayest time of it."[29] *Variety* paid special attention to leading man Lahr's development as a legitimate comedian throughout the show and said, "Ray Bolger counted almost as strongly and there is no conflict."[30] By September 25, less than a month after opening night, *Variety* reported that the show had already earned back half its investment. The announcement ran alongside a story proclaiming 1933 and 1934 to be the worst in history for performing stock companies. Also on the same page, the Public Works Division of the Emergency Relief Administration announced that it was considering staging legitimate shows in dark or abandoned theaters. Even amid real hardships, *Life Begins at 8:40* settled in for a long run.

Bolger enjoyed having opportunities to work with his friend Arlen. And although the competing ideologies of Bolger and Harburg, a lifelong socialist, would suggest that friendship might not be feasible for them, Bolger found the lyricist's company enjoyable. "Although we were at opposite ends of the political spectrum, we had one thing in common: people. We both fought against man's inhumanity. . . . You can never erase Yipper Harburg from my heart," Bolger said.[31]

The show was the first time that Bolger had interacted socially with Lahr. The five months they spent together familiarized him with the revered "nut comic's" mood swings and anxieties that plagued him offstage. Lahr had developed an interest in comedy in part because performing allowed him a way to vent his energy and neuroses. During the run of *Life Begins at 8:40*, Lahr found respite from his troubling world by playing backgammon with Gear in his upstairs dressing room. Bolger often refereed the contests. The games became comedy routines in themselves, and they proved so engrossing that actors sometimes forgot the reason they were really in the Winter Garden. "Come on Bert! Come on Luella!" stage manager Archie Thomson called out, while his assistant Jay Conley tried to hold their cues off, buying time for them to get to the stage. But Lahr could not be bothered. "Wait 'til I roll these double sixes!" he insisted.

In January 1935, a more sinister interruption threatened a performance. Thomson got word to Bolger while he was on stage that a small fire had broken out on the roof of the theater. While there was no great danger, Bolger could see audience members begin to panic. He signaled for the conductor to stop before announcing, "You can't walk out on me!" He jumped into an impromptu tap dance that kept the crowd from bolting. His bravery earned him a special citation from the New York Fire Department. He was presented with a plaque for valor at the curtain call of the following night's performance. He also received a fan letter from a doctor who had been in attendance when the fire broke out; he wrote, "Were it not for your quick thinking, clever psychology and making light of the matter, a great panic would have ensued.... [L]ittle credit was given to you, and I feel that I am voicing the opinion of many hundreds of the audience who enjoyed your bravado."[32] The show continued without incident for another two months. It closed on March 16, 1935, after 237 performances.

It is difficult to leave a success behind in the face of uncertainty. The talents who blended together to create *Life Begins at 8:40* had brought something new and interesting to Broadway. Once the show had clicked with the audience, Bolger advanced "quite a little bit" in show business, and Lastfogel had begun fielding offers from film studios on his behalf.[33] MGM, looking to compete with RKO on producing new musicals, submitted the most tantalizing offer: Bolger could travel to Hollywood and produce two pictures during the Broadway off-season. This would free him up to participate in a new stage show for the 1935–36 season. MGM was particularly interested in Bolger because studio knew he could play the Jack Donahue role in any film adaptation of the late dancer's Broadway shows that they pursued for the screen. Bolger signed his original two-picture contract with MGM on March 7, 1935, nine days before *Life Begins at 8:40* closed. Very soon after the final curtain, the Bolgers returned to Los Angeles and took up residence with Gwen's parents. Bolger reported to MGM's Culver City campus, ready to earn his first film credit. Instead, he spent the summer doing absolutely nothing.

CHAPTER 5

Broadway Goes West

MGM rallied its employees around a company motto: "Do it right. Make it big. Give it class." These words had also been used by P. T. Barnum, suggesting that the entertainment industry held on to certain guiding principles even as technology evolved. Those words weren't hollow: the head of studio operations, Louis B. Mayer, filled thirty-seven acres in Culver City with all necessary facilities to make a city within a city, a studio termed "the dream factory." Bolger had held out for a film contract from the very best purveyors of musicals and he won, but he remained skeptical about how long he and his wife would remain on the West Coast.

Not wanting to lose the wit and verve of Manhattan to the lure of materialism then running rampant in California, the Bolgers were determined not to make any purchases in Hollywood that could not fit into a trunk. The couple took up residence with the Rickards on North Martel Avenue rather than cultivate their own estate. They had no desire to own a car; after arriving, Gwen used her mother's Oldsmobile and Bolger used liverymen to drive him to and from the MGM lot. Hollywood business would be temporary, for money and exposure only. It would be a thing to do while everyone else in New York went on vacation. They were determined not to get too comfortable.

In some ways, however, the move was refreshing for the dancer and his wife. Thirty-one years old that year, 1935, Bolger had been hoofing the equivalent of two miles a night at least six nights a week since 1924. The perpetual warmth of California was salubrious for many, but particularly for a rubbery comic: it was much easier for Bolger to warm up and stay limber throughout the day. Whereas a salad in New York meant a few leaves of wilted lettuce garnished with some sickly carrots, salad in Los Angeles meant avocados, artichokes, and fennel. Gwen's aunts had sent boxes of vitamins to Bolger in New York to help him maintain his vitality through long stage runs. Now the family could support him close at hand. He had wowed them all. If there had ever been any secret doubt about his prospects in life, it was gone. They were happy to lay claim to a celebrity in the family, and the celebrity was very happy to have a family of his own.

Bolger had earned his spot as a true son, bolstered by his comfortable living as a Broadway entertainer. He was also financing Gwen's brothers. When James Rickard, two years younger than Gwen, was having a difficult time establishing himself in a career and settling down, Bolger became a partner in several of his business ventures. Robert Rickard, the baby of the family at seventeen, had lost his right eye in a childhood BB gun accident but displayed gumption in the years following and had developed a strong interest in biology. The Bolgers would later pay for his tuition to medical school. Bolger remained distanced from his biological family. He corresponded with his sister, who had married and moved to Rhode Island. Evidence suggests that after many years of wayward traveling, James had settled in Los Angeles, but how much interaction he had with his son and daughter-in-law once Ray began working at MGM is unknown.

Becoming an MGM employee meant Bolger had to adapt to a new professional hierarchy, one dominated by bureaucratic structure and specialized technicians. The MGM backlot included a film laboratory that processed 4.5 million feet of film a week; the world's largest property department, which managed more than one million items from hundreds of countries and most historical periods; and a music department with more than four million selections, making it the third-largest music library in the world in its day, behind only the Library of Congress and the New York Public Library. The makeup department, headed by Jack Dawn, could serve 1,200 actors per hour. Cedric Gibbons's art department, in charge of giving each picture "MGM's indelible association with wealth and class," curated the world's finest collection of matte paintings, backdrops, props, and settings by industry standards. It relied on the technical expertise and talent of many types of artists. All told, the studio claimed 4,000 employees by 1924.[1]

To support these creative enterprises, MGM developed a pragmatic infrastructure that remains a remarkable example of organizational planning. The studio switchboard handled 2,400 extensions and operators in prim navy suits rerouted thousands of calls a day. The studio even built its own power plant to supply the staggering wattage it used annually—enough to light 25,000 homes for a calendar year. One hundred MGM police officers were kept on hand to protect the cavalcade of celebrities on the property. The publicity department had been quick to coin the phrase that MGM had "more stars than there are in the heavens," and many aspirants wanted to get near them.

From his first day on the lot, Bolger himself felt star-struck, a new phenomenon for him. On the East Coast and more specifically in New York, while struggling to break into big-time shows, Bolger had either admired the grandest names of his generation from the balcony or rehearsed alongside them, watching them develop as they observed his own growth. In California, by contrast, no one recognized him, but thanks to the proliferation of hype in the media, he "knew" many of them. Working at MGM had its own surreal quality. "I was in a kind of dream over there," he said, "in a strange world; I found people that I'd seen on the screen and never thought that I'd ever meet in real life."[2] It became a daily occurrence for him to run into Greta Garbo, Clark Gable, and William Powell. Powell would become his first co-star, but work on a film came much later than Bolger expected. His initial contract suggested that he would complete his first picture between June 1 and August 13, 1935. For this film, he was to be paid $20,000 in seven payments. Bolger collected his salary, but he was not assigned a picture in the summer of 1935 "because it was impossible," he said later. "At MGM it would take a whole summer just to get your first character done, the costume for your picture. So it was really a mistake."[3] Photo shoots and guest appearances on MGM's radio station occupied his time. This was the way the studio generated interest in a new acquisition. Though it did not feel like it to Bolger, the studio was paying him a good deal of attention. The publicity department, whose photographers routinely shot art-quality photos of even the bit players, prepared a series of appealing portraits. Bolger projected a unique image. His unconventional face was long, thin, and glowing. His hooknose would forever keep him from being a Cary Grant, but even these imperfect features read as unique rather than misshapen with the enhancement of soft studio lights. With a full head of dark hair styled just so and his Adam's apple hidden by a plush wool sweater, Bolger radiated warmth and youth. He looked exotic. If Astaire had made good use of his receding hairline and weak chin line, Bolger might be able to overcome his aesthetic deficiencies, too. The publicity department also staged a variety of scenarios in which to shoot Bolger. They made him attempt to do everything from threading a needle to driving a golf ball. These activities seemed inane to him at the time and at first glance still do to us today. But the publicists were not as interested in the premise of the shoots as they were in the way Bolger reacted and comported himself. Trying to push thread through a tiny needle, for instance, allowed him to show off his puckered lips and big horse eyes, the expressions that got laughs on stage. In another series, Bolger swings and swings his club and never hits the golf ball, but his long torso and flexible spine are displayed well in a simple white tee shirt and golf slacks. These photos were really tests of sorts, orchestrated to discover what Bolger could and could not do well on camera.

While studio executives were willing enough to spend money by retaining promising performers who were not working on pictures, the actors quickly became embittered about losing time and prospects. Bolger soon realized that being a bit player for MGM meant sitting around and waiting, and he didn't like it. "I thought of it [MGM] as a great big motion picture factory," he said. "I'd been in factories before. I understood that end of the world. But just like you would go in a grocery store and say, 'Give me four comics, and three toe dancers, and I want five girl singers and five men singers. And I want nineteen character actors, and I want some unique personalities.' And then you just buy them, and you put them on the shelf." After signing his contract with MGM in March 1935, Bolger finally got pulled off the shelf that September to play a small part in a large musical biopic, *The Great Ziegfeld*, based on the life of the colossal impresario Florenz Ziegfeld Jr.

Although he could not be aware of it, Bolger began work at MGM just before a milestone in the history of the studio that would shape his whole experience of making motion pictures there: the death of Irving Thalberg. In 1922, at age twenty-three, Thalberg had teamed up with Louis B. Mayer and become the driving force in the merger of Metro Pictures, Goldwyn Pictures, and Louis B. Mayer pictures. The "boy wonder" was considered a genius almost unanimously in Hollywood, not only for his business acumen but also for his technical sensibilities. He was made head of production of MGM at the age of twenty-six and was its producer par excellence, although he never took screen credit for his vast contributions. Roland Flamini, Thalberg's biographer, wrote, "Today it is taken for granted that the director creates the movie and the producer handles the financing and logistics. But Thalberg did it all, from choosing Tarzan's electronically produced yell to writing Garbo's first words on the screen."[4] But the indispensable producer was racing against the clock: he had been born with a congenital heart disease, and he was not expected to live past thirty. Periodically, Thalberg's hard work would force him into long periods of convalescence, during which Mayer would plot ways to regain control of the studio that bore his name from the man truly responsible for most of his successes.

When Bolger was taken under contract, and during the filming of *The Great Ziegfeld*, Thalberg was still alive, and his influence could be felt in all aspects of film production. Flamini wrote, "He made what he called 'quality pictures,' defining quality with the equation: star (or stars) plus Broadway hit or popular classic plus high standard of production equals good box office."[5] Flamini also explains that Thalberg was the first producer to put two or more major stars in the same picture; until then, studios were of the mind that one major star—despite low-quality story or production—could carry the success of a film, and putting two stars in the same film was wasteful.

The Great Ziegfeld was not produced by Thalberg but by Hunt Stromberg, who had worked under Thalberg until 1933, when Thalberg left Hollywood for the French Riviera to convalesce after a tonsillectomy. Back in California, Mayer took away Thalberg's title, greatly diminishing his input into MGM affairs. Instead, Mayer offered Thalberg's associates full producer status and their own independent production units. This was Mayer's way to wrest control from Thalberg and to protect against the devastation the studio was all but guaranteed to experience if Thalberg did not recover from the surgery. Stromberg, like most of Thalberg's associates, defected.[6] The assignment of *The Great Ziegfeld* to Stromberg represented a real vote of confidence from Mayer, although the lavish and expensive sets and extras, and the casting of several major stars in the picture, greatly reflected Thalberg's way of doing business, as did the film's featuring three stars: William Powell and Myrna Loy, of *The Thin Man* fame, and Luise Rainer. Stromberg also continued to consult Thalberg, which the other producers, in their newfound power, refused to do.[7]

The Great Ziegfeld had initially been green-lighted by Universal Studios in 1933. When the production costs mounted, executives sold it to MGM for $300,000.[8] To make it into a lavish Best Picture winner, MGM invested $2 million.[9] The heavy dramatic and romantic parts of the film are tempered with a bevy of numbers, many of them replications of acts from Ziegfeld's real Broadway shows performed by their original artists, including Fanny Brice and Harriet Hoctor. Bolger had one solo number in the show, "She's a Follies Girl," which he sang while descending a stairway crowded with bathing-suited beauties. When he reached the main stage, he performed an eccentric tap dance. His percussion was reminiscent of Jack Donahue, who had been a Ziegfeld star, but his split routine and *pas de chat* were all his own. *The Great Ziegfeld* would continue filming into 1936, but Bolger completed his final shots in early November 1935. He and Gwen returned to New York on November 5 to begin rehearsals for a new Rodgers and Hart production.

Rodgers and Hart had also felt the allure of Hollywood. Their 1931 production, *America's Sweetheart*, lasted on Broadway a little less than four

Bolger struggled with the restrictions on his spontaneity that film work demanded. He said, "I felt I was dancing in a phone booth." Photo from the author's collection.

months. Rodgers's first child had just been born, and he needed to secure a steady income. When Paramount extended a one-picture contract to the pair for work on a Maurice Chevalier film, they accepted. The film, *Love Me Tonight*, released in 1932, so invigorated Hollywood that MGM subsequently offered Rodgers and Hart a long contract and a choice of assignments in order to lure them to the studio. Only one full-length film materialized. The two were asked to complete one-off songs for a variety of purposes, and they learned quickly that songwriting worked much differently in Hollywood. While they were conditioned to write up to twenty songs for a Broadway show, Hollywood wanted just five. Studios also had a lot more leeway in choosing who provided songs for a production, and the bosses held covert competitions among three or four different songwriting teams. Dissatisfied with the pace of work on the West Coast, Rodgers and Hart returned to New York in 1934 and launched *Jumbo*. For their next production, they would build on an idea they had hatched in Hollywood.

In 1933, RKO had announced in the trade papers that the studio was looking for a new film project for Fred Astaire and Ginger Rogers, who had just completed *The Gay Divorcee*. Rodgers and Hart wrote up an outline for a saga in which a vaudeville hoofer became a Russian ballet legend. They invited Astaire to their rooms at the Beverly Hills Hotel and pitched him their idea. He declined. Rodgers later suggested that the part was too unglamorous for Astaire to accept, that he had not wanted to tarnish his top-hat-and-tails image.[10] But Astaire was probably not interested in committing to a show that involved extensive ballet, a style he disliked. Instead, at the suggestion of Harry S. Kaufman, the Shubert Brothers' businessman, Ray Bolger was offered the lead. With him in mind, Rodgers and Hart completed the dialogue and half the songs for the show they called *On Your Toes*, and then pitched it to Lee Shubert with the idea of making it a Broadway musical. He agreed to produce the show but expressed little enthusiasm for it.

Rodgers and Hart, however, had more than enough of their own excitement. This would be the first show for which they provided lyrics, music, and the book. They went about finding actors for the cast. Monty Woolley, who had directed several Broadway shows, including Rodgers and Hart's *America's Sweetheart*, was given a featured acting role. Marilyn Miller was sought for the female romantic lead, Frankie, to star opposite Bolger, but she decided to go into retirement after her sensational marriage to Chester Lee O'Brien, a chorus dancer more than ten years her junior. She was replaced by Doris Carson. Luella Gear, who had been a star of *Life Begins at 8:40*, was cast as Peggy Porterfield.

Bolger, in his first turn as leading man, would receive top billing and share it with no one; he would have to display his full capacities as a singer, actor, dancer, and comedian and lead his cast mates with his magnitude rather than flatten them with it. Throughout the show's development, he stayed close to Rodgers and Hart, whose temperaments were quite different. Bolger likened Hart to "a little leprechaun" who would rub his hands and his nose when he was pleased and cry when he wasn't. He was also volatile, a result perhaps of his experiencing "a lot of hurt, a lot of … not … [being] satisfied quite with what he was," according to Bolger.[11] During the development of *On Your Toes*, Hart was asked to concoct great lyrics under pressure while also struggling with alcoholism.

Rodgers, on the contrary, was very emotionally disciplined, and he took nothing out of proportion. Because he had a deep knowledge of seemingly everything related to operetta, he wanted to be involved in all the components of the creative process and be heard. By comparison, "Larry was open for suggestions," Bolger said, "and Dick rather became a teacher."[12] Hart's great command of the English language meant he could write rhymes with legendary speed. However, his emerging trademark of what he called "interrhyming" was seen by some, including Hart himself, as a cheap trick.[13] Together Rodgers and Hart continued to develop their styles, Rodgers's complex melodies and Hart's clever lyrics, throughout the next decade. By the time *On Your Toes* was in production, they were well-regarded wits on Broadway.

The Bolgers, particularly Gwen, used the tryout as another learning opportunity. Hollywood stifled Gwen's creativity: in an environment as regimented and organized as the MGM studios, she was not welcomed to show up and offer suggestions or to share her beliefs about how her husband should be costumed or directed. But creating a Broadway show was different; the relatively small cast and creative team meant that responsibilities got shared and input was received more freely. She could turn up at rehearsal and weigh in on the show's production. She later considered Rodgers and Hart two of her best teachers. Both she and Bolger respected the team, but they did not believe that Rodgers and Hart understood how to write a book for a musical, which led Bolger to "battle" them on points of "literary value."[14] By literary value, Ray meant story cohesion and structure, ensuring that the book had a beginning, a middle, an end, and a plot as tight and bouncy as a new metal spring, with dialogue that came across as witty and fresh. Rodgers and Hart asked writer George Abbott and Dwight Wiman, who had been named producer after Lee Shubert allowed his option on the show to lapse, to edit the book.

The story they settled on went like this: Phil "Junior" Dolan III, played by Bolger, is the heir to a renowned family of hoofers touring vaudeville. When Junior starts acting out, his concerned mother insists on yanking him out of show business to pursue something more settled. Junior leaves behind vaudeville and becomes a Works Project Administration music teacher at Knickerbocker University. His two brightest students are Frankie Frayne and Sidney Cohn. Junior at first dismisses Frankie's heavy-handed love songs as "derivative," but he later realizes that she is using them to profess her romantic interest in him. Sidney Cohn, on the other hand, shows great potential from the get-go, as does his jazz ballet, "Slaughter on Tenth Avenue." Junior and Sidney get the ballet in front of arts patroness Peggy Porterfield with the help of Frankie, who is Peggy's close friend. The rich matron then pressures ballet master Sergei Alexandrovitch, director of the Russian Ballet, into featuring it in his company's next production. If he doesn't, Peggy will cut off his funding. This mandate brings two worlds together: the WPA students and the high-art ballerinas of the Cosmopolitan Opera House. Under the watchful portrait of President Roosevelt in the WPA classroom, a jazz-versus-classical duel ensues.

George Balanchine, the hottest ballet choreographer in New York, was brought in to apply his knowledge of Russian ballet to Rodgers and Hart's smart efforts. *On Your Toes* was Bolger's first time working with him. The show—the first to interpolate classical dance into a Broadway book musical—proved to be a setting in which a classical master and a rising Broadway personality could meet on level ground.

Balanchine, born like Bolger in 1904, witnessed many of the finest European artists of the 1920s while traveling as a ballet master with his first wife, Tamara Geva.[15] Prokofiev, Debussy, and Stravinsky scored his ballets at the Ballets Russes, and Picasso and Matisse designed sets and costumes for him. After a knee injury and the decline of the famous company, Balanchine was persuaded by Lincoln Kerstein move to the United States. He formed the School of American Ballet to train dancers in his technique and style. He also got involved in creating popular works; particularly, in staging ballets for Broadway revues. *On Your Toes* was his first book musical.

Though the ballet master, soft-spoken and contemplative, could understand Bach's fugues and Beethoven's "Pathetique" with ease, he had difficulty embracing the popular American rhythms that Rodgers composed for him. While Balanchine adjusted to the new sound, he relied on Bolger—just ten days his senior, but a native and experienced in Americana—for help. Because most of Bolger's craft was based on improvisation, his interpretations of music helped Balanchine understand its intentions. Bolger prided himself on his ability to translate lyrics with his feet, and this helped when words failed. Sometimes no language seemed useful to help translate a concept: "We were speaking in French and English and German and Russian—the language of the ballet. And it was a very vivid experience in my mind. I fell in love with this man, his personality and his humor. He was a tremendously humorous man."[16]

That humor found its way into the show through Balanchine's direction of the dance. The other major ballet piece in the show besides "Slaughter" was the "Zenobia Ballet," a spoof on *Le Spectre de la Rose* and *Scheherazade* designed to highlight the antiquity of the Russian Ballet (and its need for a modern ballet like "Slaughter") as well as Junior's apparent ineptitude in the form. "Zenobia Ballet" was danced by Tamara Geva and Basil Galahoff, and the two Russians played out the role of star-crossed lovers in an Eastern fairytale, while Bolger, as Junior, played a concubine. Balanchine never let his ex-wife or Galahoff know that he was really staging a completely tongue-in-cheek *adagio pas de deux*. He intentionally made Galahoff grab Geva in all the wrong ways, oftentimes way up near her crotch, with her hip tilted. He wanted to preserve their sincerity by hiding his comic intentions, and so they played as if it were the most beautiful dance within their capabilities. The audiences roared during the out-of-town tryouts in

Bolger and Balanchine clown around during rehearsal. UCLA Library Special Collections, Charles E. Young Research Library.

Boston. "There was great consternation," Bolger recalled, when Geva finally realized what was going on. But the company was able to convince her that she was a great satirist.[17]

Balanchine was also appreciative of the humor that naturally exuded from Bolger's dance. He said, in his imperfect English, "This Bolger...[has] amazing technique of controlling split, he got terrific muscles in leg which make him jump tremendously high, he got very individual plastic quality of the body and amazing relationship to rhythm of the music. His muscles have like the sense of humor."[18]

While making the hoax "Zenobia Ballet" appear realistic was none too difficult, Balanchine and Bolger labored together to make the grueling "Slaughter on Tenth Avenue" look as extemporaneous as possible. Halfway through the number, mobsters sent by the Russians show up to put a hit on Junior: they have been instructed to shoot Junior dead the minute the music stops. Junior learns what's going on after being slipped a note on-stage, and so he persuades the orchestra to keep playing. "I had to keep dancing until they shot at me, or until they were arrested, so it was an evolution," Bolger said. "There's a natural evolution in movement, where one movement follows the other in order to make it flow. And when you work with Balanchine, you work with your hands as well as your body. He has great expressive movements with the hands that show how you desire, how the sexual movements are done with the hands. And also with a kind of movement, a slow adagio movement with one leg over the other, intertwining, always intertwining."[19]

Night after night, this dance would have to stay as fresh as if it had never been rehearsed, while still looking impeccable. It was to take the audience on their last emotional ascension: in the course of the dance, Vera is shot dead by accident, and Bolger's character only narrowly escapes the same fate.As his idol, Fred Stone, once mused, "Sometimes I wonder whether anyone, watching a stage comedian go through an acrobatic routine, burlesquing his own efforts, has the faintest idea of the hours and days, of the weeks and months of grueling practice that go into the performance. It looks so easy. Yet the hours of hard, unrelenting practice that have gone into perfecting my stunts add up to years. The redeeming feature in my case has always been that I like work."[20] And so did Bolger.

Bolger had had some rudimentary ballet training with Senia Rusakoff as a boy in Boston, but he had never been trained as a regimented dancer. He had no working knowledge of what a ballet dancer ought to be. But this is what interested Balanchine in coaching Bolger: he was a fresh mind and a quick study. Bolger's regard for his new mentor coalesced with the fond memories he had of Rusakoff and ballet, and he stuck it out for the five weeks the company spent in rehearsal just on "Slaughter." At thirty-two, Bolger got his first serious dance training. The number Bolger created with Balanchine's patient assistance was considered masterful by audiences and professionals alike.

The "Slaughter on Tenth Avenue" ballet from *On Your Toes*. Bolger kneels in the foreground. White Studios. Photo courtesy of The Shubert Archives.

Despite the show's exquisite dancing, the cast realized in Boston that the book was suffering. Hart was nearly debilitated by alcoholism at this point. Abbott, who had originally collaborated on the book, was busy with other projects and did not want to do more work for *On Your Toes*. The Bolgers rewrote most of the second act. Dwight Wiman offered assistance, too, but his ideas clashed with those of the Bolgers. The star believed that the biggest problem with the production was that it did not stick to a "topic sentence"—one of the seven or so universal themes that categorized all of the successful popular musicals of the era. Bolger pegged this failure on Wiman's ambitious nature: "I think Tony [Wiman's nickname], in the beginning, was so overcome with all of the possibilities...that he forgot to get down to the basics. We had much too much show with too many people doing too many things in the beginning. And Tony didn't recognize that." Bolger believed that Wiman was trying to make the show too smart with high-minded literary and cultural references; he wanted to pare down Wiman's additions to the essentials. As the show prepared to enter New York, he was still dissatisfied. "I could see what was wrong with it, because I'm playing the central part," he said. "And I know all of a sudden that you'd get in the scene, and the scene went away from you. The scene walked away. Then Monty Woolley would come on with a long cigarette holder and start to do some dissertation.... I'd want to say 'What's he talking about?' And when I say 'What's he talking about?,' being the lead character in the show..."[21] Bolger's comments suggest that the book was disunified and that too much was happening at once, thanks to the hodgepodge nature of its writing. However, Bolger's criticism of scenes walking away from him also comes across as an attempt to rationalize his dislike of other actors getting attention when they shared the stage with him.

Bolger had difficulty convincing everyone that their "improvements" to the script were not in fact helpful. Despite the many experts who had gotten the story to the stage, and the competent actors and dancers who brought it to life, everyone worried the show was missing something critical, but no one knew what. It was too late. Now it was up to the reviewers to make their judgments.

In the 1920s, fifteen daily newspapers with fifteen drama critics reviewed the more than two hundred productions that appeared every season. In those days a first-rate show could be put on for anywhere between $10,000 and $20,000, and good seats went for $3 (the equivalent now of $35). During the thirties, when the number of papers and reviewers dwindled—along with the number of shows—and production costs skyrocketed, the remaining critics turned into something like butchers. Criticism had become more important as attendance declined, partly because of the Depression, but mostly because of the popularity of the movies. If a show could win the Triple Crown of New York critical support—positive reviews in the *New York Times*, the *Herald Tribune*, and the *Daily News*—it would find success. If it could earn the praise of two of the three, the show had a chance. But one positive review was not enough to save a production. The most important man to win over was Brooks Atkinson, the theater critic for the *Times*.

The opening night of *On Your Toes* was set for April 11, 1936, while *The Great Ziegfeld* was in its debut week in New York, at the Astor Theater. The final cut of the film ran exactly three hours, an anomaly for the time, but it received little criticism for its length; it was, after all, offering audiences the equivalent of two pictures for the price of one. It also spoke to Florenz Ziegfeld's legacy for producing long, lavish, and sensual shows. Instead, the reviewers targeted the biopic's inconsistencies and anachronisms. Several musical numbers were presented at the wrong point in the portrayal of Ziegfeld's career, and the script frequently mixed up which performer really originated a song in order to manipulate the plot. Bolger was billed as playing himself, which was also an egregious inconsistency: he had never performed in a Ziegfeld show. The authenticity of the biopic would have been better served if Bolger been billed instead as Jack Donahue—the Boston dancer who had found stardom on Broadway in Ziegfeld's 1925 show *Sunny* opposite Marilyn Miller, and in *Rosalie* in 1928, also opposite Miller—whom Bolger strongly resembled in appearance and style. MGM had specifically pursued Bolger to play Donahue roles, but Bolger facetiously thought they had forgotten this point by the time film shooting began.[22]

Bolger himself was given great kudos for the "She's a Follies Girl" number. The film was a success. Based on its reception, MGM decided they wanted Bolger back and offered him a very attractive contract to begin after the Broadway run of *On Your Toes*, and which could be optioned for up to six additional years as the studio desired. The afternoon before his debut as a Broadway star, Bolger went to the MGM office in Manhattan and signed his contract. Ray was at last a star on Broadway, and Gwen felt that MGM's offer was the right business move to make in order to galvanize her husband's fame.

For the first year of his salary, Bolger was to be paid $3,000 a week. It is a myth that Bolger's contract stipulated that he would be chosen to play the Scarecrow if the studio optioned to make a film version of *The Wonderful Wizard of Oz*; no such condition was included. The film Bolger was most concerned about, however, was a planned adaptation of *On Your Toes* following the Broadway run. The contract even stated that he could be loaned to another studio if MGM did not produce the film.[23]

On the opening night of *On Your Toes* at the Imperial Theatre, April 11, 1936, everything clicked. Bolger's natural star power reinforced him, giving him the strength to lead the cast through a successful performance. The script called for Junior to faint at the end of "Slaughter on Tenth Avenue," once the realization that he had survived the mobsters overcame him. In reality, Bolger recalled, he did faint, engulfed by the knowledge of having survived opening night after so much fraught preparation. He was awakened by the reaction to his performance. He said, "*On Your Toes* was a very important step in my career because it made a star out of me. The audience used to cheer the ballet at the end of the show, and that was a very thrilling experience."[24]

Like *Life Begins at 8:40*, *On Your Toes* elevated the intelligence of popular entertainment with its smart humor as well as classic dance forms. In his review, Atkinson praised the quality of writing present in *On Your Toes*: "The lines are capital. The lines are literate." He warned, "For complete enjoyment of 'On Your Toes,' it is recommended that you brush up on your Beethoven and Rimsky-Korsakoff who are mentioned not only in the book but the score. The literateurs and maestri at the Imperial assume that New York is entirely populated by students of art, which is next door to being the truth." Atkinson, not one to exaggerate, cited the entire cast and crew as being "O.K., high class, and sublime," but he gave special recognition to Bolger: "Mr. Bolger is a hoofer whose bucolic personality is so winning that for several years everyone has been hoping to have him at the head of a show. He is in great form just now—singing satisfactorily, clowning with good grace and hoofing like a house afire. Barndance Bolger leads the parade."[25]

Atkinson's review reveals his affection for Bolger's personality. While "hoofing like a house afire" suggests Bolger used more vigor than technique in performance, his comic dancing took as much thought and care as other genres demanded. The difference came from his reliance on his own experiences and emotions rather than the idioms or any particular school of thought or dance. Bolger proved, however, that being a comic dancer for the bourgeoisie held an important place in society, and that entertainment directed at the general public could be used to uplift the standards of culture. His dancing had earned him the status of an Irish prince of Broadway, and now that style was considered true Americana. The *Daily News* and the *Herald Tribune* also found much to compliment in the show, most notably Bolger's dancing, and the cast settled in for a long run. These lines from Percy Hammond's review of *On Your Toes* in the *New York Daily Herald* suggest what attracted Hollywood executives to Bolger: "Until I saw him Saturday...I did not suspect that Mr. Bolger could be so pretty and so romantic. As an actor-dancer he is to be preferred, possibly, to Mr. Astaire."[26]

Meanwhile, *The Great Ziegfeld* won three Academy Awards for the 1936 season, including Best Picture. Seymour Felix earned the Best Dance Direction award (now defunct) for his staging of the eight-minute montage "A Pretty Girl Is Like a Melody." Luise Rainer won Best Actress in a Leading Role. Ultimately, the film would earn more than $4 million in the depth of the Depression. The success encouraged Bolger to pursue additional film work. The Broadway production of *On Your Toes* closed on January 23, 1937, and the show went on the road. Bolger traveled with the company until his MGM contractual obligations forced him to Hollywood in April. He was summoned to appear in *Rosalie*, a film starring the world-famous tap dancer Eleanor Powell.

But Bolger returned to a studio that was greatly subdued by the loss of its mastermind: Irving Thalberg had died on September 14, 1936, at the age of thirty-seven. Despite Louis B. Mayer's attempt to diminish Thalberg's role at the studio while he was still alive, the organization reeled after his passing. Mayer completely shut down Thalberg's production unit. At the time of his death, Thalberg had MGM's first Technicolor film, *Maytime*, in production, starring Jeanette MacDonald and Nelson Eddy, operatic singing stars who successfully crossed the bridge from classicism into pop culture and who generated millions of dollars for the studio. Mayer had long promised MacDonald that she would star in MGM's first Technicolor film, but he spitefully trashed Thalberg's vision for *Maytime*. He ordered all footage shot to be scrapped, the script replaced, and the entire picture redone in black-and-white. Other productions halted. The boy wonder's death brought disorder to other units, too. His influence had been pervasive, and the studio needed to learn to get on without him.

As a result, the film Bolger was scheduled to work on, *Rosalie*, was subject to long delays getting into production. "I had nothing to do," he recalled. "I don't think I did anything practically that whole year. And I was so mad. I could have been on the road with *On Your Toes*."[27] Work on the film finally began five months later, in September 1937. By then, MGM was churning out films to make up for lost time. *Rosalie* was a film adaptation of the 1928 Broadway musical that had starred Marilyn Miller and featured Jack Donahue. Bolger performed the role Donahue originated: Bill Delroy, goofy side-kick to the leading man, who in the film adaptation was played by Nelson Eddy. Eleanor Powell, considered by most to be the best female tap dancer in America, and the best overall by some, starred.

Bolger struggled through the filming. He found it difficult to overcome "the lack of honesty" that motion pictures offered, as opposed to the genuine rapport he built with live audiences on stage. "Everything was mechanical," he said, "Everything can be done over and over again. If you did a tap dance, you'd have to redo the taps afterwards. I found there was a lack of spontaneity in it, because you were restricted." Bolger did not have the kind of formal training that film demanded. Until this point in his career, he had danced for as long as it took to get his idea across to an audience. Now at MGM, he was being asked to tailor routines to fit a verse and two choruses, to facilitate the scoring and sound editing. The greater technical demands of film meant greater restrictions on performers, and Bolger performed best when he had complete control of his work. "I have to be free. That's the difficult thing in the motion picture business—I felt I was dancing in a phone booth," he said.[28]

His process of creating a dance with Powell exposed Bolger's general difficulties with working within the film production model. He recalled that he and Powell were throwing around ideas for their number, when Bolger struck upon something that Powell liked. Bolger taught her the routine, and they left for the day. The next day, Powell had the routine memorized, but Bolger had totally forgotten it, so she had to teach him.[29] His extemporaneous nature proved difficult to capture on film. Bolger's dance with Powell was cut entirely from the film once the creative team realized it was unnecessary to the plot of the storyline. He did not dance at all in the final print of *Rosalie*, and the wasted opportunity frustrated him. MGM saw him as the answer to Jack Donahue, and it was irritating enough for him not to be acknowledged as a dancer in his own right. But he did not see the wisdom in standing in for a historic dancer if the dance numbers were being cut from the film altogether. Bolger, most likely backed up by Gwen, solicited Mayer's help in being cast more appropriately.

Many MGM stars had one of two opinions of Mayer: he was either a tyrant or a teddy bear. Mayer and Bolger remained on terms of mutual friendliness and respect. The studio baron had come from Haverhill, Massachusetts, and he took a shine to the young up-and-comer who hailed from Dorchester. Mayer, like the Bolgers, was a devoted Republican, having served as the vice chairman of the California Republican Party from 1931 to 1932. Mayer took special care to find out what Bolger could be doing and how his motion picture career could be ushered forward. However, even with the personal attention of Mayer, Bolger was lost in the stars.

Mayer tried to make sure that Bolger got another opportunity to perform an important dance. He insisted that Bolger's next project be a special feature in *The Girl of the Golden West,* starring MacDonald and Eddy. The film overlapped with the production schedule of *Rosalie*, and MGM was eager to rush to completion another film starring their operatic box office stars. Faced with a dictate from the boss, producer and director Robert Z. Leonard inserted Bolger into the film. Bolger knew he had been added as an embellishment and that his performance was not crucial to the picture. "It was just six minutes of a comedy bit," Bolger said, "and so when they looked at the picture, they said, 'This is funny, we love it.' But all of a sudden the picture comes up to the end, stops, and Ray Bolger does a short subject, and then the picture picks up again."[30] Once again, the number was removed from the final cut.

Bolger was next assigned to another MacDonald and Eddy picture, *Sweethearts*, which became MGM's first Technicolor film, at last. Bolger's appearance was reduced to a few minutes of screen time at the very beginning of the film: he played a Dutch boy clog dancing in wooden shoes and was totally inconsequential to the plot. Bolger felt his career was "going no place fast" and despaired at the lack of range in the roles the casting executives would give him.[31] "They had [my] image right in the beginning and lost it," Bolger said of the studio. "The biggest thing I did in *The Great Ziegfeld* was not the big elaborate dances I did. I got a lot of nice kudos. But the thing that made the people anxious to see me on the screen again was the small country boy kind of character that I played. And they never followed up on that. For a long time I was known as the face on the cutting room floor."[32] In fairness, Bolger's limited abilities as an actor in front of the cameras most likely reaffirmed to producers that he could not handle broad, challenging roles. It's notable that Bolger's greatest success at MGM at that point was for playing himself in *The Great Ziegfeld*, and that in his subsequent three assignments—when he was tasked to play anyone even slightly beyond his natural range—he was placed in films that were all directed, at least in part, by W. S. Van Dyke, who was known for his success at liberating wooden, stilted actors, and who often worked with Nelson Eddy for this reason. Bolger was compensated and working; he was by no means developing into a star. But some problems resolve themselves, like when new MGM producer Mervyn LeRoy called Bolger to discuss his taking a role in Production 1060, *The Wizard of Oz*.

In the early years of Hollywood, fantasy had been a difficult genre to break into. Then Walt Disney released his first full-length animation through RKO Pictures, *Snow White and the Seven Dwarfs*, in December 1937. Its nationwide release grossed $3 million during the Depression. MGM was eager to cash in on the audience RKO and Walt Disney had cultivated, and they believed a film version of L. Frank Baum's *The Wonderful Wizard of Oz* could achieve this. The rights to create the film were owned by producer Samuel Goldwyn, who had purchased them from the Baum estate. Goldwyn entertained many high-dollar offers for his fantasy property after it became clear that *Snow White* would be a smash hit. Louis B. Mayer won out, securing the rights for $75,000.

Mayer appointed Mervyn LeRoy, who had been hired away from Warner Brothers following Thalberg's death to become MGM's new head of production, to manage *The Wizard of Oz*. An ambitious songwriter named Arthur Freed took an uncredited role as LeRoy's assistant, the first step toward his creating and controlling the most important film musical production unit at the studio. Noel Langley, a South African–born novelist, would receive the main credit for adapting Baum's novel into a screenplay, along with Florence Ryerson and Edgar Allan Woolf.[33] It was his first credit for a complete script for MGM.

The young team approached the creation of the film this way: they would leverage the studio's Rolodex of craftsmen, artists, and electricians behind the camera. In front of it, though, they would put lesser lights. The production team feared that audiences would not accept seeing big, well-known stars in a lush fantasy film. They would need actors who were not too famous, so they called Bolger, who was still upset that the studio lured him away from Broadway for no real purpose. Now he was being offered an important role in a groundbreaking film with a $2 million budget because he was little-recognized. Bolger happily accepted the offer to re-create the Scarecrow role that had made his idol, Fred Stone, a star.

The heroine of the film, it was determined, would be a relative newcomer to MGM: Judy Garland. A former vaudevillian whose real name was Frances Ethel Gumm, Garland was the youngest of three sisters who had formed a singing group, managed by their mother. Her innate talent and unusually powerful contralto voice caught the attention of the likes of George Jessel in the early 1930s. In 1935, she was signed by MGM. The choice was unusual: studio executives found her plain-looking and pudgy. She was thirteen years old—too young to be an ingénue. One of the most fruitful jobs the studio initially found for her was to sing at Clark Gable's birthday party. Her special rendition of "You Made Me Love You" so impressed studio executives in attendance that a number in which Garland as a starry-eyed fan sang to a picture of Gable was added to the film *Broadway Melody of 1938*. Garland also tap-danced. She was then assigned to several films, including *Thoroughbreds Don't Cry* and *Love Finds Andy Hardy* with Mickey Rooney, one of the biggest box office attractions of the late thirties. After LeRoy spent some time convincing Mayer of her suitability, Garland was given *The Wizard of Oz* as her star (Shirley Temple was the early contender) vehicle. Mayer wanted to promote new acquisitions like Garland, Lana Turner, and Greer Garson. This was yet another dig at the legacy of Thalberg, whose own favorite actresses—his wife,

Norma Shearer, as well as Greta Garbo, Jeanette MacDonald, and Myrna Loy—would stop receiving career guidance from Mayer and would soon be "put out to pasture" altogether.[34]

In addition to Garland and Bolger, Buddy Ebsen was hired early on to play the Tin Woodman. Then an order came down from on high that Ebsen should play the Scarecrow, and Bolger the Tin Man. At 6' 3" and 110 pounds, Ebsen seemed the more natural Scarecrow. His brand of eccentric and soft-shoe dancing had served MGM well in films like *Broadway Melody of 1938*, in which he partnered with Garland and earned acclaim. Bolger even began wardrobe testing for the Tin Man. However, he and Gwen scheduled an appointment with Mayer's office to protest the choice, but the studio boss was not interested in the argument. Just how the matter was settled has been lost. In his later life, Bolger attributed the victory to Gwen, who may have used her business acumen to make her point with Mayer. That she stormed in demanding results seems unlikely. On the first floor of MGM's Lion Building, just opposite the casting office, was Mayer's own quarters. To ensure that irate stars and directors could not have easy access to Mayer, he arranged for three different secretaries to block the path to his door, and his own desk was built atop an imposing platform. Mayer relied so heavily on one particular secretary, Ida Koverman, that she was named his executive assistant. Koverman had formerly been an assistant to President Herbert Hoover, so she knew how to protect the interests of unpopular men. She remained a strong force in the Republican Party, and MGM employees recalled that she—as much as Mayer—had the power to make a star or to destroy one. It is safe to assume, then, that the Bolgers had a scheduled appointment to negotiate Ray's part in *The Wizard of Oz*. There was no catching Mayer unaware, and having harsh words would have backfired for the Bolgers. Bolger held out for the part of Scarecrow because he wanted the chance to display his talents to their best abilities and also to pay tribute to his hero, Fred Stone, the original Scarecrow. Though the details of the resolution are unclear, Ebsen, at least, was amenable to the idea of playing the Tin Man. He was happy just to be included in the cast. He later said, "I wanted to be in the picture because I knew it would be a very big one," he said. "And it's always good to be associated with a big project."[35]

With Dorothy, the Scarecrow, and the Tin Woodman set, there remained the question of the Cowardly Lion. LeRoy originally wanted to use MGM's mascot, Jackie, a real lion who was to be given a human voice-over in the film. Bert Lahr was the first two-legged choice to play the Cowardly Lion, and he came at the recommendation of the lyricist E. Y. Harburg, who would be writing the lyrics for *The Wizard of Oz* with his partner,

Harold Arlen, as he had for *Life Begins at 8:40* on Broadway. Based on their prior associations, Harburg knew that Lahr would bring his zaniness and his sweetness to the part of the lion in equal measure.

By the summer of 1938, scriptwriting, songwriting, and casting were well under way. The intense work needed to get a fantasy film off the ground seemed to turn the adults on the project into children and the children, like sixteen-year-old Judy Garland, into adults. The early work also showed that the opulent Technicolor musical, designed to attract children at the box office, would have a mature, satirical edge. A version of the script from June had Bolger's Scarecrow speaking this line to Garland's Dorothy: "I was crazy about a girl once—I'd have married her, only her mother told me she smoked in bed."[36] It was jettisoned, as was most of the suggestive content.

Early drafts of the screenplay also paired Dorothy and the Scarecrow's alter ego in Kansas, Hunk, as love interests. In a deleted verse of "If I Only Had a Brain," which was recorded and filmed, Bolger as the Scarecrow sings that he hopes he will "deserve" and be "worthy" of Garland's Dorothy. While none of this intrigue made it into the final film, Bolger and Garland became good friends in the course of their work, and they enjoyed a platonic, affectionate relationship.

Filming began under Richard Thorpe on October 13, 1938. The first scenes to be shot were of Dorothy discovering the Scarecrow in his cornfield. In the beginning, the aesthetic of *The Wizard of Oz* was quite different from what we think of today. Garland was stuffed into a frillier pinafore and dressed with waist-length blonde hair and heavy pink makeup. Bolger recalled seeing Garland walk on set for the first time on the first day of filming: "I saw the most beautiful child—with an unusual beauty, a special kind of beauty. And I said that's Dorothy. And I remember what a beautiful person she was inside."[37] For Bolger, Garland became a bright light during the filming, which was a difficult and often discouraging job.

Almost all of the cast members found their costumes and makeup to be uncomfortable and inhibiting, thanks to Jack Dawn, the most technically sophisticated makeup artist in Hollywood who created vivid characters without much reference to the comfort of the actors. He became a makeup man for MGM after showing Thalberg, then set to work on *The Good Earth*, a photo of a "venerable 82-year-old Chinese man" that Dawn believed would be a perfect choice for casting in the film. Thalberg agreed, and only then did Dawn admit the photo was really of him, wearing the style of sculptured makeup he had invented. Impressed, Thalberg tasked Dawn with making up two hundred Caucasian actors to look Asian for the film.[38] Dawn's one of a kind talent grew out of his unique personal journeying: he had studied the arts of making masks out of silk and lacquer in China while he was traveling the world on a tramp steamer.

After *The Good Earth*, he continued to use his "sculptured, plastic inlay make-up technique" in service to the studio. It was just what the cast of *The Wizard of Oz* needed. Everyone from the Munchkins to the flying monkeys to the principal players received the Dawn treatment. The principals reported to the studio at 6:30 each morning to be done up and ready for shooting by 9:00. The artist himself considered his makeup for Bolger's Scarecrow to be the most difficult he had ever created, "since the problem was to make a human head look like a straw-stuffed sack, without losing the general appearance of either."[39] *Wizard of Oz* historian Aljean Harmetz wrote that the solution required "a rubber bag wrinkled to simulate burlap" that covered his entire head except his eyes, nose, and mouth; "[it] took an hour each morning to glue the bag to Bolger's head and another hour to blend the brown makeup...and to paint by hand the lines that would make his nose and mouth seem like a continuation of the burlap."[40]

This very first makeup and wig test for Bolger's Scarecrow was thrown out in favor of a much more intricate—and uncomfortable—design by makeup master Jack Dawn. Photo courtesy of the Jay Scarfone/William Stillman Collection.

Makeup for the Tin Man and the Cowardly Lion required prosthetics and pastes that closed off the actors' pores, and Bolger fared perhaps the easiest of Dorothy's three companions when it came to costumes. His burlap costume was coated with asbestos to fireproof him, both from the fire used in many special effects as well as from the Lucky Strikes he smoked for stress relief. Lahr's costume was made of two real lion pelts, and Ebsen's Tin Man contraption consisted of a bamboo skeleton covered in buckram and silver leather.[41]

Filming in Technicolor required the use of rows and rows of hot arc lights, which had devastating effects on the dressed actors. Bolger said, "The mask wasn't porous, so you couldn't sweat. You couldn't breathe through your skin. You don't realize how much you breathe through your skin until you can't do it. We felt like we were suffocating."[42]

On October 24, Ebsen collapsed, unable to breathe. He was rushed to the hospital and put into an oxygen tent. Doctors discovered that the aluminum powder used to make him silver also coated his lungs when he breathed. Filming would not resume for a week, and Ebsen would be let go from the film. On the break, producer Mervyn LeRoy replaced Ebsen with Jack Haley, without telling him why his predecessor had left the role.[43]

Simultaneously, LeRoy declared his dissatisfaction with the footage he was seeing from Thorpe, who had gotten through the cornfield scene, as well as several scenes in the Wicked Witch's castle. He fired the director and brought in George Cukor on a temporary, consulting basis. Cukor disliked the idea of working on The Wizard of Oz. He did so as a gesture of goodwill toward LeRoy. Cukor said, "I was brought up on grander things. I was brought up on Tennyson." He considered Baum's novel "a minor book full of fourth-rate imagery."[44] Still, he knew how to fix pictures. While Cukor did not actually direct any of the film, with LeRoy's guidance he made several key changes to hair, makeup, wardrobe, settings, and musical numbers that were pivotal to creating the look and feel of the film as it is recognized today. His most important contribution was reimagining Garland's appearance and her demeanor. He got rid of Garland's blond wig and most of her heavy makeup. He said, "She was very young and very inexperienced—although very gifted—and so she was too cute, too inclined to act in a fairy-tale way. The whole joke was that she was this little literal girl from Kansas among all the freaks. If she is real, it makes the whole picture funny."[45]

Filming resumed November 4 under Victor Fleming, who would receive the director credit for the film. Again, the cast began with the cornfield scene. The "crow" that was to land on Bolger's shoulder in the scene was actually a raven named Jimmy. Although Jimmy was himself a screen

Bolger had been performing splits in his eccentric dancing since the 1920s. His unique style made the Scarecrow memorable for generations. Photo courtesy of the Jay Scarfone/ William Stillman Collection.

veteran, having acted in more than a thousand films in the 1930s, he was having a rough day when Fleming got to work. He got loose on the set and refused to return to his handlers. The entire soundstage had to be shut down until he was caught, and nothing else was done that day.

The quotidian frustrations and challenges of filming wore on the cast. They had expected the filming to last for around seven weeks when they were signed, but the technical setbacks and the need for painstaking perfection were stretching the production over schedule. But Fleming found ways to keep his actors engaged. As Lahr remembered,

> Fleming had a wonderful understanding of people. He knew the makeup was wearing on us. After a couple of hours it was depressing to have it on. In order for us not to lose interest in the picture, to try and keep our animation, he would call all three of us together and say, "Fellahs, you've got to help me on this scene." Well, I knew this guy was a big director, and he didn't need actors to help him. He'd say, "You guys are Broadway stars, what do you think we should do here?"... and we'd give our suggestions on how to play it.... But I always thought he was just trying to keep our interest.[46]

Working six days a week meant that the actors had very little life outside the picture. Just prior to the filming of *The Wizard of Oz,* Bolger had finally built a house with Gwen in the Hollywood Hills on Doheny Drive. It was, in Gwen's estimation, a cross between an English Tudor and Shangri-La. The couple took to calling it "Bolger Damn" because, as Gwen wrote, "it cost twice as much as originally estimated by a firm of robber-barons with 'comma, Architects' after their names."[47]

Gwen was unhappy with her domestic life in Hollywood and disliked being away from guiding her husband's work. To divert some of her creative energies, she took up sculpting in her free time. She also worried that her husband would suffer "neurologia" from his long days at MGM. Once Bolger finally got home at night, he said, he would have "two bourbon old-fashioneds. The drinks were therapeutic. I needed the alcohol to let me down, and they had enough sugar to give me a kind of a lift so I could manage to eat my dinner and fall into bed."[48] In the same interview, Bolger admitted to doing little more than getting up, going to work, and repeating this process, and half the time he could not even remember doing this.

Other stars were also relying on drugs to balance their workload. MGM gave Judy Garland diet pills—amphetamines—to keep her weight down and to increase her stamina, as well as barbiturates to help her sleep at night. These were frequently prescribed to young actors by the studio doctors, who believed that the pills were harmless. Receiving these kinds of medication so easily and relying on them probably set Garland up for her lifelong struggles with substance abuse. Photos from behind the scenes and in-between takes show Lahr on the set of the Emerald City with one hand sticking out of his lion suit, chain smoking cigarettes.

The other method the cast found for dealing with the stress of their jobs was to play endless practical jokes on each other. Lahr particularly was a worrywart, and Bolger recalled him always doing and undoing the buttons of his costume and complaining about having "gas on his stomach."[49] He also couldn't eat anything more than soup through a straw without damaging his lion makeup. Bolger ordered the most extravagant items for lunch just to tempt Lahr into eating them, which would require Lahr to endure a second lengthy makeup application procedure. Bolger succeeded at this game quite a few times.

Lahr then took his good-natured revenge on Bolger, and he recruited Haley to help him. Haley remembered Bolger's penchant for tall tales, which Bolger himself said he inherited from his Irish progenitors. Haley remembered,

Lahr said to me, "Say that you'd like to be somebody or do something. If you dwell on it, Bolger will tell you that he's done that." I agreed to go along with it. Everyday we had lunch together I'd say, "You know Ray, Bert and I worked together many years ago in a show called *Folly Town*. He was in terrific shape.... He used to box with this guy practically every day." Then you wait. And here's the line. You know this line is coming; you could lay book on it. Bolger says, "I was a boxer once." You were? "Yeah, I wasn't very good, but I had a few fights." And then he'd tell you an incident about one of his "bouts."[50]

Bolger developed a particularly close relationship with Garland—so close that he felt comfortable playing practical jokes on her. She later told the story of this particular prank: "Once I lay down for a nap in my dressing room and someone—never mind who—had put smudge pots under my bed. They slipped in and lit them, then ran out and yelled, 'Fire!' When I stumbled out through the smoke, they threw water in my face."[51] While Bolger was never directly identified as the culprit, this joke smacks of his type of humor. He was greatly preoccupied with fire while playing the Scarecrow.

Jack Haley (*left*), Bert Lahr (*center*), and Bolger (*right*) had known each other from Broadway and vaudeville for years prior to *The Wizard of Oz*. They kept sane in their overthe-top costumes by constantly pranking each other. Photo courtesy of the William Stillman/Jay Scarfone Collection.

Bolger loved children, and none of his previous stage or screen roles had afforded him the opportunity to be near them. It is clear from all of Bolger's reminiscences that he considered Garland to be a child stuck in an adult's world. The long production time required for *Oz* and the fact that nearly all of Bolger's scenes included Garland meant they spent six days a week together for seven months. Childless and yet a touch childish himself, he saw much of his own sensitive, thoughtful nature in Garland, and the two forged a friendship that would last their whole lives based on their natural sympathies. Bolger could see straight away that Garland would never get to be a normal girl. She would have no real proms or courtships or even time to discover herself. He knew her education would also suffer, as his had (albeit for different reasons), and so he encouraged her to read independently on subjects that interested her. Bolger gave Garland a pristine edition of "The Raven" by Edgar Allan Poe, her favorite author. The gift served the dual purpose of also being a gag, recalling the memories of Jimmy the misbehaving raven from their cornfield scenes.

Director Victor Fleming talks through a scene with Judy Garland and Bolger. Courtesy of Victor Fleming Scrapbooks, Margaret Herrick Library, Academy of Motion Pictures Arts and Sciences, Los Angeles.

The hard work continued on *The Wizard of Oz* through November under the direction of Fleming. He was a true he-man and drew great satisfaction from palling around with his good friend Clark Gable. Although Fleming was revered as a talented director and much loved on the set, his rougher inclinations sometimes seeped into his work. During the week of November 24, the cast filmed the "Lions and tigers and bears, oh my!" sequence. Dorothy, the Scarecrow, and the Tin Man are skipping through a dark and overgrown patch of the Yellow Brick Road when they encounter the Cowardly Lion for the first time. During the scene, the skipping, chanting trio is interrupted by Bert Lahr's stand-in, who somersaults into view. Fleming then called "Cut!" The stand-in was then replaced by the less athletic Lahr, who heckled the trembling Tin Man and Scarecrow to "Put 'em up!" before deciding to attack Toto. Dorothy steps in and slaps the Cowardly Lion on the nose. His tearful apology ensues, which reveals he's not a brave lion after all.

Garland cracked up during a couple of takes of Lahr's bawling. Lahr began his theatrics again, and Garland broke character. Fleming called "Cut," walked into the scene, and told Garland, "Darling, this is serious," before slapping her across the face.[52] He called a short break so that everyone could regroup. While this was a common form of reprimand for a child at that time, Bolger must have felt uncomfortable as he watched Garland, whom he cherished, get a scolding. Fleming was not to be challenged. Just how Bolger responded to this incident is lost, but a suggestion of his actions remains in his notes. After Garland's death in 1969, he sat down in his Beverly Hills home with a legal pad and poured out his many memories of her. Some would be for public statements, some for her memorial service in New York, and others just for him, to relive one more time. This particular passage seems to reflect the duality that Bolger always sensed in Garland, that she was a child called on to play the role of an adult too quickly: "As I write this I can feel the quickening of the pulse, the wrenching and tearing of the inner being, the torturous twisting of the mind. Withheld emotion," he reflected. And then he seemed to recount the words of solace he offered her, or at least wished he had, "Keep a smile on your face. Don't let anyone look behind your eyes into your soul."[53] The admiration Garland had for Bolger remained with her throughout her life and the many difficulties within. Whenever the two met after the filming of *Oz*, she always gave him a hug, a kiss, and lavish attention. Garland knew Bolger loved her, and she took fierce possession of and pride in that affection. Years after the filming, she would refer to him as "my Scarecrow." Fleming apologized for his behavior, and Garland maintained great respect for him. She was young and in need of love and support, but she was always aware that she had a job to do.

Garland looks at Bolger attentively between takes. Photograph by Peter Stackpole, from *The Wizard of Oz* series, circa 1939. Print courtesy of the Jay Scarfone/William Stillman Collection.

The MGM management acknowledged Garland's contributions to their enterprise by promoting her from "Featured Player" to "Star" during the production of *The Wizard of Oz*, not long after the incident with Fleming. To commemorate the occasion, Garland was given a portable dressing room trailer, which was parked temporarily in Munchkinland for the cast to admire. Bolger watched all of this, realizing that the sweet, childlike Garland was transforming into an adult harried by the big studio system. He said, "Love was a loosely used word around Judy. L. B. Mayer loved her, Arthur Freed loved her, Roger Edens, Kay Thompson all loved her. At the studio everybody loved her but never enough to give her a feeling of security, protection...so when the crutch weakens and the shield faded into the air, fear took over. Like so many artists, Judy needed to be surrounded by helping hands, sycophants, booster-uppers."[54]

Continued difficulties, including illness, injury, and the retreat of Victor Fleming to rescue *Gone with the Wind* from its own filming problems, meant that the shooting of *The Wizard of Oz* continued through mid-March 1939. Director King Vidor took over for Fleming. He filmed all of the

Bolger on set with Victor Fleming (*center front*) and producer Mervyn LeRoy (*right*). Photo courtesy of the Everett Collection.

black-and-white scenes in Kansas, most notably the sequence where Garland sang "Over the Rainbow." And then, just like that, filming ended and the cast disbanded. A week later, Garland was on the road for a five-week personal appearance tour, promoting her new status as an MGM star before returning to film *Babes in Arms* with Mickey Rooney. What little she had enjoyed of a childhood was officially over, a point Bolger must have empathized with as a man whose own childhood had effectively ended too soon.

Garland was not present at the Hollywood premiere of *The Wizard of Oz*, which was held at Grauman's Chinese Theater on August 15, 1939. Instead Bolger met his idol, Fred Stone, who attended the premiere with his daughter, Paula, a film actress. Garland had been sent with Mickey Rooney to New York City, where the pair would make a live appearance for the New York premiere of *Oz* at the Loew's Capitol on August 17. By then, the pair were the teen idol sensations of the country—250 patrolmen and 25 detectives had kept the crush of fans from the two celebrities when they made their way through Grand Central Station. For two weeks after the premiere, Rooney and Garland performed live before sold-out screenings of the film. When Rooney had to return to Los Angeles for prior film commitments, Bolger and Lahr appeared with Garland through the end of August. She was slated to rejoin Rooney in London, to give a command

Bolger enjoyed esteemed company at the Hollywood premiere of *The Wizard of Oz*. He met his idol, Fred Stone (*far right*), Stone's daughter, Paula (*far left*), and Maud Baum (*second from left*), widow of author L. Frank Baum. Photo courtesy of the Jay Scarfone/William Stillman Collection.

performance for the king and queen. England's declaration of war on Germany on September 3, however, kept the two priceless stars stateside. They returned to MGM as *The Wizard of Oz* screenings rolled out across the country.

Variety predicted the film would perform "box office magic," although the paper speculated it would be a long time before it earned out its budget, which had grown to $3 million. The film review noted that older viewers would remember the Fred Stone and David Montgomery stage production that "played for several years up and down and across the land," and that the film had captured a mix of "childish fantasy and adult satire and humor of a kind that never seems to grow old."[55] Audiences in 1939 would have recognized in the film many of the tropes and gimmicks of vaudeville. Those generations who view the film without having had firsthand experience of vaudeville or the Broadway conventions of the 1930s are fortunate to have the recorded legacy that these players left. Haley, Lahr, and Bolger all brought material from their stage experiences into the roles. Bolger contributed his iconic splits and wobbly-ankled capering. Haley's dance interlude in his solo song, "If I Only Had a Heart," featured

Following the New York premiere of *The Wizard of Oz*, Bolger (*left*) and Lahr (*right*) appeared in person with Judy Garland at the New York Capitol before screenings of the film. Photo courtesy of the Jay Scarfone/William Stillman Collection.

at least one trick from his vaudeville days: he swayed all the way to his right, defying the laws of equilibrium, and returned to standing center only to sway all the way to his left. In John Lahr's biography of his father, he identifies the Broadway origins of each of Lahr's songs in the film and notes that his famous "Put 'em up, put 'em up" challenge to the Tin Man and the Scarecrow came from *Hold Everything*, the Broadway show that had made him a star.

Frank Morgan, the Wizard, had played similar comedic parts on Broadway for many years. He had appeared on Broadway with the Astaires in *The Band Wagon* while Bolger was appearing across the street in George White's *Scandals of 1931*. Billie Burke had a long and distinguished stage career: her high-pitched matronly persona was a Broadway staple long before Glinda descended in her bubble. And of course, there are the songs by Harburg and Arlen, two distinguished Broadway tastemakers. If *The Wizard of Oz* had done nothing else than preserve for one hundred minutes a record, a shadow, of these performances, then it would still have been worth all the difficulties.

The film was well received, but many years would elapse before it became an American legend or turned a profit for MGM. Bolger was not optioned by the studio for another picture. The trade papers of the time suggested that he had been shopping around for a Broadway show prior to *The Wizard of Oz*'s release, and so it is likely that the decision was mutual. At the same time that the Bolgers wanted to return to New York, a couple among their few Hollywood friends, Robert Howard and his bride, the former Andrea Leeds, were returning to Los Angeles from their honeymoon. The Bolgers planned to lease their house to them for two years and then wasted no time getting out of town.

CHAPTER 6

Jupiter Forbid

The Bolgers settled into an apartment at the Ritz Tower, but it wasn't long before Ray was on the road again. What he wanted most was a triumphant return to Broadway, and to re-experience stage stardom he had earned with *On Your Toes*. But that would take time: he and Gwen needed to find the right vehicle, and in the meantime, he needed to re-connect with live audiences. Like citizens across the entire country, New Yorkers were bracing for the United States to enter World War II. Comedy was welcomed but not always effective at dispelling the audience's fears.

Lastfogel sent Bolger back out on the road just after Christmas 1939. He joined up with Sophie Tucker, the "Last of the Red Hot Mamas," also represented by the Morris Agency. They traveled to Covington, Kentucky, to appear in one of the lavish dining rooms of Jimmy Brink's Lookout House. While Covington might have sounded like an out-of-the-way place to recharge and reengage with small-town folks across the footlights, the secluded hamlet was anything but. Jimmy Brink, manager and proprietor, was also the local front man for the Cleveland Four crime family. Brink charmed top talent from both coasts to entertain at his Lookout House, which was a "carpet joint"—an illegal casino fancy enough to have car-peted floors and profitable enough to pay for big-name headliners. Before the formation of Las Vegas as the desert destination for gambling and glit-ter, leaders of organized crime occupied remote towns. Their criminal capitalism went unchecked in places with insufficient resources and gov-ernment dysfunction. More than 60 percent of the American population could reach Covington and its neighboring town, Newport, by train, making rural Kentucky a buzzing destination in the days before air travel became popular.[1]

At the Lookout House, Bolger perfected his patter and endeared himself to dinner show patrons and mobsters alike. He was ready for the next step in his progression to Broadway, which geographically was a three-hundred-mile jump backward: Chicago.

Bolger spent the winter appearing at the Chez Paree nightclub, the Loews Paramount, and Balaban & Katz's Chicago Theatre. Chicago had become a hub for big-band entertainment while Bolger was away at MGM. In 1938, Balaban & Katz's Chicago Theatre had dismissed its sixteen chorus girls and instituted a "band and unit policy." No longer would the theater produce its own acts for the stage. Instead it wanted big bands or ready-made variety acts. The craze for syncopation drew dance fans to the theaters to see the bands, offering great exposure for the comedians and dancers who appeared on the same program.

Variety summed up Bolger's reception at the Chicago Theatre this way: "Ray Bolger used to get laughs first with his knockabout dancing comedy, and then applause. Now he gets applause before he starts anything and then softens the audience into laughter later."[2] He had returned to dance in movie houses as a known film personality, intensifying the audience's enjoyment of his well-known material, like his dance-pantomime of a prize fight, and his newer material, like parts of the Scarecrow routine. Bitter cold temperatures in Chicago kept patrons at home, however, and the grosses were just this side of profitable.

While performing in Chicago, Bolger signed on to a new Shubert revue to debut on Broadway that spring: *Keep Off the Grass*, which he would headline with Jimmy Durante. As the leads of the show, they presided over an assemblage of sketches joined loosely with a Central Park theme. Jane Froman, a popular mezzo-soprano, and society-lady-turned-actress Ilka Chase were also featured. Bolger reunited with George Balanchine, who was brought in as choreographer.

Balanchine hoped to achieve art for the show. He was hamstrung, though, by the Shubert brothers' hard-nosed business manager, Harry Kaufman, who considered Balanchine's dances overwrought and wanted them cut down. One day in rehearsals he discovered Balanchine working on an adagio dance. "George, what are you doing? Why the slow motion?" Kaufman asked. The choreographer replied that he was building toward a climax. "Please, George, you're killing me with the slow motion. I want you to start with the climax. Give me nothing but climaxes."[3]

Bolger received a dance spot about every twenty minutes of the show, a mix of solos and partnered numbers. But his best opportunity came in the

Bolger (*far left*) rehearses *Keep Off the Grass* with Ilka Chase (*center*) and Jimmy Durante (*far right*). UCLA Library Special Collections, Charles E. Young Research Library. Photo by Jerome Robinson.

form of a satirical song performed with Chase and Durante, called "Rhett, Scarlett, and Ashley." It lampooned that *other* significant 1939 film, the one that beat out *The Wizard of Oz* for the Best Picture honor: *Gone with the Wind*. Durante and Chase also made a smashing parody of *Romeo and Juliet*, and a newly discovered deadpan singer, Virginia O'Brien, was added to the bill. But the show was long on talent and short on quality writing. After a tryout in New Haven, it went not to New York, but to Boston, where it spent a couple of extra weeks at the Shubert Theatre, getting worked out. Even there, *Billboard* forewarned, "The Messrs. Shubert apparently have been seeing too many movies. Their latest revue, *Keep Off the Grass*, looks like a Hollywood misconception of what a revue should be like. Hampered by a weak book, the show seems destined for an early demise."[4]

When she wasn't visiting her husband and the cast of *Keep Off the Grass*, Gwen stayed in New York and orbited through the social scene. As Anglophiles, the Bolgers watched the unfolding of World War II with trepidation. They gave of their spirit and cash to aid the Allies at fundraisers, such as when Gwen attended Noël Coward's Star Club at the Hotel Astor.[5]

Bolger clowns around with a signature high-jump during rehearsals for *Keep Off the Grass*. UCLA Library Special Collections, Charles E. Young Research Library. Photo by Jerome Robinson.

For the evening, Coward hoisted his usual entrance fee from $5 to $10 to benefit the Allied Relief Ball for French and British Non-Combatant War Relief. More than eight thousand society ladies and gentleman, entertainers, and public figures crushed into the club. Coward crooned "I'll See You Again," from *Bitter Sweet*, his Broadway hit that had just been adapted into another film musical for MacDonald and Eddy, and which Coward found "dreadful" in comparison with the stage show.[6] Coward introduced Eddie Cantor, a Gus Edwards protégé like Bolger, as "the Noel Coward of the Bronx." All the while, Gwen mingled with Vivien Leigh, Laurence Olivier, Alfred Lunt, and Lynn Fontanne in the most exclusive clique to form that evening.

At public events like these, when Gwen showed up sans Ray, the small talk often centered on her role in the Bolger enterprise. She wrote around this time:

> To date, I have restrained myself from answering the question with the same question: What do you do while your husband is working? Do you go to the office with him every day? But like a good wife watching the store I am polite to the customers. If the person is really interested, I make it worth her (it is usually a woman) while with a twenty minute recounting of my Herculean labors. It goes something like this: balance books, sort and prepare fan mail for answering, study market reports for discussion with broker, pay bills, read new script, re-write sketch for radio show, answer personal mail, wash Ray's special hand-made wool socks, etcetera.[7]

The relish Gwen had for being Ray's other half is palpable in her writing; she knew, but did not overestimate, her contributions to his success. Her support enabled him to focus solely on performing. *Keep Off the Grass* arrived in New York and began its run at the Broadhurst Theatre on May 23, 1940. From the beginning, ticket sales lagged behind expectations. The Shuberts wanted to close the show for the month of July, the dullest period on Broadway, and regroup in August. The chorus protested the decision to close the show, even taking the issue to the review board of Actors Equity. They preferred the management's proposition that the show stay open through the summer and that all cast members receive a one-third reduction in salary. However, Ilka Chase and Larry Adler, a harmonica specialty performer in the show, refused to accept a cut of any kind. As a result, the show ended its run after just six weeks and forty-four performances. The chorus resented Chase for the loss of their livelihoods at a time when good-paying theatrical work was hard to come by: an estimated 26 to 39 percent of the show business labor force in the United States was out of work.[8]

Bolger had little to fear. Despite the failure of the show, he at least could take satisfaction in knowing that it had lasted as long as it did, according to the papers, due to the drawing power of the two lead comics. Besides, starring in a failed Broadway show in those fraught pre-war days was better than being unemployed. And troubles at home still could not compare to the devastating carnage unfolding in Europe. Congress was debating the Burks-Wadsworth Act, which for the first time would enact peacetime conscription for men between the ages of eighteen and sixty-five. No one was sure how long the shows would go on.

Bolger was a known entity represented by a man who had grown into one of the finest agents in the country, and neither jobs nor interest dried up for him. Around the time that *Keep Off the Grass* closed, Bolger caught the attention of Harry Kalcheim, a vaudeville business veteran who, as a booking executive for the Paramount movie theater chain, scouted out acts that might round out bills featuring name-brand orchestras. Paramount was also seeing huge box office draws thanks to its band policy, and Kalcheim understood how to analyze potential talents and position them for success in his theaters. Kalcheim booked Bolger into the New York Paramount with the Xavier Cugat Band, the house orchestra of the Waldorf-Astoria Starlight Roof, and several Latin dancers at the end of July and into August.

Bolger by then did not need to perform for money. Though he received no residuals for his work, his time at MGM at least ensured him financial security for many years. In March 1940, the studio announced that Bolger's 1939 earnings totaled $87,000, equivalent to more than $1.5 million in 2018. While this was a fraction of studio boss Louis B. Mayer's haul of more than $700,000, the median income for American men at the time was $956. As long as Gwen continued to manage their fortune well, they had no reason to worry. Because of the huge sums to be made at movie studios, many known actors were disinclined to make live appearances at theaters, even at the prestigious Paramount. In-person appearances were highly taxed, which ate into their profitability, and many performers receiving Hollywood salaries threw away the grease paint for good. However, Bolger hit the boards, suggesting that he loved it and that he wanted practice. Being wealthy was important to him, but he had other priorities. His ambition goaded him on.

Bolger went next to Detroit for Paramount, appearing at the Michigan Theatre with the Charlie Barnet Orchestra. America was still technically on the sidelines of the war between the Axis and the Allies, but President Roosevelt had already signed the Selective Training and Service Act of 1940 into law. This authorized the government to draft 900,000 men, called "selectees," for one year of service. Simultaneously, Detroit's auto industry benefited from an injection of $250 million in munitions contracts. War production ramped up and new kinds of automobiles rolled off the assembly lines. This translated into larger theater crowds with extra spending money in that city; to tap into this market, Paramount was willing to spend large sums to secure top talent. The Bolger-Barnet expenditure brought big box office returns to the Michigan: $20,000 and

$24,000, respectively, for their two-week appearances. But as far as bands and comics went, the records were still held securely by Gene Krupa and Bob Hope.

America's increasing dread of the war in 1940 showed in the number of musical films and stage shows put into production that year. With drama unfolding in real life, audiences looked to theatrical entertainment for respite. This led to revivals of beloved musicals from the post–World War I era, which could bring to viewers comforting nostalgia and the hope that they would win another global conflict. At the same time, British film production of any kind all but ended. The chairman of Britain's Grand National Pictures declared in July 1940 that no further production could be expected there until Hitler had been defeated.

These conditions generated Bolger's next film project: a reimagining of Jerome Kern's 1925 hit Broadway musical, *Sunny*. The original production had starred top-shelf dancers Marilyn Miller, Jack Donahue, and Clifton Webb. Herbert Wilcox, a prominent British director who had found refuge from the war crisis at RKO Pictures, would direct his longtime protégée and secret romantic companion, Anna Neagle, in the lead role. Neagle was a versatile and bewitching blonde who had earned acclaim in England as a singer, dancer, and straight actress. As Bolger tactfully described them, "He was the Svengali, and she was the girl."[9] *Sunny* would be Wilcox's 300th film as producer-director and his sixteenth consecutive film in which he directed Neagle. The pair had already completed the nostalgia musicals *No, No, Nanette* and *Irene* for RKO. While in Hollywood for these films, they became familiar with Bolger's work at MGM and on stage. They would have understood his style's similarities with that of the "Irish prince" Jack Donahue, whose part they wanted Bolger to assume for *Sunny*. They made the Bolgers an offer, and they accepted. Wilcox then went about getting Bolger a standard three-picture contract at RKO.

The Bolgers returned to the West Coast. Ray knew that the plush conditions he had enjoyed at MGM would not be part of his RKO experience. He later said, "The personality of Metro was elegance. The personality of RKO was a very pleasant, and nice, and comfortable place to work. And it was wonderful people, and you would get your job done, only it was not going to be any Metro-Goldwyn-Mayer."[10] But in some ways, the experience must have been like déjà vu. Once again he was the supporting actor forming a trio with a film power couple. At MGM, it had been Nelson Eddy and Jeanette MacDonald. Now it was Wilcox and Neagle. Filming began on December 13, 1940. Leon Leonidoff had traveled from New York to stage the dances.

Sunny tells the tale of Sunny O'Sullivan, a sexy circus star in New Orleans. One night, while trying to rush to the tent during Mardi Gras, she runs into a handsome stranger. The two kiss before Sunny flees, trying to reach the stage in time. Her anonymous amour, unbeknownst to her, is headed ringside, where he spots his new love astride a white horse. The rest of the film is a game of cat-and-mouse with a decidedly unfeminist tone. Sunny becomes more or less a pawn between her wealthy love interest Larry Warren (played by John Carroll) and Henry Bates (played by Edward Everett Horton), the family's lawyer who is determined to bust up the romance.

Bolger plays Bunny Billings, the master of ceremonies who longs for Sunny's affections but helps her track down her mystery man, Larry Warren. Once the two are finally together, Sunny chafes under the condescension of Larry's wealthy relatives. She decides to make a break and return to the circus. Just when it looks as though she will establish herself as an independent heroine, and while she is donning an elaborate new costume in her trailer for her return performance, viewers hear a roar and soon realize that Larry is driving her trailer away. The pair end up on a yacht, where Sunny has a quick change of heart; Larry's wealthy aunt, the family matriarch, marries them at sea.

Sunny featured just three dance spots. Instead of furthering the plot, they interrupted it, much like Bolger's dancing in *The Great Ziegfeld* and *Sweethearts*. His presence in this film, as in others, is most valuable because it serves as a reference for his stage work.

His first number in the film is "Who?," the musical's best-remembered song. He receives the top-hat-and-tails treatment, which RKO was providing with such great effect to Fred Astaire, and the scene opens with Bolger, as Bunny Billings, languidly puffing a cigarette. He murmurs, rather than sings, the first three lines of the song: "Who stole my heart away? Who makes me dream all day? Dreams I know can never come true . . ." The orchestra swells and the chorus picks up the lyrics, leaving Bunny free to stub out his cigarette and pursue Sunny, who sits with her back to him across the stage. Sunny flirts with Bunny from behind her large ostrich-plume fan and then the two are off. The staging of the number is reminiscent of "Cheek to Cheek" from Fred Astaire and Ginger Rogers's RKO film *Top Hat*, made five years previously. But here, the feathers on Neagle's billowing gown seem intended to distract from Bolger's deficiencies as a ballroom dancer. His hands can't ever seem to find Neagle's, and his torso is uncharacteristically stiff as he ushers her through jumps and twirls. The romantic dance fit neither the Bunny Billings character nor Bolger's personal style.

Later, when Larry's tony relatives descend on the circus to scope out Sunny, they find her performing a comic hornpipe in drag with Bunny. In this brief dance, it's Bolger who outshines Neagle. This is Bolger's only filmed appearance in a sailor act. The costume accentuates his long legs and precise stepping, and his experience with Irish toe work is clearly superior to Neagle's. The two do not jibe comically. The beautiful Neagle fails to act like a rough-and-tough sailor, or even to parody one. Neagle comes across as the femme fatale trying, and failing, to yuk it up with Bolger, whose funny walk and slight walleye are all too naturally comical.

Bolger gets a real opportunity to display his dancing prowess with one solo number at the end of the film. Bunny is on the circus stage once again, awaiting Sunny's comeback after jilting Larry. The audience waits for the star, and suspense builds as Bunny delays them with an acrobatic tap number. Performed again to "Who?," Bolger's routine here gives us an idea of the type of number he must have performed at Radio City Music Hall for its grand opening, when he was also tapping in top hat and tails, working a giant stage with elegance and athleticism.

Production on the film ran until April 1941. Following the release of Sunny, Bolger began a second picture for RKO, Four Jacks and a Jill, with Desi Arnaz, June Havoc, and Eddie Foy Jr. The best adjectives used to describe the creation of the film are the ones Variety eventually assigned the finished product: unorganized and disastrous.

At the same time that Bolger busied himself with these B-films, the US government, knowing that war was in the offing, configured a public-private partnership to provide entertainment to troops. While Congress had voted in 1940 to enact peacetime conscription, they had voted against funding a military entertainment program. To support morale-building recreation for recruits, members of the private sector stepped in. Most notably, Thomas J. Watson, the CEO of International Business Machines (IBM), created the Friends of New York Soldiers and Sailors Inc. in 1940. This grew into the Citizens Committee for the Army and Navy, Inc. Known commonly as the CC, the Citizens Committee aspired to provide entertainment for the entire standing army, but they accomplished very little. No framework existed for connecting civilians with military leadership to provide high-quality, high-volume entertainment to American troops in the numerous camps.

In an attempt to satisfy this need, six charitable organizations agreed to consolidate their efforts and resources in February 1941 into one umbrella organization large enough to serve the entire military: the United Services Organization (USO). Representatives of the YMCA, the YWCA, the National Catholic Community Service, the National Jewish Welfare Board, the Salvation Army, and the National Travelers Aid Association met in Washington, DC. The newly named USO installed Walter Hoving, president of luxury department store chain Lord & Taylor, as chair. The business people at the helm of these early initiatives wanted to keep show business people as far from their operations as possible, to their detriment. Nonetheless, many entertainment industry leaders did what they could to support morale among enlisted men. Abe Lastfogel particularly distinguished himself with his unselfish desire and unparalleled industry connections. For example, when the Army Camps of California issued urgent appeals to the War Department in June 1941 for something to amuse the National Defense program recruits, the War Department could not get results from the CC. They got in touch with Abe Lastfogel directly. Through the Artists Managers Guild, Lastfogel was pooling an unofficial spring of talent that California military bases could draw from.

September 1941 marked the one-year anniversary of peacetime conscription, and yet the civilian morale organizations had provided almost no entertainment to the troops. The problem was that business acumen did not translate into show business knowledge. The few early shows put on by both the CC and the USO were characterized by mismanagement, inconsistent quality, and mixed reviews. An entertainment operation large enough to serve the needs of the entire American military at home and abroad, then grown to two million in number, would need to be managed by people who knew how to put on a show.

The CC and the USO met again in the nation's capital and prepared for major reorganization. This led to the creation of USO-Camp Shows, Inc. Now just one company, which would answer directly to the Department of Defense, was in charge of managing finances, securing sponsorship, organizing and funding touring companies, and maintaining relationships with the military. And for the first time, the nation's entertainment program would be managed by show business professionals. Edward Duryea Dowling, a Broadway director who had staged Bolger in *Life Begins at 8:40* and *Keep Off the Grass* and who had just acted in and directed the Pulitzer Prize–winning drama *The Time of Your Life*, was named president. Abe Lastfogel served as Camp Shows' most ardent administrator. He would be named Dowling's chief aide within the year. Now it was time for desperate attempts and big risks. The bureaucratic bottleneck could be broken only by bold action. The actors were going on the road and overseas.

Almost the entire civilian population was determined to band together and support the Allied effort. Lastfogel, with the same zeal, invested his show business expertise, his business acumen, and his reputation as the most honest agent in the world into his efforts to provide every American soldier who would be drawn into a long and bloody conflict with the gift of entertainment from home. His productions made the efforts of all the impresarios of yore—Pastor, Hammerstein, Keith, Albee, Edwards, the Shubert brothers—look like the small time. In the eyes of the entertainment industry, he had embarked on putting together the world's largest vaudeville show, for the world's most deserving audience.

As organized by Lastfogel, Camp Shows Inc. supervised four distinct circuits of morale-building touring shows. The Victory Circuit presented full-scale musicals and revues. The Blue Circuit offered smaller-scale entertainments at training centers and bases in the United States with limited theater facilities. A third circuit would bring morale to all of the army and navy convalescent hospitals in the United States.

But the fourth, the foxhole circuit, traveled overseas to more than thirty-five countries and regions. The work would be dangerous, uncomfortable, and unpredictable. Despite their star status, celebrities traveling abroad received no guarantee that they would return alive. Lastfogel needed a resolute group to send on a B-18 bomber, the mode of transportation for the project called "Camp Show Unit #1." He got his first-ever client on the phone. Without hesitation, Bolger agreed to go. Unit #1 would participate in a tour of the Caribbean islands Puerto Rico, Trinidad, British Guiana, and Saint Lucia.

Joining Bolger on the plane were comedians Stan Laurel and Oliver Hardy, Chico Marx, actor John Garfield, singer Jane Pickens, and dancer Mitzi Mayfair. They were to be the most ambitious vaudeville troupe yet: could they bring a piece of home to young men abroad? Could they delight them while they prepared for war and anticipated death?

The company got the chance to bond during a rocky flight departing from Miami. Upon landing in San Juan, they revived their constitutions with spirits at the El Morrow Officers' Club. From the moment the actors touched down, the soldiers were interested in them. On the back of his menu from El Morrow and his tab, Bolger began keeping running lists of the names, ranks, and interests of the men he met so that he could converse with them whenever they crossed paths again. Camp Show Unit #1 was the troops' first exposure to home in many months, and mutual amazement cropped up between the soldiers and the stars.

In British Guiana, the unit played to a cantonment chopped out of the dense jungle. Every new hardship Bolger encountered increased his wonder at the troops' ability to disregard their own discomforts. He described the sunburned young men as "all Americans, with eyes which say 'We have jobs to do. OK, Joe, we will do them.'"[11] Throughout the trip, Bolger felt such gratitude to the troops that it was almost palpable, humming through him, energizing him. Deep in the verdant jungle, with miles of open sky overhead, Bolger realized the young men surrounding him were the first line of defense "around our homes, lives, our individual liberties." He and his fellow performers were also experiencing a way of life completely antithetical to the one they knew. As entertainers, they were used to being wide awake at 11:00 P.M. Now they had to be rested and up before dawn, shuttling between the islands in their plane before afternoon storms obscured the line of sight. They had only cold-water showers at most of their destinations. The most extravagant meal they enjoyed came from a tiny Chinese restaurant at Guantanamo Bay, Cuba. A strict fifty-pound baggage limit meant that the men were wringing out their shirts several times a day and the women went on in wrinkled silk dresses with broken peacock feathers. But several performers attest to giving the best performances of their lives during their Camp Shows engagement, and the troops' recollections of the acts that visited them also confirmed this.

In Saint Lucia, the outdoor stage was still being built when the unit landed. The last nails got hammered in just a few minutes before the announced curtain time. Pickens acknowledged Bolger's "fine showmanship and the way the boys took him to their hearts for his brilliant performing and his very genuine desire to give them the time of their lives."[12]

The breathless enthusiasm with which Bolger experienced the tour comes through clearly in a rare telegram he sent his wife, care of the War Department:

NOW OUR JOB IS TO DO OUR UTMOST IN RECREATION FOR THESE BOYS STOP I AM SURE EVERY ONE OF US ON THIS TRIP WILL NEVER FORGET ONE MOMENT THESE EXPERIENCES STOP WE HAVE SEEN VIVIDLY CRYING NEED FOR CONTINUANCE THIS SORT OF THING[13]

After a month, the tour returned to the United States on November 27, 1941. Before disbanding, most of the entertainers vowed that this first trip would not be their last.

For a week, life resumed its normal patterns. Bolger returned home to Gwen in their apartment at the Ritz Tower and picked up a vaudeville engagement. But on December 7, 1941, as Bolger was winding down after an evening's performance with Harry James at the Paramount, the Japanese launched a surprise attack on the US naval base at Pearl Harbor, Hawaii. The next day, the United States entered World War II.

Variety, the all-knowing mainstay of show business news, foresaw the ways that the war would impact Broadway: "Due to such war conditions as blackouts, curtailed transportation facilities, rising cost of living, increased taxes, longer working hours, odd-hour work shifts, drafting of

Ray Bolger and Mitzi Mayfair dance in Puerto Rico for soldiers in November 1941. Army Signal Corps photo courtesy of UCLA Library Special Collections, Charles E. Young Research Library.

men, and more jobs and home-defense activity for women, the amusement-seeking habits of the nation will change drastically."[14] Early in 1942, a ban on the sale of tires, trucks, and personal automobiles hit both entertainers and their audiences hard. New York City movie theaters practiced turning off their neon, and the entire Atlantic City shoreline likewise pulled the plug on their marquees. It would only be a matter of time before Broadway itself was ordered to dim. Fear pulsed through the country, even in New York café society. People stayed close to home for the little entertainment they took in.

Throughout the entertainment industry a desire arose to contribute to the victory cause. Top entertainers devoted their time to selling War Bonds at rallies or otherwise raising funds. Thanks to the early experiments of USO Camp Shows, there was now a proven way of bringing entertainment to the troops. Hundreds of singers, dancers, vaudevillians, chorus girls, comedians, and specialty acts signed up for tours of duty as "soldiers in greasepaint." Despite their contributions to morale, entertainers were considered nonessential for draft classification: many actors served their country in the armed services, but evidence suggests that Bolger received a deferment.

In late 1941 and early 1942, Bolger found himself caught between competing interests. His experiences as a member of Camp Shows Unit #1 galvanized his sense of patriotism. He wanted to return to the organization. However, after his tour in the Caribbean, Bolger intended to go into rehearsals for another Broadway show.

Choreographed by George Balanchine and featuring the newcomer Gower Champion, *The Lady Comes Across* was to be another star vehicle for Bolger. Producer George Hale had secured Jessie Matthews, known as the queen of the British film musical, as the female lead, although she had not danced on stage in a decade. As the lady who came across the Atlantic for the role, Matthews arrived in New York in great distress. British ships were prime targets for the Germans, and the cargo ship carrying Matthews's luggage had been torpedoed and sunk. Bolger arrived for rehearsals with no difficulties but found his contract had been rescinded by Actors Equity. The union's rules stipulated that managers could not sign actors until a salary guarantee was deposited with the performer. As Bolger had received no money on signing, the agreement was void.

Rather than protest the legalese, Bolger entertained an offer from his old colleagues Richard Rodgers, Lorenz Hart, and Dwight Wiman to appear in their anticipated Spring 1942 production. *Hotel Splendide* was based on Ludwig Bemelmans's *New Yorker* stories of a busboy who becomes a waiter. The show promised to be a grown-up version of the kind of work Bolger did as a "juve" for Gus Edwards in *Ritz Carlton Nights* and for Rodgers and Hart in *Heads Up!* Wiman delayed completing the casting past Christmas 1941, as he was unsure of the show's ability to enter a contentious Broadway season. Top shows like *Hellzapoppin'*—at the time, the longest running musical in Broadway history—were commanding $4.40 for its best seats—a price not charged since the pre-Depression days. Competition was strong and demands were high. Increased wages from war production jobs created a strong demand for quality entertainment, as did the public's desire for an antidote to the stresses of daily life. In the end, Wiman and Rodgers scrapped their plans, although not before lining up another project. Rodgers, Hart, and Wiman knew they had to aim for a blockbuster.

They called the musical *All's Fair* and left audiences to conclude the thought: "in love and war." The musical comedy was about both, between the Greeks and the Amazonians, but it was also a veiled reference to the conflict abroad. Rodgers and Hart adapted the musical from *The Warrior's Husband*, the play that had made Katharine Hepburn a Broadway star a decade before. In their rewrite, Rodgers and Hart wanted to use the war against the Axis powers as subtext while at the same time providing fare that could relieve audiences of their wartime worries. They decided to tell the tale of the Greek army, led by Theseus and Hercules, arriving in the land of the Amazons, where they encounter women warriors and stay-at-home dads. The Greek soldiers are accompanied by a war correspondent, Homer, who is the author of a recent bestseller called *The Iliad*. Homer complains frequently about the pressures of having to make good literature from terrible source material.

The plot focuses on one of the twelve labors assigned to Hercules: stealing the Sacred Girdle of Diana from the Amazons' queen, Hippolyta. The Amazons capture the unwitting Greeks, and a romance blossoms between Theseus and Antiope, the ladies' warrior-leader. Meanwhile on the Amazonian home front, the foppish Sapiens, after several corkscrew plot twists, is forced on Queen Hippolyta by his wealthy mother, Pomposia. In exchange for Hippolyta's marriage to her son, Pomposia has pledged financial support in the war against the Greeks. As the women rush off to war, Sapiens sits at home and knits.

The material was adult, intellectual, and sometimes esoteric: with recreational travel mostly curtailed, Rodgers and Hart knew they were writing for New Yorkers rather than out-of-towners. The casting called for femme fatales and hunks. But Rodgers insisted that the star of the show, Sapiens, would be played by a dancer. The enormous success of the Rodgers and Hart musical *Pal Joey*, with Gene Kelly, convinced Rodgers that a dancing lead would be much more interesting than a singing one. Bolger was their first and only choice. The material required sweeping motion (the dances were filled with leaps, lunges, and flailing) but subtle comedy, and it would be Bolger's task to showcase his talents as an athletic eccentric dancer without coming across as silly. Before they could extend offers to anyone, however, they were going to need cash.

Rodgers had signed up to be Wiman's associate producer. This meant that a lot of the unpleasant tasks fell to him, such as tracking down investors. His reputation as a Broadway master preceded him, however, and he was able to secure a significant amount of money from Howard S. and Marguerite Cullman, the power couple of Broadway angel investments. Two of their shows, *Arsenic and Old Lace* and *Life with Father*, were current hits.[15]

With their significant outlay, Wiman and Rodgers recruited two veterans: Irene Sharaff create the costumes and Jo Mielziner designed the staging and lighting. They blended sumptuous details from ancient times with the sexiness of the present day to evoke pinup girl culture in the midst of antiquity. Mielziner hung bold striped and polka-dotted curtains and painted wispy frescoes of toga-clad gods. The motifs came from photographs of Greek and Roman urns, but his artwork recalled the warm, graceful, and distinctly American iconography that decorated Rockefeller Center. He filled the scenery with bright reds and blues—bold declarations of American patriotism in front of which the Athenians and Amazonians waged mock war. And those warriors play-fought in serious frocks. For her part, Sharaff found that the signature elements of 1940s dress could look chic and antique at the same time: pleats, ruching, and statement headware adorned the statuesque chorines and brawny choristers.

The stage was set to complement dynamic leads, and Rodgers and Wiman signed four. In addition to their dancing star, who was to receive top billing, they brought in Benay Venuta, a flashy blonde and a Broadway fixture, who had been Ethel Merman's replacement in *Annie Get Your Gun*. Bolger was not traditionally handsome, and for the role of Queen Hippolyta, the creative team needed an attractive woman who was equal parts unusual and alluring. Venuta's physique and singing voice were reminiscent of Merman's. Hart had discovered Venuta belting "Deep in the Heart of Texas" at a USO event in New York, where she stopped the show, and he wanted her for the production from that moment on. Venuta's strength complemented Bolger's weak vocals.

Constance Moore, a beautiful film star with a weak voice but legs to die for, joined the cast as Antiope, the leader of the Amazonian army. And Ronald Graham, with whom Rodgers and Hart had good luck as a supporting player in *The Boys from Syracuse*, played Theseus, the leader of the Greek army. Moore and Graham would be the juvenile romantic interests of the show. Among the four of them, the leads had singing, dancing, and wooing covered.

Because replicating the success of *Pal Joey* was the goal, Rodgers and Wiman brought in dance director Robert Alton, who had discovered Gene Kelly and choreographed him in that show. Alton had gotten his start as a dance director for the Paramount-Publix movie theater circuit. He and Bolger had known each other from the time that Alton became dance director of the New York Paramount Theatre, in 1933. The experience of creating fresh dances for the movie-going public gave Alton a particular appreciation for blending tap and ballet and for showcasing the unique attributes of his dancers rather than remaining true to a particular style. After leaving vaudeville, Alton split his time between the East and West Coasts. He favored the colorful, bright, sexy dances that laid the foundation for Broadway style as it is known in the twenty-first century. Alton was known for his physical flexibility, having begun his career as a contortionist. He and Bolger delighted in dancing together, and Bolger swore that Alton could high-kick even higher than he.[16] Because of his eclectic background, Alton was not afraid to break conventions and try something new for the benefit of his dancers. He had several tricks in mind for the star, but Bolger later declared that most of the dancing "was my own, so Bob Alton was hardly any help to me."[17] But Alton made important contributions. In keeping with his instincts to innovate the presentation of dance on stage, Alton, with Mielziner and Rodgers, devised a ramp that slanted up from the footlights into a three-foot rise, where all the dancing would take place. This would better display the dancers' footwork—and the ladies' legs—to the audience. Alton also helped to emphasize the ballet in Bolger's dancing and movements.

It is true, however, that the show lacked a specialty dance number for Bolger. He found great opportunities to distinguish himself as a comic, particularly in the mock-love ballad "Everything I've Got Belongs to You," sung as a duet with Venuta. The closest Bolger had to a show-stopping dance number was a jitterbug-like *pas de deux* with the aged Bertha Belmore, who played Sapiens's mother, Pomposia.

If Alton's contributions to the dance numbers seemed small, he was not the only member of the creative team who seemed to contribute less than the billing suggested. Larry Hart was suffering from acute alcoholism during the making of the show. Rodgers visited him frequently in the hospital, bringing pen and paper with the hope of inducing Hart to work, but Rodgers himself completed most of the writing and revision of the book. Director Joshua Logan, known for his mood instability, also terrorized the actors for much of the rehearsal period. Bolger's wife took advantage of the vacuum created by the chaos and became Rodgers's de facto apprentice. Ultimately, she rewrote much of the second act of *All's Fair* during the out-of-town tryout at the Shubert Theatre in Boston.

It was during this time, in late May 1942, that the show's named changed. *All's Fair* had been used by another show a few years prior. Even though that production did not make it to Broadway, the conventions of priority involved in naming shows demanded that Wiman and Rodgers come up with a new name. They settled on *By Jupiter* for the show's Broadway transfer, an echo from one of the show's main songs, "Jupiter Forbid."

When *By Jupiter* opened on June 3, 1942, the trade press deemed it a significant hit, if not a blockbuster. The conceit of effeminate men and belligerent women fell flat with most critics at a time when the public rallied around the heroism and masculinity of their young men going overseas to fight. Additionally, the reviewers identified the second half of the book as a major weakness of the production, without realizing that they were criticizing Bolger's wife's writing. *Variety* stated, "The first act is strong;

the second act lets down considerably. Ray Bolger is a funny man but after a while it palls to see him as the nurtured male."[18] *Billboard* likewise found the adaptation "distasteful and occasionally almost depraved" but said that in the course of the show "a faint echo of the charm of the original [*The Warrior's Husband*] is heard. That faint echo is enough to make the proceedings enjoyable."[19]

The popular press perceived many of the same flaws but also found a lot to praise for a general audience. Brooks Atkinson reviewing for the *New York Times* declared in his headline "Ray Bolger in the peak of his career." He noted how the second half of the book "reared back and passed some particular vagary of impudence" but also insisted that Bolger's performance "ought to be photographed, documented, and preserved in the time capsule for destitute posterity." He continued:

> In the last eleven years, Mr. Bolger has come a long way. When I first saw him in George White's "Scandals" in 1931 he was an amiable, bucolic hoofer in the well-loved style of Jack Donahue, whom he naturally admired. Only two or three years ago it was obvious that he had become the best comic dancer of the musical comedy stage. But after his virtuoso performance in "By Jupiter"... Mr. Bolger [is] at the top of his profession. It is all of a piece as a comedy antic— droll, sly, broad and immensely skillful.[20]

The show enjoyed a strong run. Bolger's charms kept the seats filled for months, more so than the book or the songs. The only song to transcend the show was "Nobody's Heart Belongs to Me," a plaintive ballad sung first by Benay Venuta and reprised (comically) in the second act by Bolger.

During his work on *By Jupiter*, Bolger also filmed a spot for the *Stage Door Canteen* film being shot at the Fox Movietone Studio in New York.[21] More than eighty-five stars made appearances in the revue-like musical, which attempted to recreate the atmosphere of the Stage Door Canteens all over the country, where servicemen could receive free refreshments and entertainment. Bolger appeared as a soldier and turned his tap antics into a drill routine performed to the song "The Girl I Love to Leave Behind." Rodgers and Hart prepared the number for him, based on the song "The Boy I Left Behind Me" from *By Jupiter*. Bolger burlesqued the rookie's first day at camp—learning how to handle a gun, bring his heels together in a smart-sounding click, and understand a drill sergeant's yapping. He would use this act for the basis of a new stage routine, which he called the "Sad Sack Routine," in reference to the popular comic strip character of the day that lampooned the ineptitudes of a lowly private. Bolger was itching to use his talents to aid the war efforts, in particular, the brave men he knew were defending the country.

By Jupiter could have enjoyed several hundred more performances, but Bolger informed the company in May 1943 that he would be leaving the show, citing exhaustion. Buster West was floated as a possible replacement, but in the end the show could not continue without its original star.

The entire cast was outraged by the news, but no one more so than Richard Rodgers. In his eyes, Bolger was destroying a successful show out of selfishness. Bolger ought to have known better, after suffering the closing of *Keep Off the Grass* due to the demands of Ilka Chase. And the chorus and stagehands would feel the loss more deeply than the principals would. Rodgers was so embittered by Bolger's departure that he made his personal feelings public. Responding to an announcement of the show's impending closure in Ed Sullivan's "Little Old New York" column for the *New York Daily News*, he sent a rebuttal, which Sullivan published:

> "*By Jupiter* is shuttered, so Bolger is a loafer."
> I read it in your column, and it's stuff you shouldn't go fer.
> Let's read the line correctly—
> Here's the way it should be uttered,
> Bolger is a loafer, so *By Jupiter* is shuttered.
> P.S.: Gross last week, $21,655. Performers
> out of work, nearly one hundred.
> Love, Richard Rodgers.[22]

Bolger had more complex reasons for leaving *By Jupiter*, though. One entry from his pocket agenda, looked at in hindsight, is particularly telling for its sequence of appointments. For the Friday after Thanksgiving, 1942, he had penciled in three appointments: a 1:30 lunch with Abe Lastfogel, a 2:30 appointment with Richard Rodgers, and a 4:45 meeting with the draft board. These activities outline the government secret that the Bolgers were concealing: Ray had promised Lastfogel he would go overseas with the USO after a year's work on *By Jupiter*. He informed Rodgers privately of the decision, but he could not share his true reason for leaving the show due to the USO's efforts to keep the camp show trip under wraps for security. He then proceeded to make plans, confidentially, with the military. After 427 performances, *By Jupiter* closed on June 12, 1943, the same day that Eleanor Roosevelt was in town, visiting Australian and New Zealander soldiers at New York's Aznac Club. Abroad, Heinrich Himmler, one of the most powerful members of the Nazi Party in Germany, ordered the extinction of all Jews in ghettos in Nazi-occupied Poland. The horrors of the war were spreading, and few would remain untouched by them.

Despite the public backlash for his perceived laziness, Bolger kept up his façade. *Variety* reported that Bolger was headed to Hollywood for recuperation, stopping along the way at the Marine base in the Mojave Desert to entertain troops. In reality, this was a practice run for Bolger's next stint in the USO. "Ray Bolger vacationing at Arrowhead, intent on staying in California all summer," *Variety* said on June 30. Three days later, unbeknownst to the media, Bolger boarded a military plane in San Francisco bound for Hawaii. He was now the manager and one-half of Camp Show #89. He and British-born comic and pianist Little Jack Little would tour the South Pacific, the first entertainers to do so.

Gwen stayed at her mother's home in the Fairfax section of Los Angeles and began writing letters the moment after Bolger's departure, informing her inner circle of the truth. In her message to their good friend Meyer Davis, the bandleader, she quipped, "I don't think Mr. Rodgers will be writing any more jingles for a while. I wonder if he has the grace to be embarrassed?"[23]

CHAPTER 7

Soldiers in Greasepaint

Bolger's participation in the first USO tour to the South Pacific shaped his approach to entertainment, politics, and, arguably, life. Bolger caused Gwen, his manager and confidante, considerable loneliness and even depression in this period. Managing her emotions had been difficult enough when her husband was merely touring the country for vaudeville. Now he was in active war zones, often unable to communicate for a month at a time. She wrote to him daily but received no response. She enlisted her mother, her hairdresser, her nephews, and even Broadway columnist Louis Sobol to send messages. The workaday details of their lives, she knew, would be treasures for their man overseas. No one received a reply. She tried to channel her anxiety into domestic activities.

As usual when away from her husband, Gwen made the Rickard home in Los Angeles her home and remained in the company of her strong female role models: her mother, Edna, and her aunts. From them she plucked up her resolve. She busied herself with all manner of cooking and gardening. A month passed. She wrote, "A strong back and a green thumb and dirt on my hands instead of time. The servant problem is really a blessing in very heavy disguise to the many lonely hearts in the world today."[1] She also took on, with the help of Johnny Hyde of the William Morris Agency, negotiations for a very prestigious film deal. Without the need to attend to Bolger's daily routine, she could more actively shape his long-term prospects. British director Victor Saville wanted Bolger for a supporting role in his forthcoming adaptation of the play *Heart of the City*. The film would be a Technicolor musical, telling the story of a London variety theater that refused to close for even a single performance during the Blitz. Saville was best known in the United States as the producer of

MGM's *Goodbye, Mr. Chips*, Bolger's favorite movie, which was filmed in London. Like Herbert Wilcox, with whom Bolger worked at RKO, Saville took refuge in the United States during the war, only he made Columbia Pictures his base. As in his role in *Sunny*, Bolger would be cast as the short side of a love triangle between the romantic leads played by Rita Hayworth, the top pinup girl for the men overseas, and Lee Bowman, who had been Hayworth's co-star in her smash hit the year prior, *Cover Girl*. Bolger knew Hayworth from golfing together. Both were also devout Catholics.

Gwen negotiated with Saville to rework a major plot point for the film. In the original script she was offered, Bolger's character was to be jilted in the end by Hayworth's character, and then, with a stiff upper lip, carry on without her. Gwen requested that Bolger's character instead die in the bombing of the theater, as a means to throw the audience's sympathy to him. Saville agreed. He went back to the scriptwriters and, giving Gwen credit for the idea, had them rewrite a fade-out scene as she had recommended. She marveled that her input had been incorporated so freely into a major picture and began to desire a place of closer contact with the creatives of the entertainment sphere. She put aside the gardening gloves and started going out more and seeing people.

Gwen filled her subsequent letters to her husband with news from all her industry friends, including Jack Warner, Sol Lesser, Harold Arlen, and Danny Kaye. How closely the Bolgers' lives were wrapped in each other is especially apparent in Ray's absence. Without her husband, Gwen continued to hone her skills in scriptwriting and producing, in the service of their future collaboration. But as of August 12, 1943, Gwen had still not heard a word from Ray. She had seen him off on July 15 to Travis Air Force Base and had no idea what had transpired since then.

As the ranking star of Camp Show Unit #89, Bolger was declared the operation's manager. USO-Camp Shows Inc. provided him with $1,800 in traveler's checks to see him through the tour. Bolger was to pay himself $70 a week. He was responsible for managing the funds, maintaining bills and receipts from any hotels along the way, and keeping track of incidentals. These were all responsibilities that Gwen normally managed for him at home, and it remained to be seen what sort of a job the dancer would do as an administrator. Bolger also had no idea if he would like the man the USO had paired him with. John J. Leonard, better known as Little Jack Little, traveled from New York to San Francisco to report for duty. A songwriter, comedian, and radio broadcaster five years Bolger's senior, Little would serve as Bolger's piano and accordion accompanist as they toured the South Pacific.[2] The two had never met before, and Bolger knew just a little about Little: he had been born in London but grew up in the American Midwest. Best known for his song "In a Shanty in Old Shanty Town," Little had toured the country with an orchestra after becoming a pioneer of radio crooning in the 1920s. His wife had died in 1940. The trip abroad offered him one way to put his loss in perspective. Bolger looked forward to learning more about his accompanist on his arrival, in the day scheduled for rest at their hotel in San Francisco. Once the duo united, Bolger called the airfield to check in and Little went to the hotel to shower. Bolger got the airfield operator on the line and told him they were ready for their scheduled departure the next day. The airman corrected him, saying, "You've got forty minutes to get out here if you want this plane." As Bolger remembered it, "Jack dressed in the taxi."[3] They were on their way to a constellation of islands so underdeveloped that soldiers were still slashing at the jungle foliage with machetes to make way for make-shift stages.

The USO sent just Bolger and Little to the South Pacific because many of the territories they would tour were still considered unfit for women, even for female nurses. The two would be sharing some of the islands with the Imperial Japanese Army. There would be no buffer between Little and Bolger if their personalities did not jibe. But from their first day together at Travis Air Force Base, Bolger judged Little to be easygoing and unflappably Midwestern. They would need to depend on each other, and fortunately neither had any reservations about doing so. They both soon realized how many forces existed in the world that wanted to destroy them and the American troops serving all around them.

The United States was the most powerful presence in the South Pacific. At the time of Bolger and Little's tour, there were three million active military personnel there.[4] The United States' large aircraft carriers stood like bastions in the sea, fending off the smaller and faster Japanese ships that kept the Americans on the defensive. To the Allied powers, Germany still seemed the bigger threat, and many troops were being ordered across the European theatre. But the Japanese were fighting with ferocity in the South Pacific. While Japan lacked a serious infantry, its navy allowed it to make all-out attacks on the Pacific islands. Japan also benefited from an extensive fleet of fighter planes, and it had invested in state-of-the-art research for bombers. The Japanese would use these bombers to exhaust their target, then swoop in with heavy artillery and fighter planes to finish the attack, creating thousands of American casualties even in short battles for small islands.

After the attack on Pearl Harbor on December 7, 1941, and the Axis powers' declarations of war against the United States, the Japanese had launched several coordinated attacks in the South Pacific. They had taken over most of the Philippines, Singapore, and Malaysia by 1942. By the end of 1942, however, the Japanese were almost out of their famed fighter planes, and the United States had started its invasion into the lands the Japanese had captured. They began at the Philippines. Japan had conquered most of that nation's territories in a single summer. Unlike the ease with which the Japanese had succeeded, the US Army faced huge losses as the Japanese fought to the last man standing, intent on shutting down the munitions trade between the United States and its ally, Australia. Meanwhile, the Americans wanted to push the Japanese back to Tokyo. Between June 4 and June 7, 1942, while Bolger was busy with *By Jupiter*'s Broadway debut, the Imperial Japanese Navy attacked the American Navy at Midway, an atoll roughly equidistant from Asia and North America. The US military inflicted horrific damage on the Japanese and won the battle. In the aftermath, the Japanese turned their attention to capturing the Solomon Islands, a crucial connection between Australia and the United States. Beginning in August 1942, the Japanese and the Americans fought the Battle of Guadalcanal, the largest of the Solomon Islands. Both sides wanted control of the strategically important Henderson Field airway on the island. The battle was waged by land, sea, and air nearly every day and every night.

The Americans fought the Japanese in disease-ridden jungles, in extreme heat and rain. Dehydration and malaria were persistent concerns. Clothing rotted. Constant infighting meant supplies could not always be replenished. But the greatest threat of all came from the Japanese snipers. The Americans were not psychologically prepared for enemies as cruel as the Japanese and won the battle for Guadalcanal only after half a year of savage fighting. The victory spurred the American military's new strategy of island-hopping: Americans would seize Japan's major island bases throughout the South Pacific, and each conquered island's resources would be used to support the next offensive, until the Japanese had been pushed back to Tokyo. Bolger and Little tried to offer relief to as many of the men on these islands as possible.

The first leg of their journey took them from the mainland to Hawaii. Bolger recalled, "The seven hours to Honolulu left no doubt that Jack and I aren't what you could call creative 15,000 feet over an ocean whose limits the eye couldn't trace."[5] Instead of planning their routine, they took the time to steady themselves before the adventure swept them into action. But when they touched down at Hickam Field in Honolulu, the performers received their first request for a show: would they entertain five thousand GIs that afternoon, on an improvised platform? They obliged, despite feeling ill-prepared. Bolger walked on stage and told the crowd, "We haven't got an act, but it's certainly a delight to be here with you in this South Sea Paradise."

The assembled soldiers offered up some good-natured booing. While these islands have come to be associated with vacationing havens, at this time they were dangerous jungles isolated from all the soldiers' cultures and family members back home. The performers soon realized that the troops enjoyed being kidded about the lives they were leading. They had found a fail-safe routine. They also learned how eager their audience was to interact with live entertainers. The soldiers had had their fill of movies on their bases, and they weren't shy about singing and talking back to Bolger and Little. The first performance turned out to be 105 minutes of ad libbing.

Unit #89 continued on to Fiji and New Caledonia for a couple of short visits, before arriving in Brisbane, Australia, which was to be their home base and travel hub, in late July for nine days. Brisbane's population of 350,000 swelled to more than a million with the arrival of American troops in December 1941. At the start of the war, the Australian government admitted its fears of being unable to defend itself from the persistent threat of Japanese invasion. They were willing to submit to an American supreme commander for the southwest Pacific and received General Douglas MacArthur. The servicemen who came with him were billeted in Brisbane for training before being sent to the Pacific front. The lucky men returned there from the front for rest and recreation. The unlucky men were sent there to convalesce in hospitals. Bolger and Little found the city packed with soldiers. They received two of the last hotel rooms and decided to flip a coin to determine who got the room with the window. Bolger won, but they spent very little time away from the troops and were all but embedded with the enlisted men. They ate with them, listened to their stories, and provided some news of home. Bolger mostly assured the men that the States were still filled with women of all shapes and sizes. On the backs of envelopes and stray papers, he again made lists of men's nicknames, ranks, hometowns, and interests.

Shortly after their arrival, Bolger and Little came up with new material and a stage show they would use for most of their tour. They always incorporated the details of the men they knew would be in the audience. They also fell into a schedule. On their first afternoon, they visited the Greenslopes Military Hospital and spent twenty minutes in each of the hospital's six wards, talking with the men who couldn't get up and around and offering entertainment. Little would play the accordion, and Bolger would sing and dance. They learned quickly that the troops were most interested in nostalgia. Even in July, "White Christmas" was the most requested number. Bolger said, "The hospitalized lads constituted an entertainer's dream audience—every line was sure fire."[6]

Little and Bolger put on their first stage show in Australia at the end of July 1943. The army engineers had built an open-air theater with benches to accommodate four thousand men sitting and another four thousand standing. The stars were slated to perform for an hour before dinnertime. The theater filled up for their first performance. On his piano, Little rattled out the melody to "Stardust," and then canted, "I wanna tell ya a story." Bolger and Little alternately extemporized the tale of their arrival from San Francisco, peppered with references they had picked up around Brisbane. Bolger took the lead on dance and comedy. He offered up his prize-fighter sketch, his Sad Sack routine from *Stage Door Canteen*, and his Scarecrow number. Drawing from Little's immense knowledge of local radio stations back in the States, the pair satirized various small-town radio hosts. Men from the region being lampooned would identify themselves in the audience by yelling "Yahoo!" The stars took requests for songs, dances, and gags. Then Bolger asked the audience if anyone wanted to come up on stage and dance with him. The commanding officer, in the wings, sent word to Bolger and Little that the show was running over time, and that the men had to move on for their evening meal. When Bolger tried to explain to the audience that they had to wind things up, they booed vehemently. "To hell with chow, go on with the show," someone in the audience yelled back. A cheer went up, and the show continued. The commanding officer acceded that dinner would be served whenever the show was over.

Bolger recalled that from that first day on, their afternoon performances meant late dinner. After dinner, Bolger and Little performed an evening show, which would run until eleven o'clock or so, depending on how involved the audience got. Occasionally, a soldier made a wisecrack that neither Bolger nor Little could handle or top. They would then stop the show and ask the audience to give the slyboots a hand. After the night show, the celebrities would then visit around the camps. Bolger discovered that many men had never heard of him before, but that they could be won over to his side quickly after he began swapping tall tales with them. Bolger reported that many of the men also confided their greatest wish to him, and that it was often the same: to go home, get married, and never leave their country again.

In the spare moments Bolger and Little had for themselves they improved their act. A couple of times, their audiences had requested songs that they did not know. "Pistol Packin' Mama" and "Sunday, Monday, and

Always" had become popular after the two had left home. They listened to the radio for several nights, taking down words and music, so that they could teach themselves the numbers and add them to their repertoire. Bolger also continued to write home. From Australia, Bolger sent some unnecessary civilian clothing back to Gwen in Los Angeles. On a long piece of toilet paper he wrote, "Dearest Darling, These clothes are about as much use to me as this Australian tissue. I feel fine—All my love."

Gwen's many letters remained unanswered, and she was hurt. She was still working with Johnny Hyde to land the *Heart of the City* deal, but she wanted more money than producer Sol Lesser was offering. Johnny recommended they wait it out, and Gwen agreed. When not negotiating the movie deal, she relied on getting out in the sun and exercising to stabilize her moods. "You should see me in a bathing suit and your sun helmet— motivating a lawn mower!"[7] she wrote to her husband. She reported all the news of home, but in her heightened anxiety she focused on the many ways she thought the country was changing. Even Broadway—the physical street and the lives that revolved around it—looked very different. Gwen wrote of the passing of theatrical critic John Anderson, who had given her husband his first notice in a major New York theatrical review. Burns Mantle, another major critic, had retired.

All of a sudden, thank-you letters started to arrive at the Rickard home from soldiers who had seen Bolger's performances in Hawaii and Australia. This is how Gwen first learned that her husband was safe and making a very positive impact on his audiences.

One soldier wrote,

We are familiar enough with the entertainer who comes up to see us and doesn't have any prepared script, so he says, then proceeds into a stilted, time-worn act. Bolger and Little really did an impromptu show. They did anything and everything asked for. During the evening performance the mike went dead and the talented Bolger, who is to me one of the greatest dancers of them all, really went to town. He did imitations of Hitler, Musso, Hirohito and anybody else requested, any dance you could think of, mugged, and even sang. Little sang and played all requests, and told plenty of good stories.[8]

She was thrilled that her husband was so well received abroad but hurt that he would not send word of his accomplishments himself. She did the only thing she could do. She waited.

In early August, Bolger and Little flew 1,300 miles northwest from Brisbane to Papua New Guinea. Just seven months before, in January 1943, a combined American and Australian force had wrested Papua New Guinea from the Japanese. The territory had seen some of the worst brutality of the war, and the men stationed there had little relief. Unit #89 went first to Port Moresby, the Papua New Guinea force's headquarters, on the west coast of the Papua territory. It was here that Bolger wrote his first letter to Gwen that passed the censor successfully. "Dearest Darling," he wrote on August 2, from atop a broken ammunition container he had confiscated as a desk inside his tent, "I've written before this but the letter came back to me." He had written on both sides of the paper, and this was against the strict rules set for military personnel writing letters back to the States to keep secrets from being intercepted. He reported that he had not yet received any mail from her and that "it's a strange world without you." He promised to send little scribbles as frequently as possible, although he knew he was sworn against providing any details. As if to acknowledge that the censor, rather than his wife, would be the first to read his romantic words, he signed his letter, "Have you heard? I love you, Ray."

A few days later, Bolger and Little flew to Milne Bay, three hundred miles east. The Battle of Milne Bay in 1942 had been the first outright defeat of Japanese land forces in the war. While performing there, Bolger and Little Jack Little met then-Lieutenant General Walter Krueger, who commanded the Sixth US Army. The men of this field army would be heavily involved in operations to neutralize Japan's major base in the South Pacific, Rabaul, which was also located on Papua New Guinea. Krueger approached the entertainers with a special request: to travel north to Kiriwina, in the Solomon Sea, where his men of the Sixth Army were preparing for hellish battle against the Japanese at their other stronghold, Arawe. The general was concerned for his troops, who were in a very remote location and had little to occupy their time; the only entertainment they had received since leaving the States was movies. Krueger requested that Unit #89 spend eight weeks with his men, which would require the performers to extend their planned tour by that amount of time. Bolger and Little were willing, even eager, but they needed clearance from their overseers in Brisbane before they could alter their route. In order to obtain this green light, they had to travel back to Australia to make the petition themselves: a 2,400-mile-round-trip, when Kiriwina stood less than two hundred miles from Milne Bay, but they got the approval.

"That was where we learned how many different outfits it takes to fight a war," Bolger said of Kiriwina. "We got to understand what officers meant when they told us it took four to seven men behind the lines to keep one man fighting up front." Bolger and Little played to bomber commands, which were continually moving in and out on missions against the Japanese. In return, they were given impromptu lessons by the troops in subjects like meteorology and radio operation.

On Kiriwina, the celebrities met the Seabees, the men of the 15th Naval Construction Battalion (initials "CB"). The Seabees' motto was "Can do!" and they were responsible for transforming the jungle islands into functional shops of war. They built roads and causeways, which were so filled with trucks when a ship came to unload that traffic crept along at five miles an hour. They had even built out of coral the airstrip on which Bolger and Little's B-18 landed. They completed another airstrip on the island in thirteen days, working twenty-four hours straight until it was finished, even when they were under fire. The island was pelted by heavy rain, which also impeded their hard work and depressed their morale. And still they persisted. Bolger had never been more impressed with a group of people. These men worked, surrounded by dumps for ammunition and oil. They had little to cheer or comfort them, and yet they never shirked or rebelled. They kept at it for the sake of the men laboring on either side of them. Bolger believed they represented the very best of American ingenuity and camaraderie, and he saw them as a model for society.

Though he admired the Seabees' patriotism, Little viewed their situation from a different perspective, which he worked into the act on Kiriwina. He saw that along with periods of intense activity, these soldiers also fought off boredom and anxiety during long stretches of inactivity while they awaited new assignments. In a risky move, Little told some of the soldiers that they reminded him of a friend he had once, who was detained in an insane asylum: one day when Little visited, an inmate started clapping his hands. Little asked him why. "Gee, you got to do something around here to keep from going screwy," the patient replied. The men of Kiriwina took the story to heart, and for the remaining five weeks of Bolger and Little's stay, the soldiers would spontaneously clap in the course of the day as an expression of their situation. Bolger said, "These boys don't want to come home but can't understand why they're kept on desolate islands so long with nothing to do."

Bolger and Little left the Sixth Army in early September 1943. They headed from Kiriwina to Milne Bay on a Patrol Torpedo boat, hoping to catch a flight at Milne Bay that would take them back to Port Moresby. After their long wait, a plane arrived, but it was so heavily packed that Bolger and the other men looking for a lift had to climb over a mountain of freight and luggage to get to their seats along the wall. The plane took off and struggled to get altitude, confirming the passengers' fears

Bolger and Little Jack Little especially enjoyed performing for the 15th Naval Construction Battalion, or the "CBs," in the South Pacific. UCLA Library Special Collections, Charles E. Young Research Library.

that it was overloaded. When the weather closed in on them, the pilot took a short cut, flying so low that Bolger could see the whitecaps on the waves beneath. For a moment, he was sure he was on a ship rather than a plane. It was Bolger's first brush with death on the tour.

The show went next to Oro Bay, Papua New Guinea, where Bolger and Little figured on entertaining for a few days before making an easy hop back to Brisbane. They were touched at how soldiers lined up with ten shilling Australian bank notes, which they called "short snorters," for autographs after shows. As some of the first performers in the South Pacific, Bolger's and Little's signatures headlined what would become a long list of celebrity signatures acquired during later tours from entertainers such as Bob Hope, who came after Unit #89 had broken the ground. Leaving Oro Bay was not as easy as the entertainers had anticipated, because the United States had launched a paratroop attack on nearby Lae, another major Japanese base on Papua New Guinea. Most of the region's planes were tied up, but Bolger and Little were able to find a general on his way to Australia. His bomber was not yet commissioned for combat, but the entertainers were willing to hitch a ride. They christened the plane "Pistol

Packin' Mama" after the hit song back home. Once on board the plane, Bolger and Little knew they had about four hours before arriving in Australia, and they settled in for a nap. Not long into the flight, however, fog closed in and the pilot lost sight of the sun.

The night chill awoke Bolger around the time he had expected to reach Brisbane. Looking out his window, he saw neither land nor sea. He and Little, also awakened by the cold, moved to the front of the plane for warmth. They heard the pilot say, "Navigator, have you any idea where we are?"

"No," came the reply. The pilot then called for the passengers to put their parachutes on. The plane was starting to ice up. He brought the plane lower to de-ice and to look for stars. The passengers rushed to the back of the plane and donned their parachutes. Because Bolger had learned how to operate interphones with the Seabees, the pilot gave him a headset to wear. He would give Bolger the signal when it was time for everyone to jump. Instead, Bolger got word from the pilot that the moon had broken through. The navigator got his bearings and announced that they would land in Brisbane in an hour and a half. Time passed, but the destination that the passengers saw beneath them seemed too small for that city. An Aussie with them identified the location as Amberley, fifty miles from Brisbane. Some heated back-and-forth exchanges ensued over the radio. The pilot didn't know whether the airfield could take a plane as large as his bomber, but there was no time to find out: they had fuel for just twenty minutes more of flying time. The passengers braced themselves. Bolger recalled, "Finally, . . . [the pilot] set down in the cleanest landing I ever made."

While Bolger was preparing to bail out of an airplane over the Coral Sea, Gwen in Los Angeles felt desperation of her own. She had at last received a brief message from Bolger, in late August, bearing the news that he planned to extend his trip by another two months. He could not tell her why due to his oath of secrecy. He did not seem to have received any of her mail, or her news, which was that she had finally settled the negotiations on *Heart of the City* with Bolger's original October return date in mind. Saville wanted to begin shooting on November 1. On learning of his plans, she wasted no time insisting he put his professional considerations first, writing back immediately:

> I know this will be a disappointment to you . . . but we must be practical and you can go out again to boost the boys. It isn't every day that the right thing comes along and I think you have earned the right to take advantage of it.[9]

On the day he was originally supposed to return home, Gwen received another letter from Ray. "This morning I opened a V letter from you with eager anticipation," she wrote on October 1, "only to find a revolting picture with not even hello written on it, from you. Maybe I've lost my humor, but it simply irked me." She destroyed the picture, leaving no record of what she had seen to upset her, and she took to opening Bolger's mail. From overseas friends of Bolger's writing to him at home, Gwen learned that he had vacationed for two weeks in Australia, and had even met General MacArthur, his wife, Jean, and their only son, Arthur MacArthur IV. Young Arthur was just five years old. When the boy offered Bolger his hand to shake, Bolger's instantly went limp. He collapsed to the ground in a heap, transforming without warning into the Scarecrow of Oz. But this didn't amuse Gwen. "I can't understand why you failed to sit down and write me a real letter," she fumed. "I got a hasty, type-written note signed Ray Bolger asking for news of your business, and that is all.... Whoever is responsible for failure to provide your correct address ought to be hung."[10] What Gwen had not told her husband was that her health had been strained over the autumn, and that in a week's time she would be undergoing a tonsillectomy. She wanted her husband's comfort.

Meanwhile, Bolger remained ignorant of his bungling a film deal by extending his tour. Unit #89's next assignment, in late September, sent them to Guadalcanal in the Solomon Islands. It was their most dangerous assignment yet. The United States had wrested the airfield from Japanese control more than a year before, and the Japanese were eager to reclaim it. The American commanding officers warned Bolger and Little on their arrival that the full moon would attract action from the Japanese.

While Bolger lacked the support of his relations in these difficult days, some measure of home seemed to be all around him. He found himself hosted in the tent of USMC Major Irving Robert "Bob" Kriendler. As a civilian he owned and operated the 21 Club, which stood guarded by wrought-iron gates and an array of jockey statues on West 49th Street in Manhattan. The club was one of the Bolgers' favorites when they were in town. Somehow, Kriendler had also managed to secure a wrought-iron gate for the front of his tent on Guadalcanal.

Having a friend on Guadalcanal was a comfort to both Ray and Kriendler. Bolger and Little gave a performance on their first night after arriving and went to bed around one in the morning. Sirens woke them shortly after. A Japanese plane was dropping bombs on the island, but the radar could not locate it. The plane left without causing damage. But the next night, twelve planes approached. Bolger and Little ran to the trenches. The island was alive with searchlights blazing and anti-aircraft guns exploding. They saw a light bounce off a plane at twenty thousand feet. It looked to be about as big as Bolger's thumb. He saw the whole plane glow and realized that a bullet had found its way to the plane's gas tank. The pilot tried to maneuver in such a way that the fire would be extinguished, but he was doomed. The plane blew up in the air. Three minutes passed. A light bounced off another plane and a tracer caught it. This pilot, too, tried to save himself, and landed just three city blocks' distance from Bolger and Little in their trench. The men on Guadalcanal took down two more planes: one landed on an adjacent island, the other crashed in the sea. "I thought I'd be nervous after my first bombing, fearfully lying awake expecting another. I was surprised to find myself relaxed—and I slept soundly," he wrote. These attacks continued for three more nights.

In the hush of the evenings, before the planes arrived, Bolger and Little picked up Tokyo broadcasts on their transistor radio. On one occasion, they tuned in and heard Little's "In a Shanty in Old Shanty Town." The Japanese played American music, particularly love songs, in an attempt to psych out the GIs. They tried to manipulate the soldiers' strong sense of nostalgia for the music and then insinuate that all their loved ones at home had moved on without them. This angered the American entertainers, and it encouraged them to leave everything on the stage for the troops every night and to move on to more obscure and dangerous locations. Bolger and Little understood that for many of the men, the entertainers were the men's first interactions with home, and, more poignantly, sometimes the last.

Where death seemed ubiquitous, there also was love. The loss and destruction made Bolger think on what was most important to him in his life: Gwen. She would turn thirty-four, without him near to celebrate her life, on October 7, 1943. Bolger followed General Krueger's men to Kiribati, on Canton Island, and would remain there for most of the month. The Marine Corps were preparing for the first American offensive against the Japanese, at their stronghold on Tarawa.

Bolger finally got word from his wife of his planned involvement in *The Heart of the City*. Despite how much he missed her, and how much promise a picture with Rita Hayworth offered, he would not leave Krueger's men. He and Little wanted to remain with them until the fighting began in late November. But in early October, Japanese raids intensified on the island. The Marines continued to down "Jap Zeros" and maintain control of the area, but the USO, at Krueger's insistence, ordered Bolger and Little out of the territory. They left for New Caledonia in the first hours of October 8, 1943. Back in Los Angeles, it was still October 7, and Gwen was celebrating her thirty-fourth birthday in the California Hospital of downtown Los Angeles.

Gwen's thoughts had been filled with her husband the week before her birthday and her tonsillectomy. She vacillated between great love and great disappointment. On the afternoon before her operation, she lay in her mother's living room when the doorbell rang. Her mother answered: it was the postman, bringing a small package addressed to Gwen, from Ray. Gwen ripped it open. She found a cat's eye ring.

The surprise shocked Gwen back into equilibrium. She went to sleep wearing the ring. She kept it around her finger as a talisman when she checked into California Hospital, although the staff insisted she remove it before her surgery. A great deal of fussing ensued, but Gwen relented. After the operation, on the morning of her birthday, she received a letter from her husband, wishing her a happy day, and explaining his recent close encounters with the Japanese.

"Dearest Miracle Man," she wrote to him the next day, thanking him for his comforting gesture. She ended on a conciliatory note,

> As the end of the third month rolls around I find myself missing you every second. There is real pain in loneliness and instead of dulling with time it worsens. It may be wrong for anyone to love a person as much as I love you, but there it is and I'm not sorry. You are indeed my better half and without you I'm a pretty incomplete creature. So please come home pretty soon, darling. Until then I'll wear the cat's eye as . . . another reminder of how dear you are to me.[11]

Her husband spent an additional six weeks away, turning down the chance to appear in *The Heart of the City*, which was renamed *Tonight and Every Night*. Dancer and choreographer Jack Cole filled the role that Bolger was to play. The fighting in the Pacific was ramping up, and Little and Bolger felt valuable. They made appearances in the New Hebrides and returned to Guadalcanal for most of November.

Bolger returned to Travis Air Force Base in California on Thanksgiving Day, 1943.[12] When his plane landed, he emerged in a Panama hat and a trench coat, beaming. Gwen stood at the bottom of the stairs of the plane, a new trotter-length mink coat draped across her shoulders. She sought to dazzle him, and she succeeded. He handed her a souvenir he had kept near him since departing Oahu: a fresh coconut. They laughed and then kissed. The partners were back in business.

The travels arranged by USO Camp Shows were so secretive that Abe Lastfogel could not release statistics for overseas outfits during his tenure as aide de camp to Eddie Dowling, the organization's president. Subsequently, many Camp Show records were destroyed. It is known that the overseas program covered far more territory than the domestic programs. According to the Hollywood Victory Committee, which tracked the contributions of film players to the war effort, movie stars traveled a total of 886,000 miles for the cause in the United States alone.

For their part, Bolger and Little completed a 27,000-mile journey for the USO between July and November. The only injury Bolger sustained overseas was an infected blister on his heel, which he received from tap dancing on one of the makeshift stages slapped together along the way. Their audiences had ranged from fifty to four thousand military personnel. For one memorable performance in the New Hebrides, an audience of 2,500 hospital patients was willing to sit in a deluge of rain to catch their show. Bolger's participation in the USO enhanced his sense of patriotism and his interest in participating in political life. He would find more ways to engage with the Republican Party and with the social causes they believed in.

The consternation and unhappiness that Gwen had experienced as a result of Bolger's lagging letters soon melted away. While she unpacked his luggage at North Martel Avenue, she found a neat bundle of letters: every one she had ever sent. Their prolonged separation taught each of them just what the other brought to their relationship and professional partnership. They would look for a project they could make into a true collaboration.

Bolger, at the wheel of the boat, visits with men of the V Bomber Command in Port Moresby, New Guinea, 1943. UCLA Library Special Collections, Charles E. Young Research Library.

CHAPTER 8

Where's Charley?

On returning from his duties with Camp Show Unit #89, Bolger wanted to volunteer for reassignment with the USO. Gwen, however, insisted that her husband devote his time to a project that would expand his newfound acclaim. MGM was rapidly signing up available talent as the studio had announced the 1944–45 season would be the most ambitious musical schedule in its history. Most of the available chorus boys and chorines, those who were not in the service or in the defense plants, were put under contract. Industry experts predicted that the studio would also put the biggest name bands around the country under contract. While Bolger had not always been pleased with the work given him at MGM in the prior decade, he signed a two-picture contract with the studio.

In spring of 1944, Bolger was announced to star in *Holiday in Mexico*. Xavier Cugat and his orchestra, with whom Bolger had appeared in vaudeville, would support him in the film. At the same time, Bolger's former co-star and young friend, Judy Garland, would star in *Week-End at the Waldorf*. Neither Bolger nor Garland ultimately landed these roles. Bolger's contract was about to expire when MGM decided to throw him in their next big-budget musical, which by chance *would* star Judy Garland: *The Harvey Girls*. The film was being produced by MGM's prestigious Arthur Freed unit. During the filming of *The Wizard of Oz*, Freed had just been starting out at the studio as an assistant to producer Mervyn LeRoy. Now he was the producer in charge of the premiere musical-making operation in the country, creating many hit films. Some of his creations, like *Girl Crazy* and *Meet Me in St. Louis*, had made Garland a bona fide star.

MGM had at first intended *The Harvey Girls* to be a straight vehicle for Lana Turner. But the musical arranger Roger Edens believed an Old

West–style musical would be more popular: Rodgers and Hammerstein's *Oklahoma!* was approaching its second year on Broadway with no sign of slowing down. The Freed Unit produced *The Harvey Girls* with no expense spared. Garland, following up on her smashing success in *Meet Me in St. Louis*, was cast in the lead role of Susan Bradley, a wanderlust beauty from Ohio headed to Sandrock, Arizona, the latest whistle-stop in the great expansion west.

Bolger's role added little to the plot of *The Harvey Girls,* but he provided the film with two of its most entertaining numbers: Bolger and Virginia O'Brien, with whom he had worked in *Keep Off the Grass,* performed the comic song "In the Wild, Wild West," and he also performed a tap routine to "On the Atchison, Topeka, and the Santa Fe" solo—or just about. He took character actress Marjorie Main, who had played the gravel-voiced Ma of *Ma and Pa Kettle,* for a quick spin on the dance floor, a move that hearkened back to his dancing with Bertha Belmore in *By Jupiter.*

Bolger grew friendly with Main, who was fourteen years his senior and a rumored lesbian, during the shooting. He loved flirting with her, escorting her to her seat to rest between takes of their dance, and kissing her hand. He would tease her that "the rest of the world could have all their Hedy Lamarrs and Betty Grables, because he'd have his Marjorie, who was just as graceful."[1]

The casting also enabled Bolger to reconnect with Garland while they shot the film at MGM's Culver City studios and on location in Chatsworth and Monument Valley. But he could see that the child he adored had grown into a distressed, anxious woman. She had married the orchestra leader David Rose in 1941, just two months after his divorce from actress Martha Raye. And she had undergone at least one abortion at the insistence of her mother, MGM Studios, and her husband, which led to their divorce in 1944. When *The Harvey Girls* began filming in January 1945, Garland was engaged to Vincente Minnelli, who had directed her in *Meet Me in St. Louis.* He had begun his career directing stage shows for Roxy Rothafel at Radio City Music Hall and was now an auteur at MGM. But Bolger could see that this would end unhappily for her as well. He later wrote, "What was the escape [from the MGM workload]? Sex. . . . Doesn't work. Despair. Try again. A softspoken, quiet director [Vincente Minnelli]—a child [Liza]. You work her through the marriage. Suddenly she bursts wide open."[2]

Bolger and Garland's mutual affection endured during the shooting, but she was distracted by her personal life. She delayed production considerably by showing up on set late or, some days, not showing up at all. Bolger understood the limitations of their friendship. He could not protect her from the many anxieties she was experiencing, but he made their professional reunion as pleasant as possible.

Bolger's work on *The Harvey Girls* earned him $65,000 (more than $900,000 in 2018 dollars), which he gratefully bankrolled before returning to the nightclub stage at the Chez Paree in Chicago and eventually to the New York scene. Gwen and Ray resumed their old habits. They went to their favorite supper clubs in the evening to dine with friends, and on rare 1:00 A.M. excursions to El Morocco, they even danced together. They were happy to mingle with many diverse members of New York's creative class. One such chum was Jerry Wald, a heavyset, balding film executive. Wald began his career as a New York radio columnist and eventually became a producer for Vitaphone, the radio division of Warner Brothers. By the mid-1940s, he had transitioned to working on movies for the studio. Wald ran into Bolger more than a dozen times in New York during the mid- to late forties. Wald always hoped he would get Bolger to play Jack Donahue in a Marilyn Miller biopic for his studio. When they ran into each other, they would kid about this: Wald would say a script was in the works, or Bolger would ask, "What about that script?" Wald did end up delivering a draft to the Bolgers, but neither Gwen nor Ray was happy with it, so Wald went back to the drawing board, and Bolger proceeded to Broadway. He had had enough of movies for a while.

Broadway in the last days of the war was a different place from the one Bolger had known during the run of *By Jupiter*. Audiences were more discerning than ever, as the success of *Oklahoma!* and *Carousel* attested. Strong books, integrated lyrics, and sophisticated choreography were the hallmarks of quality musicals. The revue format started to show its age and had lost favor. Cole Porter's *Seven Lively Arts*, starring Beatrice Lillie and Bert Lahr, closed in May 1945 after 183 performances. The Shuberts' revue *Laffing Room Only* left town in July 1945, after 232 performances. Another revue did not arrive until March 1946, when Bolger led the cast of *Three to Make Ready* onto Broadway. But even Nancy Hamilton, the show's writer, did not have stellar notions of her creation, summing up her thoughts on the format, "Revues are the answer to a lazy writer's prayer."

An actress, lyricist, and writer, Hamilton had created two other revue shows. *One for the Money* appeared in 1939 and *Two for the Show* in 1940. They were best remembered for giving early opportunities to the newcomers Gene Kelly, Keenan Wynn, and Betty Hutton. For *Three to Make Ready* Hamilton secured backers—among them Gregory Peck who contributed $1,500, and Katharine Cornell, who chipped in $1,000—plus support from the Shuberts to fund the final show in her trilogy, and then she signed up Bolger. Because of the amount of shows playing on Broadway at the time, *Three to Make Ready* had to wait for a theater to become available. In the meantime, the show enjoyed three-and-a-half lucrative weeks on the road, spending ten days in Boston and the balance of the time in Philadelphia.

Hamilton's sketches, directed by the great Shakespearean director Margaret Webster, gave Bolger more opportunities to mug than to dance. He led the ensemble through "Kenosha Canoe," a ballet parody of *Oklahoma!* that imagined how Rodgers and Hammerstein might adapt Theodore Dreiser's novel *An American Tragedy* for the stage. In a sketch originally titled "Cold Water Flat," and later retitled "Housing Shortage," married couple Joe and Mary, played by Bolger and Rose Ingraham, struggle with a gushing, broken toilet. Joe wakes up and realizes it was all a dream—and then goes and breaks the toilet. Audiences were appalled that a sketch with Ray Bolger took place in a water closet, although the only toilet on-stage was painted onto a backdrop.

Bolger also integrated his Sad Sack routine into the show. In this episode, Sad Sack, an army private, finds himself stuck on a ship due to a misunderstanding. He is approached first by a sergeant, then a captain, and then a colonel as the situation escalates. When asked if he can read signs that suggest he shouldn't be there, he quips, "If I could read, I'd be in the Navy!" Sad Sack gets accused of desertion, coercion, and espionage before finally extricating himself from the situation. The character still resonated with wartime audiences. (Coincidentally, much of the Broadway run of *Three to Make Ready* would occur between VE Day and VJ Day.)

In "Shoe on the Other Foot," Bolger appeared as a flustered shoe store clerk, opposite a daffy customer played by Brenda Forbes. Bolger spends several minutes tearing apart the store for the lady, until she realizes that nothing really interests her and she had only stopped in to kill time before an appointment.

The show's original songs included "If It's Love," "It's a Nice Night for It," and "A Lovely, Lazy Kind of Day." The last of these was sung by Gordon MacRae in one of his first show business appearances and danced by Bolger. This number brought back elements of his Scarecrow dance, as he alternated between complete bodily tension and relaxation to emphasize "the lazy" day. The loose-jointed Bolger fell into a split as he did in his solo for *The Great Ziegfeld*. Also, as in that routine, he hoisted himself up and up from the floor by his hamstrings and nearly returned to his feet, before he sank back down again and repeated the process, to the amazement of the live audience.

Bolger's best spot came in "The Old Soft Shoe." Donning a bowler hat, a flannel suit with a carnation, and spats, he appeared in front of a pencil-sketch backdrop of an elegant old hotel and sang of the day when he and his Alice were playing the Palace. The dance started romantically but then morphed into a spoof of soft-shoe dancers of the days of yore. An ensemble of dancers, representing samba and jitterbug, joined Bolger on stage before he lyrically dismissed them in preference to his own style. This nostalgic homage to vaudeville offered him a routine to garnish with all his favorite old tricks and aerial leaps. Bolger's soft-shoe routine to "On the Atchison, Topeka, and the Santa Fe" from *The Harvey Girls*, filmed a year prior to the production of *Three to Make Ready*, preserved a record of many of the elements Bolger incorporated into "The Old Soft Shoe."

Three to Make Ready opened on Broadway at the Adelphi Theatre on March 7, 1946. It generated little enthusiasm outside of Bolger's performances. "During most of the sketches, *Three to Make Ready* comes to a distinct halt," the *New York Times* proclaimed the next morning.[3] All the critics agreed that Bolger appeared in top form and that the weight of the show rested on his shoulders. Lewis Nichols in the *Times* wrote, "Anyone who suggests that he [Bolger]...is lower than genius deserves to be driven through the streets by a pack of snapping dogs. He is in the highest bracket of the revue. Easy and amiable, he drifts in and out of an evening....And it is only fair to say that this one player's surroundings are not cut to his dimensions."[4]

The critics agreed that Nancy Hamilton's sketches ran too long, and, according to George Jean Nathan, the original songs she introduced with music writer Morgan Lewis had already been written "a thousand times better" by Oscar Hammerstein, Lorenz Hart, and Cole Porter.[5] Despite the lackluster quality of the material, the show fared well financially. Bolger's personal appeal was by then a reliable box office draw. And while the pressure to carry an entire show put great physical strain on him, both he and Gwen agreed that he should remain in the show until the backers had earned a profit. It makes sense that he would want to prove himself a valuable investment asset for future projects, since *By Jupiter*, his last show on Broadway prior to *Three to Make Ready*, had given him a reputation for cutting and running, even for a noble pursuit. Bolger stayed the course over nine months and three theater changes—*Three to Make Ready* was subject to rather more disassembling than most Broadway shows. Its sets were carefully laid out on the sidewalks of New York three times, initially to install them in the Adelphi, then in the Broadhurst Theater after a May 1946 transfer, and finally in the Adelphi again after the show returned there in October.

Bolger not only continued to exert himself to his physical limits in the show, but he also displayed great intellectual curiosity and agility in the way he revisited the material during the run. After the show had transferred to the Broadhurst, he updated his routine for "The Old Soft

Shoe," which had by then been proclaimed as one of the finest pieces of performance then on Broadway—a high compliment, considering Ethel Merman was then debuting *Annie Get Your Gun* at the Imperial Theatre on the other end of Shubert Alley. As an encore, he parodied a vaudevillian leaving the stage, only to about-face before stepping behind the curtain, yucking it up for more applause. From the breast pocket of his coat he took out a paper bag and sprinkled the stage with sand. He then shuffled along in a "sand dance," his clear taps hushed by the grit into a lulling patter. He made an homage to Joe Frisco by performing the locomotive step. With massive post-war railroad strikes shaking the country and halting transit in the year following V-J Day, he found a great comic opportunity in abruptly stopping the Frisco routine and saying, "Can't do that—we're on strike!"

By this time, Bolger was a known quantity on Broadway for his athleticism and versatility. He was also rich: projects up to and including *Three to Make Ready* had earned Ray more than $2 million. He was rich in social connections at this point as well, and there was a high demand to be known to Bolger. Bolger's dressing room was like an extension of the dance floor at El Morocco, or another banquette at the 21 Club: interesting show business types and regular joes wafted in and out. One night after a performance at the Broadhurst in the fall of 1946, Bolger received a young CBS executive as a guest in his dressing room. He introduced himself as Ernest Martin, the head of radio programming for CBS. He was based in Los Angeles and worked extensively with comedy writers. He wanted to branch out. He was planning to write a Broadway show based on George Gershwin's composition "An American in Paris." Would Bolger be interested in playing the lead? "Sure!" Bolger responded affably. Martin took his single-word response to be a promise. Bolger continued with his evening, and with his life.

Three to Make Ready transferred back to the Adelphi to make room for a previously arranged commitment: a straight play produced by Rodgers and Hammerstein, *Happy Birthday*, starring Helen Hayes. It was late October. *Three to Make Ready* had already distinguished itself as the longest running of Nancy Hamilton's trilogy, and Bolger felt the wear of the show. Before the Christmas rush, he requested a vacation from December 16 to 24. Gwen had arranged a trip to Nassau to allow him a proper recuperation. But the management refused his request, insisting it would disrupt the run.

Bolger continued to perform, hiding his fatigue from his audiences. He mustered through both performances on Saturday, December 15. After the final curtain of the evening performance, the Bolgers took a cab to

Harkness Pavilion in Washington Heights, where Ray was admitted for treatment of jaundice. The *Three to Make Ready* management suspended the show. He remained in the hospital for almost a full month—until January 12, 1947. His doctors then cleared him to travel to Palm Springs with Gwen and complete his convalescence through the end of the month. He spent the rest of Spring 1947 playing *Three to Make Ready* on the road, in Chicago, Baltimore, Philadelphia, and Boston. The financial success of the touring engagements meant that the investors turned a profit and that Bolger's star power was back in the national consciousness. His health was restored, his wife remained by his side, nurturing him, and his talent was more pronounced and valuable than ever in the eyes of the public and industry professionals alike. While he was out on tour, the lead attraction in a tired musical revue, he was committed, verbally at least, to Ernest Martin's show for the next Broadway season. The young producer kept in touch and guaranteed the show would be the antithesis of *Three to Make Ready*: new, strong, smart, and fast. Bolger took the summer of 1947 to rest. He would begin making nightclub appearances again in the fall. But for now, it was up to Martin to do the spadework.

Not yet thirty, Ernest Martin radiated unqualified confidence. He had secured the position of head of radio development for KNX, CBS's flagship radio station in Los Angeles, in his early twenties. He specialized in comedy and was promised a big role in producing television shows with his comic talents when the medium came of age. But corporate life did not excite him—he was an irrepressible optimist, and he dreamed of striking out on his own in the world of entertainment management. While socializing at a cocktail party, he met Cy Feuer, the short, blunt, bespectacled head of the music department at Republic Pictures. Feuer himself had a touch of restlessness: he had just left the army. While on leave in New York, he had been able to catch Broadway shows such as *Something for the Boys* with Ethel Merman. Now he wanted to create his own. Neither Feuer nor Martin knew anything about musicals, but by the end of the evening, the two decided they would keep their day jobs while creating a Broadway show together.

Because Martin was on friendly terms with Ira Gershwin, he first wanted to make a musical of George Gershwin's "An American in Paris." Ira agreed to let Martin proceed, although he never signed away any rights. That gave Martin and Feuer enough impetus to pursue the challenge of adapting Gershwin's composition. "An American in Paris," a tone poem, did not even have lyrics. They would be starting from scratch, creating an original story. Martin thought the composition could be broken into four or five songs, which they would integrate into an original libretto. As if that wasn't enough work, they also wanted Fred Astaire to be their star. The dancer was in the midst of a busy Hollywood career, but the producers believed they could lure him back to Broadway with a Gershwin vehicle. Astaire had first made a name for himself in New York in the 1920s as the star of two Gershwin musicals, produced by Vinton Freedley and Alex Aarons. They got to Astaire through Ira, and he expressed interest in seeing the written product.

Next, Martin and Feuer went to New York for a meeting with Freedley. They went to the Plaza Hotel's Oak Room. The old impresario showed up to lunch in a flannel suit, black homburg, and spats, cluing in Martin and Feuer that the legend may have been stuck in the past. Their conversation did not go well. A few days later Astaire formally declined. He had no interest in returning to live performance. While he still had Ira Gershwin's interest, Martin began thinking of another big Broadway dancing star they could approach. He quickly thought of Ray Bolger. Through Martin's friend Bill Paley, the CEO of CBS, Martin was introduced to Howard Reinheimer, theatrical lawyer extraordinaire whom Rodgers and Hammerstein kept on retainer. Martin and Feuer were looking for some guidance, and they ran their idea for the *An American in Paris* show past the famous lawyer. Reinheimer disliked the idea and encouraged the young novices in a different direction. He knew of a better property to use as a vehicle for Bolger.

For years, Reinheimer said, he had tried to secure the rights to *Charley's Aunt*, one of the most lucrative and long-enduring British farces, for several different American clients interested in adaptation. The play by Brandon Thomas had broken all theatrical records for any sort of show when its original London run in 1892 lasted for 1,466 performances. *Charley's Aunt* takes place at Oxford University right before the turn of the twentieth century. Two students of the men-only university, Jack Chesney and Charley Wykeham, want to invite their girlfriends to attend a school theatrical event. This will require the girls to stay the night, and so they need to have a chaperone. Charley's long-lost aunt, Donna Lucia D'Alvadorez, is en route to Oxford to see the show. Charley invites the girls, assuming his aunt will chaperone them.

The day the girls are to arrive, Charley receives word that his aunt will be delayed for a few days, and the boys are devastated. While they sulk, Lord Fancourt Babberley, their neighbor down the hall, arrives in his costume for the production: he is a perfect Victorian dowager. Rather than break the news to their girlfriends that the date will have to be called off, Jack and Charley persuade Babberley to pose as Charley's aunt. Their hijinks unfold over four acts.

It was rumored that since the play's debut, not a day had gone by when *Charley's Aunt* wasn't playing somewhere in the world, and this wasn't much of an exaggeration. Reinheimer had approached the estate of Brandon Thomas with many musical adaptation offers from different clients, most prominently Jerome Kern. But the estate guarded rights to the show carefully. They received between $50,000 and $100,000 each year in revenue from stock and amateur rights. The British had a reputation for closely guarding their jokes, and no one in the Thomas family wanted to see their beloved property butchered at the hands of Broadway types. The estate had told Reinheimer that they would allow the show to be performed in New York only if either Ray Bolger or Danny Kaye starred as the eponymous aunt. But even if Bolger could be enticed, Reinheimer and Martin knew that securing the rights would be difficult.

In the fall of 1947, Martin contacted Bolger with the news that *An American in Paris* was off, and *Charley's Aunt* was on. Bolger, after consulting with Gwen, demurred. A four-act pantomime was not the right format for him, and the story as it existed did not work as a musical. Bolger also believed the role of Lord Babberley was too small. Martin and Feuer seemed destined to lose their star. They decided that Feuer would try to rewrite the book and offer a new script to the Bolgers. Feuer believed the central problem with the role was how restrictive the aunt's costume and persona would be for Bolger. While keeping him in drag as a "painfully unfeminine" woman was "essential to the comic core of the play," Feuer knew that Bolger couldn't dance in the dress. And then he had a breakthrough:

> The solution was pretty risky.... Charley would play both roles—himself and his own aunt. This would lead to an infinite variety of complications and setups and awkward situations. When Charley was in the room, the aunt was offstage resting; when the aunt was present, Charley was gone. His girlfriend, Amy, would ask plaintively, "Where's Charley?" Hence the new title, plus the new structure.[6]

The Bolgers approved of the edits, which meant that all Feuer and Martin needed to proceed was permission from the Thomas estate. Together, the producers agreed it was time to take the risk: Feuer would quit his job as music director of Republic Pictures. His experiences in the war had given him some familiarity with the basic geography of England. After the New Year, he would go abroad and make the petition for permission to do the show. To help Feuer stay afloat with no steady employment, Martin would send him freelance composing gigs from CBS.

Feuer arrived at Claridge's Hotel in London and began wooing Thomas's heirs, Amy, Sylvia, and Javon. After taking their time to make a decision, they agreed to let Feuer and Martin produce *Where's Charley?* if three conditions were met: Bolger needed to be the star, the show had to play in a first-class Broadway theater, and Feuer's edits to the original Samuel French edition of the play had to be the basis of the finished musical.

By the time Feuer and Martin got the green light from the Thomas estate, Bolger was in Chicago, again appearing at the Chez Paree. While he was there, Jerry Wald came to meet him. Wald was ready to move forward with a new draft of his script for *Look for the Silver Lining*, the Marilyn Miller biopic. Casting had taken some time. Vincente Minnelli and Judy Garland had put up a tough fight for the property; they wanted to be loaned from MGM to Warner Brothers so that Minnelli could direct his wife in the lead. The MGM brass would not have it, and Wald instead secured David Butler to direct and June Haver to star. Bolger remained Wald's first choice to play Miller's mentor, Jack Donahue, and Butler was similarly interested in seeing Bolger in the role. Gwen and Ray reviewed the new script and found it satisfactory. Bolger signed on and was able to secure his *Three to Make Ready* co-star, Gordon MacRae, to play the role of Miller's love interest, Frank Carter. They would need three months to shoot the picture. From Chicago, Ray went west, to Warner Brothers' Burbank studio. Gwen flew east to New York to work out the details of *Where's Charley?* with Reinheimer, Feuer, and Martin.

Once in New York, Feuer and Martin formalized their working relationship with Gwen by forming a production company. Reinheimer handled the paperwork, and Gwen received an official associate producer credit. Henceforth they were known as Feuer, Martin, and Rickard. The men agreed to the arrangement mostly to ensure Bolger's loyalty throughout the production and to relieve themselves of half the responsibility for fundraising. Gwen was tasked with raising $100,000, and she impressed her co-producers with her ability to tap into the coffers of her well-off acquaintances. Socialites, dentists, businessmen, and fans were all asked, and many responded with enthusiasm. She described her methods: "You must brush up the old charm technique, learn resistance-smothering tactics, glibly recite glamorous facts and figures, get a romantic angle on the limited partnership agreement, smiling all the while."[7] As none of the producers wanted to surrender any artistic control, Gwen concentrated not on big donors but on a large number of small donors, those willing to put between $500 and $1,500 toward her goal. In fundraising, she outstripped Feuer and Martin, who also had to come up with $100,000 between them. When they were $10,000 shy of their goal, she offered to make up the difference—in exchange for more points in the profits. Being new to the business, they agreed. Ray wrote this vivid description of Gwen's fundraising efforts:

> She is fast becoming a feared and noted woman around town. Her salesmanship is something to behold....She never "lets up" on her victims until they're screaming for help and grasping their last dollar in a tightly clenched fist, and agree to come into the show for one or more units! The wife of one of our better known Feudal Barons was known to have some "scratch" lying loose in her boudoir. Gwen hearing about this called her immediately. "Hello darling," purrs Gwen, "write out a check for $5,000 and send it down to me this morning. $4,000 is for one unit of our show and $1,000, call money. Hope to see you soon. Goodbye." Before dear Mrs. Pew—or Pugh?—could recover her senses the check was in Gwen's hands along with a little reminder: Please don't tell my husband. Ha! Ha![8]

With money in hand, Feuer and Martin needed to find a theater, a first-rate one to make good on the terms of their agreement with the Thomas estate. Not content with being only a fundraiser, Gwen inserted herself into these decisions as well. She had known the Shuberts for almost twenty years and proved to be invaluable in securing a property from Elias Weinstock, the Shuberts' manager for real estate bookings. Based on Bolger's reputation, Weinstock offered the *Where's Charley?* Company the St. James Theatre, where *Oklahoma!* was finishing its nearly five-year run.

Knowing what theater they would be working in and what sets could be accommodated, the producers engaged a scenic designer. They agreed on David Ffolkes, who would also design the costumes. Ffolkes's background included numerous productions of Shakespeare for Broadway, but he also showed the producers sketches he had made for Alan Jay Lerner and Frederick Loewe's magical musical set in the Scottish Highlands, *Brigadoon*. Ffolkes came up with tasteful, cost-effective designs that captured the Victorian era and yet were not too ornate to draw attention away from the cast. Then came the task of hiring those who would execute the designs. Of this process, Gwen wrote, "If you have ever bargained in the Orient or in the souks of Tunis you have a slight edge in the situation. Screaming 'Robber!' you accept the best bids and start cutting expenses somewhere else."[9]

Everyone's first choice for director was George Abbott. A bald man with the face and perception of an eagle, Abbott had performed in Broadway plays from his teens through his mid-twenties before he transitioned to writing and directing, two tasks he did for *On Your Toes*. Abbott had two musicals—*Look, Ma, I'm Dancin!* and *High Button Shoes*—on Broadway when Feuer met with him to discuss *Where's Charley?* Even with new sensibilities emerging on Broadway in the post-war world, he was still revered as the master of farce-comedy. Abbott was pleased with Feuer's updates to the *Charley's Aunt* script; he expressed interest in directing the musical but withheld his final assent until the company chose a writer for the music and lyrics.

Feuer approached two friends from Hollywood: Harold Arlen and Frank Loesser. Arlen, an old friend of Bolger's from their days in Buffalo, had written music for *Life Begins at 8:40* on Broadway and *The Wizard of Oz* at MGM. Loesser was a lyricist for Paramount Pictures who had made big hits with the songs "Praise the Lord and Pass the Ammunition" and "Baby, It's Cold Outside." These choices pleased Abbott. Before Arlen could get to work, however, his Beverly Hills home burned to the ground. He lost everything, and his wife, Anya, suffered a nervous breakdown. Arlen bowed out of *Where's Charley?* to maintain domestic stability.

The tragedy offered Frank Loesser the opportunity to write both the lyrics and the music for the show, a double duty he had been interested in pursuing for some time. Abbott got wind of this and balked. He knew nothing of Loesser and was unsure whether he could pull off both responsibilities with the requisite aplomb. He insisted on meeting with Loesser in person to determine whether his music would be compatible with the book.

This proved costly, as Abbott preferred working at his Long Island estate and Loesser was still based in Hollywood. Agreeing to meet with Loesser on the West Coast, the old Broadway legend refused to travel any way other than first class, and arriving in West Hollywood, he checked into the expensive Sunset Tower. Back in New York, the producers waited for word of the outcome. Gwen said, "Frank is fiery and fierce and George is icy and calm. The attracting of the opposites instantly manifested itself. The two went to work at once."[10]

While many of these initial selections were made peaceably among the troika of producers, Gwen's imperiousness became more apparent as the work intensified. In June 1948, Bolger finished filming *Look for the Silver Lining* and went east. He vacationed at Lake Placid and returned to Manhattan in August "fat and sassy." He wrote to his relatives, "Had my gums and teeth all fixed up and am in fine shape to go to work." Before starting on his new Broadway show, though, Bolger took a brief and educational digression into the nascent world of television broadcasting.

TV was still very much a novelty, even in the country's major cities, although post-war prosperity fueled a new consumer demand for television sets. The two major radio-broadcasting networks, the National Broadcasting Company (NBC) and the Columbia Broadcasting System (CBS), had been experimenting with television stations in New York City since the 1930s. The American Broadcasting Company (ABC), being younger and smaller, was late to join the party, but by 1945, it had acquired an experimental station in Newark, New Jersey, WJZ. In 1948 ABC finally committed to a bold pledge: it would invest $5 million in making five television stations across the country operational by the end of the year. WJZ would serve the New York City market.

The medium was new and exciting, but when it came to messaging, ABC wanted to serve up nostalgia. It would inaugurate the new TV station by broadcasting a salute to vaudeville, live from the Palace Theatre. It was as if the network wanted to make sure this beloved tradition made the leap into the new wave, or at least wanted to bolster the new wave by means of a beloved tradition. The Palace itself had adjusted to the new modes and preferences in entertainment. In 1932, it had become the "RKO Palace"—a movie theater. But ABC would be sure its stage was decorated once again with as many of the great variety entertainers of the 1920s as it could secure, before beaming them out to the city as well as to its affiliates in Boston, Philadelphia, Baltimore, and Washington.

The network offered Bing Crosby $10,000 to sing one song on the broadcast, but he declined. George Jessel and Jimmy Durante were asked, but prior commitments kept them away. Instead, comedienne Beatrice Lillie, vaudevillian Pat Rooney Sr., and the band leader Paul Whiteman, who had become ABC's vice president and musical director, flashed across the nation's eighteen-inch plate glass screens, which were mounted in wooden boxes and controlled by tuning knobs. Bolger was brought in as the master of ceremonies, a role dating from his days as a member of the Gus Edwards troupe. He also danced in the production.

The day after the musical spectacular was broadcast, WJZ began airing routine—albeit primitive—programming for New York audiences. *Cartoon Teletales*, *News and Views*, and variety programming played out between 5:30 and 9:00 P.M. every night. If you turned on the little wooden box when a show wasn't being broadcast—that is, the other nineteen-and-a-half hours of the day—the screen merely glowed with gray and white static. Most Americans were still satiating their entertainment diets elsewhere. "The American Broadcasting Co. is deeply aware of a high responsibility to the people in its approach to television," declared Edward J. Noble, the bow-tied chairman of the board, during that inaugural ABC broadcast. "Television imposes on us the profound obligation to use it with dignity, with skill, with honesty, and with care. We shall discharge that high obligation to the very best of our ability." While Noble and the other executives broke their heads over how to do that—and at the same time earn big money and prestige—Bolger slipped away from the television scene. He had a new show to put on Broadway.

Bolger returned to New York in time for auditions. Together the creative team viewed thousands of dancers and singers before selecting sixteen of each. From the cattle call they also discovered Allyn Ann McLerie, a doe-eyed brunette with plump lips and apple cheeks. She had come with her male performance partner looking for chorus work. Gwen noticed first that her sweet, unusual beauty would complement Bolger nicely as his leading lady. McLerie was put through her paces and found to be a capable dancer and singer. The management offered her the role of Amy Spettigue, Charley's girlfriend. McLerie, who had hoped to get any work as a dancer, walked out of the audition hall with an offer to be a Broadway star. However, the three producers were not in agreement on every big decision.

Martin's involvement in the day-to-day affairs of *Where's Charley?* grew after he quit his day job at CBS. It also meant he had more opportunities to clash with Gwen. Their differences arose during the selection of the dance director. Her first choice for choreographer was George Balanchine, a man who had a great affinity for Bolger and vice versa. He was brought in, but Feuer and Martin made it clear that he did not get the final say in the selection of the dancers. This was an affront to the renowned choreographer, who had proven through his career with New York City Ballet to know a little more about Terpsichore than the hotshot young producers. Balanchine quit. Feuer and Martin brought in Al White, who had staged Bolger's dances in *Look for the Silver Lining*. White was supposed to pursue another assignment at Warner Brothers but extricated himself from that to work with Bolger again. Gwen took issue with this choice. She began commenting on White's dance staging very early in the work, and he could not tolerate this. Then, Gwen insisted that he be billed as Albert White Jr., because "Al White" would not look dignified enough in the program. White walked out on the night of August 21. George Balanchine returned as choreographer on August 22. The management told the *New York Times* that White had been "called back to the Coast."[11] The insights of Katherine Reeve, a chorus girl who met and married Gwen's brother during the Broadway run of *Where's Charley?* and who came to understand the family's dynamics, suggest that the Bolgers convinced Balanchine, whom Ray dearly loved, to return to the fold. Reeve said, "George Balanchine was very quiet, and no big spectacular thing. . . . Ray liked a family show, and he liked to know his people. I know Gwen would say, 'Ray, you've got to have control of these things, or it's going to end up crazy.'"[12]

The company rehearsed out of the Adelphi Theatre during the day and on two floors above Al and Dick's Restaurant, across the street, when performances of *Look, Ma! I'm Dancin'!* kept them out of the theater. The bones of the show were laid out and put together. The musical numbers were scrutinized. Reeve recalled one of them, "The Train that Brought You to Town": "We got to be a train all over the stage and chug along in big lines with everyone going all around. It was fun! It was a cute, cute song."[13] But the entire creative team knew the show was too long, and songs would have to go. They would have to condense the book when the show went out of town for tryouts. The cast and crew of *Where's Charley?* boarded a train bound for Philadelphia one hot, sticky August afternoon. They were trying to keep their expenses as low as possible. The production company couldn't afford the union per diem for taking the entire orchestra from New York to Philadelphia, so they brought just a few key players to work with a road orchestra.

Everyone checked into the Warwick Hotel—except the Bolgers. They insisted on having accommodations separate from the rest of the company and instead holed up at the Barclay. *Where's Charley?* would be the first new musical of the season opening in town, at the Forrest Theatre, on September 15. Competing for attention in Philadelphia's other theaters would be return engagements for two Shubert shows—*Brigadoon* and *For Love or Money*.

Shortly after arriving in August, the *Charley* cast embarked on a "stop-and-go" rehearsal. They started from the top but stopped each time they discovered a problem in dialogue, staging, or direction. It took them four days to make it the entire way through the show. This was followed by one dress rehearsal—with no stopping—for backers and friends before the sets were fully hung or properly lighted. At this time Gwen wrote of "the electricians yelling, stagehands hollering, musicians singing away, actors valiantly trying to remember their lines."[14] Abbott and Loesser shouted corrections across the stage and into the pit. The company achieved some order, but more work remained.

After the rehearsal, all three producers, Loesser, and Abbott met in a coffee shop to offer their criticisms. No one thought the stylized "Pernambuco" ballet worked, but the number was essential to the plot because it explained how Charley's aunt had become a D'Alvadorez, and it would have to stay. They contemplated cutting "The Woman in His Room," a song written to convey Amy's insecurity that Charley is having an affair with a woman whose picture is in his bedroom because he seems to be flitting in and out all the time. Everyone except Abbott thought the show was far too long, and he would not commit to any deletions at the meeting. Although the producers appreciated working with an icon of Broadway, in moments like these they found him to be hidebound. He put a dime on the table for his coffee and left. "There's a lot of work to be done, mostly on Mr. Abbott's book," Gwen wrote home to her mother and aunts after the coffee meeting. "It's been hard work for everyone. Just keeping my mouth shut takes a lot out of me! There are many laughs in the Aunt costume but we need more and I'll get them in if I have to wall Mr. A up in a chimney somewhere."[15] She called the ticket broker the next day, anxious to know if tickets were selling.

Pre-sales for *Where's Charley?* drew strong emotions from the other two producers as well. Feuer had come from a film background. He had produced many pictures and he trusted that people went to see them, but he remained far from his audience. Martin worked in radio, releasing programs seemingly into the ether. One day before the Philadelphia premiere, he dragged Feuer out of a rehearsal and took him to the box office. A woman was buying two tickets to opening night. Neither Feuer nor Martin had ever watched someone lay down money for something they created before, and they felt gratified by it. They had built the show, and people were coming. But this by itself was not a guarantee of success.

Before the war, multi-year shows were rarities. During the war, they became commonplace. *Life with Father* ran for more than three thousand performances; *Oklahoma!*, two thousand; and *The Voice of the Turtle*, one thousand. By the time *Where's Charley?* came to town, only one show that had opened during the war years, *Harvey*, was still playing. Industry insiders predicted that shows with any kind of longevity would go back to being exceptional. Lewis Funke of the *New York Times* wrote, "Nothing ever is normal on Broadway and Broadway hates the idea of returning to normal."[16] The *Where's Charley?* Company did not think very highly of the proposition, either.

The box office turned out all right for opening week in Philadelphia, which played to capacity. Popular opinion was on the show's side. It was then time for the company to learn what the critics thought. "In and out of skirts from start to finish," *Variety* declared, Bolger "never worked harder."[17] It was true. Bolger drank a quart of orange juice and a quart of water during the course of each performance, to keep hydrated through all the quick-costume changing, running, door slamming, and sauntering required of him in the aunt's crinoline dress. The reviewer was particularly taken with the chorus, which he called "eye-filling to the nth degree and tastefully yet seductively gowned in styles of the period." He had less enthusiasm for Ffolkes's set design but conceded that the "colorful atmosphere, well-doused in nostalgia…covers much of that admitted corn" that was endemic to a production adapted from a fifty-six-year-old farce. The leads, especially

McLerie, were given fine notices. *Billboard* even praised "Pernambuco" as snipping "smartly at the Katherine Dunham tropical terping."[18] But those first reviews weren't Valentines: according to *Variety*, *Where's Charley?* was "by no means ready for Broadway...but with a half-hour pruned and Ray Bolger's presence and terrific ability as the star, it should eventually make the grade without much difficulty."[19]

The press was so enthusiastic over Bolger's performance that they failed to notice that he spoke-sang his solo number, "Once in Love with Amy." He was worn down by the laborious task of leading an athletic show on a shoestring, but he also adhered to the old school of theatrical comportment. He treated his audience members like guests of honor and hid his ailments.

Abbott got the notes on his book loud clear. He began trimming. The cast prepared the next day to run a revision of the show that night. Then came word from Feuer and Martin and Rickard that the next performance was canceled: Bolger had come down with full-scale laryngitis. They could not risk further damage to his voice. They would also skip the Wednesday matinee. Gwen put Bolger to bed. But as producer, she could not linger at his bedside. She was expected to make appearances at several parties across town, coddle and reassure cast and crew, and prepare for the transfer to Broadway that everyone hoped would still happen.

Bolger returned to the show Wednesday night, and the box office picked up considerably. At a time when $30,000 a week was considered sensational money, *Where's Charley?* earned $25,000 that first week, with just six performances. Chorus girl Katharine Reeve recalled preparing backstage during those early performances when changes were coming rapidly: "They would cut something and [the stage manager would] say 'that's not in tonight,' and you skipped it."[20] By the second week, the show had been trimmed by that recommended half-hour. The Forrest Theater played to near-capacity and hit the company's goal for revenue. By the end of week three, the run had made a profit.

Then the show transferred to the St. James Theatre at Forty-Fourth Street, between Seventh and Eighth Avenues. It opened on October 11, 1948, with steady advance ticket sales. Following opening night, five of the six reviews by major New York critics panned the show as too old-fashioned, too corny, too predictable. The reviewers agreed that the only bright spot—and a very bright spot at that—was the appearance of Ray Bolger. Even so, he received more opportunities for comedy than dance with this show. Perhaps the most revered contemporary critic, the *New York Times*'s Brooks Atkinson wrote that Balanchine's two grandest dances in the show, "Pernambuco" and "The Red Rose Cotillion," were "too austere to introduce Mr. Bolger's satiric flourishes." But Atkinson insisted that Bolger's presence redeemed the show when he wrote: "'Where's Charley?' is a rhetorical question. Where's Bolger? is more to the point. Fortunately, he is all here at the moment, and in fine fettle, too."[21] Bolger would create his best moment in the show, however, after the opening night.

His solo number, "Once in Love with Amy," came at the beginning of the second act. Charley receives his first kiss from Amy, who sashays away, and he blurts out a rhapsodic ode to love. Originally, Bolger capered about for seven minutes. But during the first matinee in New York, the song evolved, thanks to Feuer's seven-year-old son, Bobby.

A music lover like his father, Bobby had acetate demo records of the entire *Where's Charley?* score, which he played on a portable toy phonograph. He also knew Bolger from visits the star would pay Feuer. Bolger liked kids, and he acquired a little buddy when he met Bobby. Feuer brought his wife, Posy, Bobby, and one of Bobby's friends to the first *Charley?* matinee and got the boys third-row center seats. The Feuers stood in the back and watched.

When it came time for "Amy," Bolger came out and started his usual dance, but he sang the first word and then stopped. He blanked on the rest of the line. "Hold it! What was the lyric? How did it go?" he asked the audience.

From the dark, Bobby piped up, "Ray, it goes like this—" and, standing on his seat, fed the star the line.

Bolger's eyebrows arched in surprise and he laughed, unable to see who had spoken. "Do you know it?" he asked.

"Yeah," said the mysterious little voice.

"Why don't you sing it with me?" Bolger asked in challenge.

"OK," said Bobby, as if Bolger were back in the Feuer living room. They started to sing together, although Bolger grew upset with the kid taking all the laughs from the audience. "Why doesn't everyone sing with us?" he asked, trying to regain control of the number by completely surrendering it.

He managed to pull the song together, leaving the audience in raptures. Then he went backstage fuming. "What the hell was that going over?" he asked the stage manager. "For Christ's sake, these goddamn kids in the audience—" In the meantime, Feuer made his way backstage and was able to say, "It was Bobby," before Bolger tore an artery.

"Jesus!" Bolger said, and kept muttering. When at last he calmed down he said, "You know, there's something to that. Maybe I ought to try it tonight."

"Don't," Feuer advised. "Saturday night audiences are always miserable. Try it on a matinee."

Bolger started to experiment, and within a couple of weeks, the original seven-minute version of the song was lost amid a twenty-two-minute showstopper. Bolger would have the orchestra, the mezzanine, the men, the women, the servicemen take a line, according to his whim, and the audience never tired of it. In fact, even after Bolger exhausted every demographic breakdown and assigned parts every which way, the audience still demanded more. On several occasions he had to break character altogether and say, "Folks, this is a musical show—there's more we have to cover!" and the audience would at last let him off.

Word of mouth spread the news of Bolger's interactive sing-along far and wide, and ticket sales remained strong. The floor and the balcony wanted to have a part in a Broadway show, and Bolger was not afraid to vamp. He would stop the orchestra and make jokes with the conductor. The conductor would play the *Poet and Peasant* overture, and Bolger would break into spontaneous eccentric dance before bucking right back into "Amy."

"I'm flying!" says Bolger as he launches into an improvised dance during a performance of "Once in Love with Amy" at the St. James Theatre. Photo by Philippe Halsman. © Halsman Archive.

Popular opinion sustained the show, even though the critics had been cold. Gwen also stayed on top of opportunities to boost ticket sales. Thousands of tickets to *Where's Charley?* were sold to brokers who served convention attendees in New York. In the spring of 1949, the New Haven & Hartford Railroad introduced its Silver Whistle train service, bringing Connecticut commuters to Manhattan in time for Broadway shows and returning them home after the final curtain fell. *Where's Charley?* became one of the shows the railroad promoted, resulting in more than seven hundred additional ticket sales for the summer, usually the slowest months on Broadway.

But the best sales pitch for matinee seats at the St. James was the family-friendly quality of the show and the way that Bolger's personal magnetism enraptured young children. John Martin wrote, "To sit in a matinee audience composed in large part of small children and hear them laugh as loudly and as genuinely as their sophisticated elders at points they could not possibly understand, is to realize just how fundamental a medium he [Bolger] has found."[22]

During one Saturday matinee, Bolger glanced into the front row while performing "Once in Love with Amy." He saw on one end of the aisle an elderly couple who seemed in the throes of a happy, fifty-year marriage. On the opposite aisle, there were two five-year-olds. He thought that all age ranges seemed to be represented in between the two couples on the ends like notes on a musical scale. The children leaned forward in their seats and, as the audience members ascended in age, they leaned back farther in their seats. Bolger didn't take for granted the enthusiasm or fan letters from his child fans. He said that, for them, his dancing at Saturday matinees was worth $2 million whereas for the other performances he gave only about $1.75 million. He had arrived at a place in his career where he felt himself becoming the Fred Stone–figure of his youth to young audience members. If he could give those children a touch of what *Jack O'Lantern* had given him, he would be satisfied.

The role, in fact, gave him back much more. He received recognition from the press as a first-rate dancer at a time when Broadway was teeming with talent, seemingly fresher and more exciting than his. The way Broadway entertainers were being trained was changing drastically. Bolger had come up through vaudeville, which had since passed away. Younger Broadway comics had had to learn in nightclubs, which did not give them the same depth or scope. Dance training was also becoming more academic: the month before *Where's Charley?* opened on Broadway, the country's—and the world's—first public high school for the performing arts, with dance as curriculum, opened its doors: there was competition now for the "hoofing" generation.

Sophisticated dancing could be found up and down Broadway. *Kiss Me, Kate* was being choreographed by the modern dancer Hanya Holm, who dialed back the public's notion of modern dance as highbrow without dumbing down her choreography. Her work on the show would be considered "gay, witty, and stylish." *Inside U.S.A.*, a revue that opened in February 1949, featured an acclaimed romantic dance by Valerie Bettis, set on the San Francisco waterfront, to a new song by Howard Dietz and Arthur Schwartz, "Haunted Heart." Gower Champion choreographed a fresh, youthful revue, *Lend an Ear*. And another musical revue, *Along Fifth Avenue*, showcased the work of American Ballet Theater alumni. "Hoofers" were old news. Bolger belonged to the fast-fading class of performers who had come up the hard way.

While Bolger's work came from deep-rooted traditions, he remained fresh in the eyes of the audience because, it was written, his was a style all his own. As a forty-five-year-old man, he stood as the exemplar of the vaudevillian, suggested by an old line in the boilerplate contract: "You are unique, extraordinary, and cannot be duplicated."

After their initial round of reviews, many members of the Broadway critical establishment were drawn back to *Where's Charley?* They were stunned by the steady ticket sales, but not so surprised when they realized that what kept the show running was the way Bolger mesmerized audience members, who then went out and evangelized for him.

In fact, just about a week after *Where's Charley* opened at the St. James, Brooks Atkinson returned to reassess. The star's singular talents were the subjects of his contemplation. He conceded that many of the comedians then working in the theater had come up through nightclubs. They lacked "size, scope, and gusto" because they were used to working on small stages and using microphones to project themselves into the audience. He believed they lacked talents sufficient to command the authority of a one-thousand-seat Broadway house. Not so with Bolger. Atkinson wrote, "Having come up the hard way through the rough-and-tumble of show business, he can command the whole stage. That is one thing that a dancer learns in the apprentice stage, and it is essential to everything that is theatrical."[23]

The Bolgers also enjoyed the attention of elite artists who congratulated Ray on his impressive success and sought social access to him. Irene Selznick, daughter of Louis B. Mayer, got to see Bolger in his element in *Where's Charley?* and she declared, "Ray is so inventive and superb that I was quite overcome."[24] Alfred Hitchcock invited the Bolgers out to dinner with his daughter. Margo and Eddie Albert invited the couple to their housewarming party after moving into a new Beekman Place townhouse. Also in attendance that night were Adolph Green and Betty Comden, as well as Judy Garland and her then-husband, Vincente Minnelli. Garland had suffered an extreme mental breakdown in 1947 and had recovered at the Austin Riggs Center in Stockbridge, Massachusetts. Bolger was impressed by how good she looked at the Alberts' party, like "the old Judy." He said, "A large Steinway stood in the middle of the living room...the old carpet was up, the floor bare. Leonard Bernstein sat at the piano and played. Judy sang.... Suddenly Judy broke out 'On the Sunny Side of the Street.' My feet could take it no longer. No one will ever see that dance again. I never touched the floor once. That was the magic Judy had."[25]

The 1949 Broadway season would become part of the legacy of American entertainment. The American Theater Wing seemed to sense the way history would receive these shows as the season drew to an end.[26] The third annual Antoinette Perry Awards, known as the Tonys, honoring the best Broadway had to offer, would celebrate that year with a brand-new prize. At the first two ceremonies, award-winning women had received gold bracelets inscribed with their initials and the name of their prize; men received gold bill clips. This year's winners would be the first to take home the enduring indicator of Broadway stardom: a silver medallion featuring the masks of comedy and tragedy. The likelihood of the contests being close—and of nominees' egos being hurt—inspired the American Theater Wing to announce, through the *New York Times*, that the organization, "avoids any 'firsts' or 'bests' and presents the prizes for a 'notable contribution to the current season.'" The statement continued, "Anything that enlivens the theater may win a 'Tony.'"[27]

One thousand guests dressed in black tie arrived at the Grand Ballroom of the Waldorf-Astoria Hotel on April 24, 1949, for the ceremony. Brock Pemberton, the late Antoinette Perry's professional partner, cofounder of the American Theater Wing, and a member of the Algonquin Round Table, hosted the event. Despite the American Theater Wing's planned restraint on superlatives, the organization could find no better way to describe its awards. Pemberton presented the medallion for Best Director to Elia Kazan, for his work on the original production *Death of a Salesman*. Gower Champion was named Best Choreographer for *Lend an Ear*. Rex Harrison won in the category of Best Actor in a Play for *Anne of the Thousand Days*. Jo Mielziner won in the Scenic Design category for his work on all of those shows. *Kiss Me, Kate* won the honor of Best Musical. And then, Pemberton called out the award for Best Actor in a Musical. The song-and-dance man who had enlivened Broadway that year was Ray Bolger, star of *Where's Charley?*

The celebrities who filled the four stories of the Grand Ballroom applauded him especially. Since the early twenties, Bolger had appeared in their midst. First, he was a vaudeville dancer, performing splits and high kicks between motion picture shows at the Paramount and Loews theaters in New York. At the same time, for spare money, he danced on kitchen tables for celebrities' personal parties. In the thirties, he achieved star billing on Broadway in *On Your Toes*. Now Bolger's contribution to Broadway was galvanized by winning the 1949 Tony Award for Best Actor in a Musical.

But his wife was not finding as much fulfillment in their shared project. Gwen began to have doubts about her talents and her budding career. She had spent nineteen years watching people like Rodgers and Hart, Dwight Wiman, and the Shubert brothers go about their work. She had managed her husband's career by day and shadowed him in the wings and his dressing room during performances. Many of the *Where's Charley?* management team encouraged her pursuits with sincerity. But she hesitated under the weight of the pressure she placed on herself. She wrote to herself in frustration, "What is next on your agenda, Madame Producer? Or are you a morning glory: A One-Shot Aggie? Are you afraid to try it alone? Can you do it without Bolger? Are you only half-safe?"

Several months into the run of *Where's Charley?*, Gwen met up with, Irene Selznick at a party. Selznick was the first female producer of a Broadway drama for her work on *A Streetcar Named Desire*, which opened in December 1947 and became a huge success. Selznick sensed that Gwen was depressed and fatigued, and she asked if Gwen were suffering from "hit-itis." She explained that she had experienced an endorphin crash after her work on *Streetcar* had come to an end and she was left with nothing to do. "I woke up with a Pulitzer Prize–Winning Trauma," she said. Gwen laughed and felt her mood lifting. She would continue to work, even if the Broadway show no longer required as much from its producers.

She continued to devote herself to her husband, whose stamina was tested greatly during the run of the show. He continued to suffer bouts of laryngitis, and his workload also increased with the loss of his dynamic leading lady. Allyn Ann McLerie left the show in June 1949, after almost a year in the role, to accept a part in Irving Berlin's new musical, *Miss Liberty*. She was replaced with Joan Chandler, a sweet-looking brunette who had been a founding member of the Actors Studio and who had appeared opposite James Stewart in the Alfred Hitchcock film *Rope* the previous year. The night before her debut, Bolger canceled the evening performance of *Where's Charley?* due to another bout of laryngitis. His new co-star lasted just a month in the production before illness forced her from the role. Chandler's understudy, Marie Foster, became Amy in July 1948 and was replaced in August with Beverlee Bozeman.

Gwen kept a close eye on these replacements. Her co-producers, Feuer and Martin, had headed to Los Angeles that summer to work on their next Broadway show with Frank Loesser, *Guys and Dolls*. Their current show took a backseat to their new endeavor. Gwen felt that none of the replacement Amys lived up to McLerie's interpretation and that the romance of Charley and Amy was no longer believable. And she noticed how her husband broadened his portrayal of Charley, adding more horsing around to accommodate for first Foster's and then Bozeman's deficiencies. [28]

These additional demands further strained Bolger. He was never an extreme socializer, but for the run of *Charley?*, he and Gwen tried to ensure that everything he did offstage enhanced, rather than detracted from, his two hours and ten minutes onstage for each performance. They moved into a $666-a-month suite at the Waldorf-Astoria Hotel, where they had fewer household chores and concerns to attend to. He awoke at noon each weekday and completed a half-hour of seated stretches and sit-ups in pajamas, followed by the five position exercises of ballet. He breakfasted on easily digestible foods: orange juice, hot cereal, and toast. In the afternoons, the Bolgers went out for a stroll through Central Park, and when they returned, a Swedish masseur named Bengty Seashore stopped by daily to give Ray a massage. He was especially anxious about his feet, and aside from his walk, he would keep completely off of them while at home, remaining on the couch with his feet draped over the back of it, or tucking his feet beneath him while he sat, reading the New York newspapers. He would eat another simple, light meal at 6:30 in the evening and would arrive at the St. James Theatre by 8:00 P.M. for the 8:40 curtain. He spoke as little as possible and had special stationery created that was stamped with the words "I can't talk!" across the top in blue letters.

At the start of 1950, Bolger felt the urgency of improving his voice to keep up with the demands of the show. The box office continued to bring in profit, and *Where's Charley?* celebrated its five-hundredth performance just after the New Year. There could be no slowing down.

Help came from an unexpected avenue: Robert Baird, a baritone in the men's chorus, hoped to make a career as an operatic singer. As such, he had undergone extensive voice lessons in techniques foreign to musical comedy singers. He recommended that Bolger try one of his methods. By manipulating his thyroid cartilage, Bolger could lift his hyoid bone, the only bone protecting the vocal cords, to emit louder sounds. Bolger and Baird worked together four hours a week, for six months. Gwen marveled at the results: "the range and quality of his voice is growing in power and beauty and he has gained a few pounds, mostly in the upper torso!"[29]

Bolger gave strong performances throughout the spring of 1950, allowing the producers some breathing room and the ability to make future plans for *Where's Charley?* as a property and for its star. Feuer traveled to England to negotiate the sale of the show's film rights with J. Arthur Rank, owner of the Pinewood Film Studios. Feuer also teamed with Gwen to launch a Swedish production of the show in Stockholm, while Martin made arrangements for a production to move onto London's West End.

Gwen also imagined a life after *Charley*. She purchased the dramatic rights to *All the Ships at Sea*, an anthology of nonfiction short stories written by naval captain William J. Lederer. In the stories, Lederer paints himself as the good-hearted underdog who wins the day with a combination of self-effacement, determination, and patriotism. She made an astute choice; Lederer's character smacked of Bolger's persona. For instance, Lederer enters the Annapolis Naval Training Station hoping to rise in the ranks. He soon learns that his lack of a high school diploma will keep him from making any significant progress, and he is assigned to maintain the men's lavatory, or "head." Lederer is bitter, but he decides, "If this is to be my career, the Navy'll have at least one shipshape head. I don't suppose I have to have a diploma to clean up this crummy hole!"

He spends months cleaning the residual muck and comes up with comical, inventive ways to train the three hundred men using the head to be neater. At last he passes a demanding inspection by the admiral. He has done a better job than the admiral has ever seen in forty-one years. He has proved himself worthy of promotion, and the captain waives the high school diploma requirement for him to study at the Naval Academy. He tells Lederer, "Some day, maybe, you can tell people you got into the Naval Academy by using your head."[30]

Gwen thought of producing a comedy, without songs, based on the book. Her husband would play Lederer. Alternatively, they might produce the show together and cast another actor. They thought of commissioning a script for *All the Ships at Sea* as a long-term project. In the short term, Gwen hoped to find the right script to bring directly to the stage.

Accordingly, she jumped between both coasts to investigate three plays and their playwrights for her next project. When the deals fell through, she took to writing. Frustrated and doubtful of her abilities, though, she would write a play, tear it up, and begin another. The fear of being unable to replicate her success without her husband held her back.

In August, Bolger's doctor advised him that he could not continue working at his current level for much longer. While the show consistently brought in $35,000 to $40,000 per week, that summer's receipts had hit as low as $24,000. Feuer and Martin did not believe it could last through the entire next season, which would officially begin in September. The closing date was set for September 9, 1950, after the show's 792nd performance.

Once the news broke, Bolger fans flocked to buy up remaining seats at the final performances. The star himself received reams of fan mail from children, adolescents, and adults around the country who had caught the show on vacations to New York. They grieved because they would not have a chance to see the show again before it left Broadway.

The Broadway run may have been over, and Bolger may have been enjoying a much-needed rest, but the cast and creative crew knew the disbandment would be only temporary: the producers had announced that a road show reuniting Bolger and McLerie would begin in November. In December, Warner Brothers purchased the film rights for $200,000, with the original Amy and Charley slated to reprise their roles. David Butler would direct.

On Christmas night, 1950, *Where's Charley?* opened at the Shubert Theatre in Boston to sold-out capacity. The city had come to welcome its most beloved dancer home. The show ran through January 27 and immediately returned to New York. It opened at the Broadway Theatre on January 29, 1951, for a three-month engagement at popular prices. With the highest seat in the house set at $6, the producers believed they would make between $40,000 and $50,000 a week. The competition on their return, however, was steep. Their greatest challenge came from Feuer and Martin's new production of *Guys and Dolls*, which had opened on Broadway the month after *Where's Charley?* left town.

The company had been barred from the St. James due to a prior booking, and they found adjusting to the Broadway Theatre difficult. Larger than the St. James, the theater relied upon an "obsolete public address system with foot-mikes only," and Bolger's voice still had its limitations.[31] The Warner Brothers production company had hoped to record a performance of the return engagement in order to plan for the film adaptation. However, the idea had to be abandoned because of the challenging acoustics of the Broadway and the production expense required. The show would transfer to the West Coast for engagements in California, and they hoped to make a recording later. Unfortunately, this never came to be. Likewise, the original Broadway production of *Where's Charley?* never recorded a cast album due to the rules of the musician's strike then being waged by James Petrillo, head of the American Federation of Musicians. His most famous—and contentious—actions as a union boss were the Petrillo Bans, during which he halted all commercial recordings by union members from 1942 to 1944 and then again in 1948, in an attempt to pressure recording companies into providing better royalties to musicians. The Warner Brothers film would be the only vestige of Bolger's most important role.

Where's Charley? went first to the Curran Theatre in San Francisco, where it played to standing room only capacity, and then to the Philharmonic Auditorium in Los Angeles. Following the final performance on May 26, 1951, Butler's assistant director, Phil Quinn, took Bolger's special breakaway aunt costume to the overnight theatrical dry cleaners. On May 27, the cleaned dress was his carry-on item as he boarded a plane to London. The American cast members of the Warner Brothers film would follow.

CHAPTER 9
The New Triple Threat Man

The Bolgers arrived in London in July 1951 and found it a study in contrasts. They brought their traveling trunks to Claridge's, the luxury Art Deco hotel in the heart of Mayfair. Following tradition, the cast members spread out among London's finest hotels to ward off the discomforts of overexposure to each other. Director David Butler took rooms at the Dorchester, Claridge's most prestigious rival. Assistant director Phil Quinn holed up across the way from Butler, at the Baker Hotel. Allyn Ann McLerie and her husband, the lyricist Adolph Green, resided in Radlett Place, three miles away from most of the party. But the Bolgers received the best situation. A great brown-brick fortress, Claridge's had been Queen Victoria's favorite hotel. More recently, it had sheltered members of the royal family during the war, which had ended almost six years before. In the city, the Bolgers could still experience the damages and privations of war. Whole city blocks—with the exception of a single surviving restaurant or building—were leveled in the aftermath of heavy bombing.

The cast decamped from their luxurious safe havens to the Elstree Studios in Borehamwood, where interior scenes were shot, and to the campus of St. John's College at Oxford University for exteriors. Butler was the first director granted permission to shoot on the venerated campus; everything with the exception of the faculty burying ground was available to his crew. The cast recognized the privileges of being on an American film studio's payroll at once. Their new local crewmembers, they soon realized, had very little. During the summer and autumn of 1951, when *Where's Charley?* was filmed, the British were still experiencing the rationing of food and clothing. Some of the grips, gaffers, and other assistants received the *Where's Charley?* group frostily. They were used to arrogant Americans storming in and making demands for beef at lunch, or for cream and sugar at tea—items the British had not seen in years but which they were expected to procure because the visitors wanted to feel at home. Butler and Bolger worked actively to engender their friendship, giving their food ration coupons to the men and women on set. Butler explained, "We could eat at the hotels and charge it to Warner Brothers.... They're the gamest people I ever saw in my life. They had very little to eat, and they smiled with it. They made a joke out of it."[1]

The director and the star also made it a point to pass small gifts to their coworkers, hoping to come across as caring rather than condescending. Bolger would buy coffee and rolls for the men at break time. Butler even gave the crew a special dispensation from working on Saturdays so the men could take in the important soccer matches. Shooting would shut down for the day, and as an expression of thanks, the crews worked happily on Sunday without overtime pay.

The Americans further integrated into their British surroundings by hiring large quantities of real Oxfordians. Two hundred summer students were used as extras on campus, and they, too, exceeded Butler's expectations of humanity. Because of the frequent bursts of rain, the cast would often need to wait around for the sun to return before a sequence could be filmed. Butler would ask that the extras hold their places during the rain showers, rather than go milling about and getting lost. They would sit around for hours at a time. When Butler at last announced, "Roll 'em," they stood up and performed.

The first sequence shot at Elstree was the "Better Get Out of Here" song-and-tap-dance number. Michael Kidd, the thirty-six-year-old choreographer who had just achieved fame for his work on Feuer and Martin's *Guys and Dolls,* served as dance director. This was Kidd's first experience directing dance for film. The Bolgers and Kidd had traveled together from New York on the *Queen Mary*, and they had become friendly on board. Kidd later said of Bolger, "I thought he was wonderful.... [I]t wasn't just the eccentricity of his movements that attracted me, but he created a character. And he used the eccentricity of his movement to enhance the character that he created."[2]

The "Better Get Out of Here" number represents Bolger's best dance work on film. He is at the height of his dancing prowess (he had honed the routine over two years on Broadway) while also appearing very fit and refreshed. His costuming and staging may not make him look as young as a true collegian, but he does look better than his forty-seven years. The six-minute number encompasses not only his famed eccentric moves but also his Irish soft-shoe dancing. Kidd succeeded in capturing a sweeping dance

Bolger, dressed as Charley's Aunt, takes a break from shooting to speak with director David Butler (*standing*). From the Everett Collection.

with breadth and gaiety, rather than stifling the movement with the constraints of a soundstage.

Despite Kidd's originality in staging this number, Gwen insisted that "Once in Love with Amy" would have to be shot outdoors. Gwen had the idea to shoot the number at an inn on the banks of the Thames. Although she was a producer on the stage show, Bolger's wife had no official decision-making capacity with the Warner Brothers movie. That role belonged to Gerry Blattner, head of Warner Brothers European Film Productions. But Gwen ruptured the collegiality on set by challenging Butler on many matters and causing several dust-ups. After the first few weeks, their heated arguments cooled. They even became friends. She convinced him to join her on a reconnaissance trip to the bank of the Thames, where she wanted "Once in Love with Amy" to be shot. With Butler under the sway of Gwen, Blattner, the film's actual producer, had to intervene. He wrote to Steve Trilling, studio boss Jack Warner's second-in-command back at the Warner Brothers Studios in Burbank, of the incident. Blattner had been overseeing other pictures in Italy and was away from set for several days. When he returned,

> I found myself faced with a detailed plan worked out for this number requiring a minimum of four days' shooting on this location in September. The chance of getting four consecutive days of sunshine at that time of year is very risky. Plus the carrying of all Studio overheads, plus cost of maintaining the Unit in hotels, plus extensive water construction for camera cranes, plus heavy transportation charges, decided me to stop this whole idea, as I was convinced that we could get as good results building a suitable exterior set in the Studio and shooting same under controlled conditions, without running the great risk of almost certainly going over budget, schedule, and the possibility of not being able to complete the number on location after all. I mention all this as I think that Gwen and Ray were very disappointed at the time.[3]

A fake inn and a river beside it were created at Elstree. While the Bolgers were unhappy with the arrangement, Kidd's ideas pleased them. The number's success on Broadway, Kidd knew, stemmed from Bolger's making it an interactive sing-along. With no audience to prime, the magic effect would be lost, so to recreate the audience effect, Kidd installed a few extras in boats on the soundstage's river. Once Bolger, as Charley, finished capering around the grounds of the inn, oblivious to everything but his growing affection for Amy, the boaters applauded his routine. Startled, Charley conducted them to sing another stanza of the song before pattering off into the sunset.

On an evening just before Bolger and McLerie were scheduled to film the "Pernambuco" Latin ballet, the leading lady came down with a 105 degree fever at her hotel. Her condition only deteriorated, and the next day she developed severe ulcerations in her mouth. Blattner had her admitted to the hospital, where she remained for a week. Doctors determined that she was suffering an infection caused by germs from her teeth caps. Filming of

"Pernambuco" was rescheduled to September 27, 1951, just two days before Bolger's official end date on the picture.

While filming pickup shots on the Oxford lawn one afternoon near the conclusion of the shoot, Bolger, in his aunt's costume, observed a well-dressed man smoking a cigarette and observing the proceedings. Bolger said the man reminded him of a distinguished New England gentleman. They began conversing, and the man asked questions about the cameras, the sets, the actors. Then he introduced himself as Dr. A. J. Poole, president of Oxford University. Poole invited the entire cast to the presidential mansion for a dinner party. Though he never could affect the pose of an all-out intellectual convincingly, Bolger's childlike curiosity, contemplative nature, and strong, straight bearing made him a favorite among learned men. He listened with an attention that made conversationalists feel they were the only people in the world; Bolger, always looking to expand his knowledge of art, languages, and literature, wanted in on their world. Even when he was bogged down by academic discussion, his well-developed faculty for listening helped him remain interested. The starlit ambience of an Oxford garden party, silent except for the sounds of coffee cups clinking and the cognoscenti's discussions, offered him a comfortable rest from his acting. At the party, Butler said, Poole produced a venerable old register, containing entries of all the significant happenings at Oxford since the Year One. The president of the college flipped to the most recent record: the descent of the Warner Brothers *Where's Charley?* cast and crew upon the campus.[4]

The film company was charmed by working on location. The actors ate in the campus tearooms, and Butler set up shop in a study, where everyone gathered to watch the daily rushes. The Bolgers and the studio brass thought the film was promising. Blattner wrote to Trilling, "If I am typical of the general public reaction, then I am convinced that we will have a real hit with *Charley*, as going to daily rushes to see Bolger's comedy is like a tonic."[5] From Claridge's, Gwen wrote to her mother:

> The picture is coming along well and judging from the rushes we are catching the same speed and comedy the play had. Ray's make-up is wonderful and for the first time he looks like himself, except about 20 years younger. I worked with the make-up man and we solved all the problems together—*he* was willing to try mascara on Ray's eyes (in Hollywood they insisted it was impossible!) and it does the trick. And our boy is much more natural and relaxed. He says it is because I'm on the set and he is confident I wouldn't let him do

anything wrong. I think it is because at last he is doing what is right for him on the screen.[6]

Even as filming wrapped, there was more work to be done: Feuer, Martin, and Gwen were eager to send a tour of *Where's Charley?* throughout the United States. Gil Lamb and Eddie Foy Jr. were being considered for the role of Charley in the touring production. They also wanted to mount a production for the West End with Bolger, but Warner Brothers wanted to put him immediately into production on a new feature film and give him a starring role. Additionally, Bolger was aging. For as prestigious as a West End credit for his defining role would have been to him, Bolger loved America, and he knew what the physical demands of an additional turn as Charley would mean, particularly far away from home. So in England, Feuer and Martin were actively pursuing Norman Wisdom, a little-known pantomimist and singer whom Bolger and Loesser had seen on an early episode of *Toast of the Town*, which most viewers referred to as *The Ed Sullivan Show*. If either production got off the ground in 1952, Warner Brothers would likely not be able to release the film until 1953. Though everyone looked forward to the release of the picture, not even Warner Brothers was sure of when that would be. When the studio purchased the rights to make a film of the musical, their contract included a clause that would keep the release date from interfering with any theatrical productions then occurring.

Bolger returned to New York in early November 1951 and then proceeded to Hollywood. Warner Brothers wanted Bolger to fulfill his three-picture contract with them quickly, by starring in *April in Paris* with Doris Day. It, too, was directed by David Butler. The film wedded an idea of Jerry Wald's—to make Bolger a leading man—and the studio's attempt to keep picture goers from tiring of its tried-and-true pairing of Doris Day and Gordon MacRae, who had already appeared together in *Tea for Two*, *West Point Story*, *On Moonlight Bay*, and *Starlift*. The assignment switch was a coup for Bolger, as Day was the leading female box office draw at the time. He played S. Winthrop "Sam" Putnam, the Assistant Secretary to the Assistant to the Undersecretary of State. Sam is a sexless Yankee blue-blood who descended upon Washington with a dream of becoming president. After ten years with the State Department, he is still a minor bureaucrat, but he has a hopeful future: he's engaged to the daughter of the Secretary of State, and their impending nuptials have been printed in the *Congressional Record*.

Sam's chance to prove himself professionally comes when he is asked to organize the International Festival of the Arts in Paris. It's his job to make sure the best and the brightest America has to offer end up in the City of Love for the exposition. He gets off to a bad start when instead of inviting Ethel Barrymore to represent "theatre," he sends her invitation to a chorus girl, Ethel "Dynamite" Jackson, played by Day, and must resolve the whole situation aboard an ocean liner as the delegation heads to Paris for the festivities.

Filming for *April in Paris* began in February 1952. The shoot was relatively relaxed compared with Bolger's previous film, as he worked entirely at the Warner Brothers studio close to home, and he was working with a familiar director. However, challenges emerged as the two stars—a hoofing phenom and a songbird—struggled to find common ground and a good working relationship. Bolger was not used to working with a star bigger than he; he was used to being in a family-style cast where he was the clear patriarch.

He had not shared top billing with anyone in *Where's Charley?*, and partnering with Day was a big adjustment to make. She was a contralto known for her sweetness and clarity in delivering lyrics; she had perfect pitch and perfect rhythm. Bolger, despite the vocal training he had received during the run of *Where's Charley?*, was not a good match for her vocally. Likewise, Day could not keep up with Bolger on the dance floor. Her tapping had to be dubbed by Dian Myles. Day wrote in her memoir,

> I never worked harder at anything than I did at the dances. . . . Hours and hours and hours. A film dancer does not have the freedom of a stage dancer. She must dance precisely to a mark. Her turns must be exact. She must face precisely in the camera direction required while executing very difficult steps. And to learn those steps! . . . I would drag myself home at night, too tired to move another step, but I kept practicing in my head.[7]

Director David Butler also took issue with the way Bolger interacted with Day on the set. Butler had been working with Day since 1949. Their first picture together had been *It's a Great Feeling*. At the time of the *April in Paris* filming three years later, he still believed she was green. He said, "She used to come in a door and run across a set so fast you couldn't pan with her."[8] Day's greenness also meant, in Butler's view, that she allowed her co-stars to upstage her. Butler himself had been an actor, and he didn't let other actors get away with taking advantage of Day in scenes. Day, like Bolger, was not quite comfortable on camera. Unlike Bolger, she was shy and very self-critical. Bolger, in contrast, was used to performing on stage, and he put himself out front—he was not a retiring performer. In their scenes, he inadvertently upstaged her with his energy. Butler called Bolger out multiple times for this, making dynamics between the director and the leading actors uncomfortable at times through the completion of shooting, in late May 1952.

Immediately after filming wrapped, the Bolgers decamped to Lake Placid, New York, to relax at the summer home of their old friend Leon Leonidoff. They needed time to rest and reassess. While the Bolgers were on the East Coast, the *Where's Charley?* film at last received its movie premiere at Radio City Music Hall, on June 26, 1952. The *New York Times* immediately christened it "as inane a lark as ever tossed logic to the critics— and, as clearly as we remember the show on the stage, it is as near to a carbon copy as the cinema craftsmen could achieve."[9] *Variety* was more enthusiastic in its praise, proclaiming in its stylized lingo, "Ray Bolger repeats stage triumph in sock tunepic; surefire b.o."[10] *Variety* took the picture less seriously than did its newspaper counterparts, hailing the film as a "gay spoof" and a "delightful romp." McLerie also received high praise, and the industry magazine projected that she would emerge a film star. She had been signed to a long-term contract with Warner Brothers based on the strength of her performance as Amy. The supporting cast and the Technicolor, the review said, brought out the best in the leads.

The public took to the picture at once. Due to popular demand, it remained at the Music Hall for five weeks before being released nationally. It would go on to be a top-grossing picture for the year 1952, earning

Ray Bolger as Charley Wykeham and Allyn Ann McLerie as Amy Spettigue in a still from the "lost" Warner Brothers film, *Where's Charley?*, 1952.

$1.5 million. This modest success, however, was dwarfed by that of the most profitable musical of the year: MGM's *Singin' in the Rain*, which earned $3.3 million. Nonetheless, acclaim for Bolger as Charley came from all directions, and "Once in Love with Amy" rang out from radios across the country. He seemed to have finally gotten all he could hope for out of the role. But, unfortunately, the memory of Bolger as Charley Wykeham would not endure in the popular consciousness. After the film's initial release, it got locked away in Warner Brother's vaults for a couple of nebulous reasons: first, the show's producers feared future showings would conflict with future stage tours of *Where's Charley?*, and so it became unofficially embargoed. Second, Jo Sullivan, the wife and later estate representative of Frank Loesser, who had a controlling interest in the film, felt that it did not represent her husband's work well; she refused to allow the film to be released on television and, later, on video for home viewing. Today, only collectors who get their hands on bootlegged copies see the film. Although it is believed that Warner Brothers has once again received permission to release the film, it is now so poorly remembered that the studio does not want to invest the massive sums required to restore the original print and release it to the consumer market. The irony remains that, although Bolger committed just one of his Broadway roles to film, this performance is lost almost as completely as those that were never recorded.

Six months after Warner Brothers released the family-friendly *Where's Charley?*, the studio released *April in Paris* on December 24, 1952. Like many of Bolger's film musicals, *April in Paris* is pleasant but forgettable. The picture is a colorful mélange of garish showgirl costumes and chintzy stock footage of Paris (the entire film was shot in Burbank). None of the songs from the film seeped into the popular culture. Its reliance on slapstick and farce was reminiscent of *Where's Charley?* But that film was driven by prudish mirth, and the entire undercurrent of *April in Paris* is sex. It was the most risqué film either Day or Bolger had appeared in up to that point, which is not saying much. However, the Catholic Legion of Decency had demanded many excisions from Warner Brothers, and the final shooting script was riddled with double entendres.

After Bolger's new picture appeared, concerned parents wrote to Jack Warner himself to say how ashamed they were for two stars who usually represented stalwart virtues to be associated with smut. But both Day and Bolger survived the filming without lasting damage to their reputations, at least in the public's eye. It made a respectable $2.75 million throughout 1953, although this figure is almost half the earnings of the most popular musical film that year, *Gentlemen Prefer Blondes*, which earned $5.1 million and proved that the year's audience was fine with a sexy musical if it was performed by stars known to be provocateurs, like Marilyn Monroe and Jane Russell.

Bolger's participation in the brace of Warner Brothers pictures cemented several aspects of his reputation. First, he was a charming throwback to the dancers of a generation before, like Jack Donahue. Second, he could be considered a comic in his own right for his portrayal of Charley Wykeham. And third, he could appeal to adults as well as to children, as his slightly risqué turn in *April in Paris* proved. He was officially a pop culture figure, and he could use his exposure to try something new.

Throughout his career, Bolger's primary interest remained to entertain. He knew what he did well, and he wanted to keep doing it: he could charm, he could high kick, he could tap and split and bumble around the stage. Sometimes he decided he wanted to be more comedian than dancer; at other times, he wanted to be more dancer than comedian. But his purview never stretched much further than that. Gwen, for her part, had been most interested in reputation management: would this stage role, say, in *Life Begins at 8:40*, allow her husband to emerge as a Broadway star later? The answer was yes, as was proved when he won acclaim for his portrayal of Junior Dolan in *On Your Toes*. Should Bolger appear in such-and-such nightclub? No, because it would over-expose him for later stage work. Only Bolger's agent and agency, Abe Lastfogel of the William Morris office, was concerned with how Bolger would adapt to new media over the decades. Lastfogel saw to it in the 1950s that the "new triple threat man" was the king of entertainment: he had to be able to star in film, on television, and in nightclubs.

It wasn't that Lastfogel was much more visionary. He and Bolger had come from similar humble beginnings, and as they both aged, they grew more conservative. Where in the good old days Lastfogel was referred to as "honest Abe" for his unprecedented moral scrupulousness, in the fifties and sixties he was more likely to be called "the Pope." His character hadn't changed, but his belief system was received with slightly more cynicism as entertainment became more corporate and less personal. He did not try to force his views on the clients he served and who made the agency prosper. As the agency's historian, Frank Rose, wrote of the organization, "In the thirties, his office built Jimmy Cagney into a star and Mae West into a sex siren. In the forties, it made Rita Hayworth a love goddess and gave Marilyn Monroe her start. In the fifties, it took Frank Sinatra when he'd hit bottom and put Elvis Presley on television."[11] Lastfogel's integrity had driven the firm's growth over time, even though the entertainment industry in which they operated was often underhanded and dirty. But Lastfogel allowed himself to be guided only by his dedication to the legacy of William Morris Sr. His own business sense and talent for recruiting and developing agents with diverse specialties and interests enabled him to pursue, and lay claim to, a string of "next big things".

It had been Bolger's good fortune to find Lastfogel at the very start of his career, before Lastfogel built up the most successful and influential talent agency in the country. It helped that they fostered a close friendship. Even if the comic dancer was not totally enthusiastic about the new media of the twentieth century, his agent-friend would fold him into some of the most important developments in twentieth-century entertainment: the development of the Las Vegas Strip and the wide-scale roll-out of national network television.

In 1931, about five thousand people lived in Las Vegas, a dusty, sleepy railroad town. Then the Nevada legislature passed the Wide Open Gambling Bill, legalizing all sorts of gaming. The El Rancho Vegas resort opened a decade later and introduced the prospects of luxury vacationing and high-stakes gambling to average Americans. Across the street, the rival Club Bingo—a three-hundred-seat bingo hall—lured patrons. The possibilities of the new desert oasis attracted the interest of mobsters. Bugsy Siegel opened the $6 million Flamingo Resort in 1946 with the help of his child-hood friend Meyer Lansky. Then came competitor hotels and entertainment centers on the Strip: the Desert Inn, the Sands, and the Dunes. Big-money entertainment mingled with government interests in Las Vegas. The Nellis Air Force Base trained fighter pilots for World War II, and the nearby Nevada Test Site began conducting atomic bomb tests after Harry Truman gave his okay in 1950. Vegas became a new wellspring of money, power, mystery, crime, and intrigue.

Fall 1952 saw the opening of the Sahara resort, a $5 million operation, on the site of the old Club Bingo. It boasted two hundred rooms, the larg-est pool in the city, and a six-hundred-seat theater with proscenium stage called the Congo Room. Stan Irwin, a former comedian who was responsi-ble for booking talent into the new Sahara, wanted a major comic to appear in the Congo Room for the grand opening bill. His first choice was Milton Berle, so he contacted his agency, William Morris. Berle demanded $40,000 a week, an unheard-of figure for nightlife entertainment. Irwin considered it, but he was unable to give an official opening date for the Congo Room. By the time the plan was finalized, Berle was already engaged elsewhere. His second choice was Danny Thomas, but he already had alle-giance to the Flamingo in Vegas, and it was considered very bad form for entertainers to hop from one Vegas resort to another. Irwin's third choice was Ray Bolger. He extended an offer of $20,000 per week to the comic dancer in September. Lastfogel told Irwin that Bolger refused to do nightclubs. Irwin appealed to Gwen directly, who decided that the engagement was classy enough for her husband to accept. He signed for the October 7 opening.

When the Sahara opened, the new hotel's lobby and gambling parlor were filled with flowers from well-wishers. Wall-to-wall crowds turned out for opening night, and hundreds were turned away from the doors of the Congo Room theater. Sharing the bill with Bolger was Lisa Kirk, a raspy alto singer who had created the role of Bianca in *Kiss Me, Kate* on Broadway. The Sa-Harem Dancers, a dozen tall, sultry white women bedazzled the audience and reinforced the tenuous "East Indian fantasy" theme; the Shyretto Trio trick cyclists supported them.

Bolger earned praise for crooning a few songs from his past shows, like "Life Is Just a Bowl of Cherries." He also spent forty minutes going through his usual repertoire of comedy dances to great applause. *Variety* wrote, "Moving forward in time cycle, he spreads a nifty batch of yocks through a nostalgia kick of 'Charleston,' 'Blackbottom,' 'Conga,' 'Rhumba,' and jitterbug."[12] He also performed the Sad Sack and prize fight routines. For his finale, he offered "Once in Love with Amy," which forced him to beg off from the stage so that Kirk could go through her repertoire.

There were some opening night glitches. Both entertainers, particularly Kirk, were hampered by a faulty microphone system. The reviewers posited that the Congo Room's format—smaller than a Broadway theater but too large to be an intimate café setting—would make the audience feel removed from the entertainers. But for the opening bill, the electricity in the air suggested otherwise. Bolger learned that his star power worked perfectly well in Vegas. He signed a lucrative, long-term contract with the Sahara for seasonal appearances. Lastfogel had other ideas for how he could fill the balance of his year.

Bolger had sat out television's development between 1948 and 1951. But by 1952 the medium could no longer be ignored. CBS and NBC remained the dominant players. ABC, where Bolger had made his true debut, was still playing catch-up. NBC's *Colgate Comedy Hour* executives rang up Abe Lastfogel. They wanted a very popular comic who could appeal to children and parents alike for their Christmas episode. Bolger tried to resist, but he accepted when the network offered Gwen the opportunity to write the episode.

Gwen dove into the writing with zeal. Ray mostly grumbled. She set the episode in a snowy street, where Bolger would admire Christmas window displays and bump into Santa Claus and happy children. She built her husband's best-loved dance and comedy routines into the episode. She left time for two Christmas songs—"O Little Town of Bethlehem" and "I Hope You Have a Very Merry Christmas"—and four commercial breaks. For the finale, Bolger would perform "Once in Love with Amy" and have the studio audience join in the song. The *Colgate Comedy Hour* executives approved the script, and Bolger was scheduled to appear on December 21, 1952.

Bolger planned to wear his original costume from *Three to Make Ready* for "The Old Softshoe" routine. However, because he wasn't concerned that it might not fit, he didn't try on the six-year-old suit until the night before the show. When he did, he realized it was far too tight, and he fussed to find something else. Bolger was slowly getting larger, losing the physique of a young and over-active Broadway dancer an inch at a time. Although his level of preparation reflects his lack of interest in television, his vaudevillian work ethic showed up when he arrived on stage. He was comforted to see that Al Goodman, who had conducted George White's *Scandals of 1931*, was out in front of the studio orchestra with his baton. Broadway was all around, in a new configuration. Bolger got in his performance zone for his audience, and the evening whisked by.

The *New York Times* the next day welcomed Bolger's appearance as a triumph and noted, "His presentation was a small revue that had wit, grace, and style perfectly attuned to the intimacy of the home screen. From the moment the curtain went up until just before the final commercial, Mr. Bolger did not spare himself."[13]

Most surprising to the Bolgers, though, were the floods of fan mail they received directly after the performance. Ray said, "The spontaneity of the reception, letters from people from Coast to Coast, warm, friendly, living room guest type letters these were. You just don't get them in the theatre. It takes years for so many people to see your show. Even in the movies."[14] Bolger had found a use for television: to bring his personality to millions of families across the country, and receive their endearment in return, the payoff for any actor.

Bolger warmed up to television just as ABC hit a growth spurt. It was after all the youngest network: NBC had begun television broadcasting in 1939 and ABC in 1941. Things had not been going so well for ABC since its triumphant roll-out of WJZ in 1948. It had invested too much in buying and building individual stations and still had just five network-owned-and-operated stations and nine full-time affiliates. There were rumors of bankruptcy, but after a corporate merger, the network was in a position to lay out serious money for new programming. Leonard Goldenson, president of ABC, wanted to flesh out its evening broadcast with situation comedies. He also had a different production model in mind for his new programs: whereas most shows, like *The Colgate Comedy Hour*, were televised live from New York, ABC television shows would be filmed before studio audiences in Los Angeles, and then broadcast. This ground had been broken by *I Love Lucy*, the smash-hit CBS sitcom produced by Lucille Ball and Desi Arnaz at Desilu Productions, their Hollywood outpost. Filming television episodes rather than broadcasting them live allowed for the possibility of reruns and residuals, which would increase revenue. Goldenson was determined that ABC would use its third-place finish behind NBC and CBS as an advantage rather than a liability. Since the network was already lagging behind the two front-runners, it would experiment with new formats to reach new audiences, the sort that made advertisers willing to pay big money. Then it would catch up to the other networks.

To stay in the black with advertising dollars, ABC needed to develop the shows and front the money to pay the industry's top comics. Then the corporation would engage in powerful salesmanship, selling the television shows as well as their timeslots to advertising agencies, who were buying on behalf of multimillion-dollar companies. Sales of consumer products could rocket with television exposure, the executives figured, if trusted Hollywood stars could convince the viewing public to buy more of them.

Although he took the futuristic view, Goldenson came from the movie theater world. He had done business with the William Morris Agency since the 1930s, when he was booking talent into Paramount theaters between films. As ABC ramped up its television programming, Goldenson wanted one of the most famous comic dancers to emerge from the Paramount stages for his network: he asked Lastfogel if Bolger would develop a half-hour musical comedy show for ABC. Goldenson also expressed interest in some of Lastfogel's other comedian clients: Danny Thomas, George Jessel, and Sammy Davis Jr.

For once, Bolger didn't try to refuse the offer. Not only had his experience with NBC buoyed his faith in television, but he and Gwen also desperately wanted to work together. Their attempts to adapt *All the Ships at Sea* had stalled. They had launched a confectionary company together, the Hollywood Candy Company, which sold a very waxy grade of chocolate. They had fallen off from their glamorous heydays as producer-and-star of *Where's Charley?*, but television offered them a second chance to achieve that kind of satisfaction.

The Bolgers pitched a concept to ABC. Their show would be called *Where's Raymond?* as an obvious play on the popularity of *Where's Charley?*, and it would focus on Raymond Wallace, a Broadway star who was always delayed in getting to the theater. Raymond's antics with his brother, his girlfriend, or other rotating characters would provide the comedy. And when Raymond Wallace finally arrived at the theater at the last possible second, the routine he performed with his waiting dance partner would give the audience the song and dance they expected from Bolger.

ABC approved the concept for the 1953–1954 season in late March 1953 and paid Bolger $150,000 to star in his series for thirty episodes. The program was scheduled to air at 9:00 P.M. on Friday, as part of ABC's attempt to establish a "comedy night." When Lastfogel negotiated the deal for Bolger's show to run on ABC, he also insisted that another client of his get the greenlight. ABC agreed. Thus came *The Danny Thomas Show*, which concerned the domestic life of Danny Williams, a successful nightclub entertainer. With Williams keeping late hours at the club, the burden of caring for his two children fell to his wife.

Programming decisions, including length of television shows, genres, and stars, were made by the networks in the service of making the best deals possible with advertising agencies. Though earlier forays into television, like Ed Sullivan's *Toast of the Town* and the *Colgate Comedy Hour*, had preferred the hour-long format, production costs of television shows in the 1950s were exorbitant. Advertisers were more willing to back half-hour shows, or to share sponsorship credit on a one-hour show, than to finance an entire hour-long program on their own. Each half-hour episode of *Where's Raymond?* would cost $39,000 to produce.

Networks also learned during their expansion that they could generate more revenue by selling two half-hour programs than one hour-long program. Advertisers paying such high prices wanted to ensure that their investment would net out. In their offices, they conducted market research and collected data to figure out what kinds of programming their key demographics wanted and at what times they were most likely to watch television. Frequently, an advertiser would be interested in a program but would make the network move it to a spot the advertiser preferred. Networks, not wanting to lose the cash, would begin rearranging their timetables like chessboards, balancing their own needs to retain traffic and drive ratings with the demands of their clients. They also had to pay attention to other television shows competing in the same time slots on different networks.

But securing one large-if-finicky advertiser could also lock in other sponsors, who wanted to catch the viewing audience before or after an important show. *The Danny Thomas Show*, airing Tuesdays at 9:00 P.M., had this kind of impact on ABC's advertising sales. American Tobacco bought it up on behalf of Lucky Strike cigarettes almost as soon as it hit the market in July 1953, which led to the company's sponsoring alternate weeks of

Where's Raymond? with advertisements for its Pall Mall brand. ABC sold the other half-interest in the Bolger program to Sherwin-Williams Paint Company, which agreed on the condition that the show would in fact air on Thursday nights at 8:30 rather than Friday night at 9 o'clock.

The William Morris Agency helped both of its clients secure space for production at Desilu Productions' studio in Hollywood. *Where's Raymond?* would be produced by the Bolgers' new company, B&R Enterprises (for "Bolger" and "Rickard"). It was appropriate, then, that they would work in the proximity of the reigning Hollywood power couple and their wildly successful television show: Lucille Ball and Desi Arnaz, and *I Love Lucy*. With this venture, Gwen received more professional control over her husband than she had ever had before. B&R Enterprises was structured in such a way that, for the life of the company, Gwen would be leasing out Bolger to television studios to make appearances. B&R took advantage of being able to observe Desilu's operations and innovations.

Desilu was pioneering the three-camera method before a live studio audience, but *Where's Raymond?* would have to forego filming in front of people. The song-and-dance routine for each episode would take at least three hours to shoot each week, even though the number would run only about three minutes. A studio audience was used to seeing an episode being shot sequentially; for a half-hour program, they were expected to stay seated for no longer than an hour and a half. Episodes of Bolger's show would need to be shot over the course of three eight-hour days, using as many as eleven sets. There would be no room for any audience on the soundstage. With time and space working against them, the production team decided that a laugh track would have to be dubbed over the filmed program.

Marc Daniels, who worked on *I Love Lucy*, directed the pilot episode of *Where's Raymond?* The first show consisted of a flimsy patter-and-horseplay plot and emphasized the dance routine that would become a staple of each program. B&R recruited a dance director from Universal Studios, Harold "Hal" Belfer, to stage the number for the pilot. For the Spanish-style dance, a take-off of the "Pernambuco" routine, Belfer brought two women: his assistant, Sylvia Lewis, and a chorine looking for a big break films, Rita Moreno.

Privately, Gwen was considering both women for a role in the show—a dancing female lead had not yet been cast. The two professional dancers learned in the course of the afternoon, though, how limited Bolger's range was. Moreno made the most of her day on set—a *Life* photographer came to shoot promotional photos, and a headshot of Moreno made it on the cover of the magazine almost a year later, which brought her to the attention of legendary Hollywood producer Darryl Zanuck. But even before that development, she was uninterested in working with Bolger. She didn't feel he had the potential to succeed in a dance variety format. Of her experience she later said, "That wasn't his thing. That wasn't his métier . . . but he tried to go along with the dance choreography instead of saying, 'Listen, I'm a big star. I don't need this.'"[15]

But Gwen was more interested in Lewis; her long body's proportions matched Ray's well, and her angles—high cheekbones and arched eyebrows—complemented his billowy looseness. Gwen also saw that Lewis's diverse background—including ballet, Latin dance, voice, and piano—could stretch Bolger's limited range in ways that would benefit the demands of a weekly television show.

B&R offered to sign Lewis as choreographer of the show, a decision that Belfer generously cheered, even though it meant he was losing his assistant. When the show premiered on October 8, 1953, the cast featured Richard Erdman as Raymond's landlord, Pete Morrisey; Allyn Joslyn as Raymond's brother, Jonathan Wallace; and Betty Lynn as Raymond's girlfriend, June. Lewis also received a role in front of the camera: she would play Raymond's dance partner, Sylvia Sedgewick, in the fictional revue.

The weekly adventures of Raymond Wallace would include his finding the courage to fire his wardrobe mistress, investing in a vague oil deal, and landing in jail for destroying a police summons. Critics were willing to accept the program as light fare, but the shortcomings of the format for Bolger were apparent. As the *Billboard* review for the program noted, Bolger was at his best during the physical performances, but the show suffered from "radio-vintage dialogue. . . . Bolger is a great impromptu comic but in the tight half-hour he didn't get any opportunity to run wild."[16]

The Danny Thomas Show had debuted the night before. Together, the two programs were considered the strongest comedy offerings of "the new ABC." However, their initial Trendex viewer ratings disappointed their sponsors. *The Danny Thomas* show scored just 9.6 in October 1953, and *Where's Raymond?* scored 11.5. Neither number was good enough to enter the network's own Top 10 listing. By comparison, the most-watched episode of *I Love Lucy*, in which Lucy has a baby, had aired in January of that year and received a Trendex score of 68.8. Not only were the new ABC comedy shows proving lackluster for their own networks, but there was little indication at first that either of them could help to bridge the gap between ABC and its main rivals, NBC and CBS. But these were early days; the network believed both shows would pick up viewers.

Bolger recognized that some of the shortcomings of the program stemmed from his own limitations as a performer. This vexed him. His style of acting, his persona, and his exuberance were so larger-than-life that on the small screen he appeared stilted. The work was hard. On Friday night, the script for the following week would be given to the cast to review over the weekend. On Monday, Bolger and Lewis would meet at a rehearsal hall off the Desilu lot with a pianist and the songs for the week in tow. All of Monday was allocated to the musical number, and all the choreography was completed by the time they wrapped. The three would talk about the number, with most consideration going to whatever Lewis had in mind. The ideas would flow; the pianist would pick up an introduction. Lewis would take a few steps. Bolger vamped a little. They went back and forth and set the dance before lunch on Monday, hoping they would retain everything they had decided through the break. Every week, between three- and four-and-a-half minutes of original choreography had to be created. Tuesday through Thursday were spent rehearsing and blocking scenes. On Friday there would be a dress rehearsal before filming that evening. As Lewis said, "We got into a routine, and you just have to work at that level and that speed, and you can't be a perfectionist. [You hope] your technique serves you well and you just do what you do, and hope it comes out well, and that's it. That's the best you can hope for."[17]

Although Bolger put in ten- to twelve-hour workdays like the rest of his cast, hard work was not enough. He needed to expand his range to include types of dance he had never tried before. Lewis devised routines that used Bolger's repertoire as a launching point but pushed him in new directions. Together they performed a pseudo-salsa, a Gypsy dance, the march of the wooden soldier, and dozens of character dances. She found it challenging, as a trained ballerina and tap dancer, to work with an artist as spontaneous as Bolger. Though she never expressed it while the show was being produced, she later admitted she was frustrated by his lack of formal training and his limited knowledge of technique and conventional choreography—aspects of his craft that a formal education would have provided him. It did not take long for her to realize that Bolger sold personality, not expert dancing.

The show lumbered along with Bolger's popularity as both the selling point and the sticking point, though tensions backstage threatened the show's health. Broadway, though traditionally liberal, tolerated the conservative point of view. However, in Hollywood, Bolger's politics were unpopular. Always closed-mouthed, Bolger socialized minimally with his cast. When he did speak, he generally kept the conversation simple. Lewis recalled that he reminisced about working with Balanchine for *On Your Toes*; she had not been the only choreographer bewildered by Bolger's style. The star himself recalled the grueling weeks of nonstop training for the dramatic jazz

One of the dozens of numbers Sylvia Lewis, *right*, choreographed for herself and Ray Bolger was a ballet to "Under Paris Skies," which began when Bolger, as the artist, realized his creation came to life. Photo courtesy of Sylvia Lewis.

ballet "Slaughter on Tenth Avenue." During those first rehearsals, in his rich Russian accent, Balanchine lamented to Bolger, "Everything you do comes out funny!"

Bolger liked to take the cast even further back in time, recounting his days as a youth in Boston and telling jokes and tall tales about the city's Irish Catholics. But sometimes nostalgia carried him into politics. Bolger showed his Republican sympathies in his discussion of James Michael Curley and the great Kennedy dynasty in Massachusetts. The conversation topics would veer from Democrats and Republicans to capitalists and communists, and sometimes the cast began arguing. Bolger viewed his country as a meritocracy, where individuals should be free to pursue and enjoy their own successes. He viewed himself as a self-made man who contributed generously. He was a libertarian who believed that a minimal government should be in place to prevent harm but not to promote good: private industry and private charity would be the best remedy for society's ills.

In 1953, Senator Joe McCarthy hijacked the House Un-American Activities Committee to make allegations of communism against hundreds of Americans. In total, he would blacklist 320 artists and writers. They were kept from working and traveling. Many would never recover their careers from the taint of this association. Though Bolger seemed to hold no grudges against any of his employees' beliefs, one day, in the midst of rehearsal, a flutter of paper and hushed tones descended on the soundstage. "Loyalty Oaths" were handed around the set. Each employee was expected to sign the document, which stated they had no communist sympathies. Any cast member that did not sign would lose his or her job. Lewis said, "Whether it came from D.C., or whether it was pressured by Bolger, I don't know. I have no idea. But it was very tense around there at that period. And he was a very outspoken right-winger."[18]

Gwen also irritated the cast members. Although she was a partner in B&R Enterprises, she had no official capacity to make decisions on the production of each episode of *Where's Raymond?* She shared her opinions forcibly. The cast had little good to say about her, and behind her back they mocked her dowdy clothes, her hair style, and especially the way she mothered Bolger. The cast members frequently speculated about the private life of the Bolgers, who seemed so unknowable to them. Lewis said,

> It's amazing that those two individuals [Gwen and Ray] found each other. Nobody could deal with either one of them other than each other. Because, aside from a few times in rehearsal, even situations where he was with just three or four of us—if a lot of people were around, he seemed to feel obliged to behave a certain way, he had a guard up in his body language, in his verbal language, in everything. But to see him let his hair down, we could have a laugh— those things were rare, they were in rehearsal. And then when Gwen was present he became something a little different yet. And I really did try to visualize them hanging out in the kitchen and just, you know, letting it all out and leveling about something. I just couldn't imagine it. I guess they must have sometimes.[19]

Lewis's greatest concern, though, was Bolger's lack of rhythm. The film editors were challenged with putting together the dance footage in a way that would complement Bolger's efforts. The difficulty here, Lewis said, was that the structure of a piece of music never guided his performances— serendipity and improvisation did. Consequently, there was a lot of cursing in the editing room. Lewis remembered getting frequent calls from the technicians, who would view Bolger's dance for the week and be at a loss for how to cut the film. "We can't find the beat," they would tell her. Eventually, they devised a helpful system: "Okay, when *Sylvia's* foot hits the floor, that's the beat."

Danny Thomas's ratings picked up strongly toward the end of his first season, whereas Bolger's show never got very high up in the charts. As a result, both American Tobacco and Sherwin Williams withdrew their sponsorship. ABC was willing to renew the program for a second season, but a protracted search for replacement sponsors began.

Even with the television show's uncertain future, the Bolgers felt the their sense of "home" shift from the East Coast to the West. Ready to give home ownership another try, they had purchased a mansion in Beverly Hills prior to the launch of their show. This afforded Bolger the opportunity to play golf more regularly, at the Bel Air Country Club, where he began to make the acquaintance of key members of the Los Angeles political and business scenes. Performing was no longer merely a means to stardom; *Where's Charley?* had secured that for him. Bolger began to crave influence and, to some degree, money. Over the course of the 1950s, he made several children's and novelty recordings for Decca, one of the first media companies to catch the renewed uptick of interest in *The Wizard of Oz*. These lacked artistic merit, but they were a means of expanding revenue and fame. By the time he launched the second season of his television show, his newfound interest in merchandising was clear.

Big changes at the rocketing ABC shook up the 1954–55 season. The network had cut an impressive deal with Walt Disney for an hour-show, *Disneyland*. The weekly anthology series featured an assortment of productions all created under Disney's supervision, including original cartoons, feature-length films divided into one-hour segments, and educational documentaries. Sponsors swarmed ABC for the opportunity to catch the *Disneyland* viewers, and the lift in prestige that the new series provided the network helped attract new sponsors for other programming, including two sponsors for the second season of Bolger's show. The 1954–55 season would begin filming in July.

Until then, Bolger returned to the Sahara in Las Vegas. Increasingly, comics were taking the second-banana spot at the Las Vegas nightclubs, with singers becoming the headliners. He offered a seventy-minute show with the operatic prodigy Anna Maria Alberghetti and Muriel Landers, a comic standing five-foot-two and weighing two hundred pounds who had appeared on Bolger's television show. Bolger planted Landers in the audience before the show and later called her out for a seemingly impromptu burlesque of a ballroom number. The tall, lanky star with his short, squat partner amused audiences. Bolger performed a new bit: he impersonated the stripper Lili St. Cyr, who was also performing in Las Vegas. The seventeen-year-old Alberghetti sang classics like "Italian Lullaby" and "Showboat" and more contemporary pieces like "That's Amore" in her lilting soprano register. Her mother played piano for her, and her father led the Cee Davidson Orchestra, highlighting the sweet tone of the show. Surprisingly, the Sahara found that Bolger was one of the few celebrities who could consistently bring in the volume of gamblers necessary to fund lavish entertainment. His courtly nostalgia shows held the attention of Vegas audiences more effectively than they held television audiences.

Bolger managed to make a splash on television that summer, though, by becoming the substitute host of an episode of NBC's *The Buick-Berle Show*. Milton Berle, the first major American television star, who was known simply as "Mr. Television," had been a mainstay of major network comedy programming since 1948. He was also represented by the William Morris Agency. When Berle had to miss one of his own programs for the first time due to the death of his mother, Lastfogel's instinct told him to get Bolger. With very little rehearsal time, Bolger managed to make a success of his guest appearance. He brought Muriel Landers from Las Vegas and corralled the other stars appearing on the program with just the right amount of buffoonery. It augured well for his television series' return in the fall.

Bolger returned to work for ABC at a time when it was experiencing a massive growth spurt. By fall 1954, ABC was operating at a profit for the first time thanks to *Disneyland*. It had also rolled out full-scale daytime and weekend programming, in which it had invested $34 million. *The Danny Thomas Show* had found its niche and was doing well. All portents indicated that a revised Bolger show held great potential that season.

Executives from New York traveled to Los Angeles. They met with Bolger to discuss some changes. They were retitling his show *The Ray Bolger Show*, to play to his personal appeal. Additionally, they wanted to leverage Bolger as a brand in service of their sponsor, Dorothy Gray cosmetics. They would use his image on promotional displays in department stores nationwide. The change in sponsorship also brought about significant technical changes in the show. Viewers had rebelled at the use of the laugh track on *Where's Raymond?*, and so the production team completely overhauled their process so that the series could be filmed in front of a live studio audience. They believed this would also improve Bolger's performances, as he played best to real people. The entire cast also got together and requested that Mrs. Bolger be barred from the set. They won.

The cameramen experimented with a new kind of film from Eastman, called Tri-X.[20] The major appeal of the new film was that it cut down on the amount of light needed to film segments. From the days of filming *The Wizard of Oz* onward, Bolger had struggled with performing in high temperatures. He was now fifty years old. Every effort that could be taken to cool the soundstage would increase his comfort and stamina.

On January 4, 1954, on the Desilu soundstage, Bolger's co-stars had surprised him with a fiftieth-birthday cake. The public still revered Bolger, but not because of his newness: he was a nostalgic comfort in the Cold War era. As a review of the revamped second season of his television series read,

It may not always be a funny program, but it is a happy one. And, Mr. Bolger gets to sing and dance to the viewer's content. Let's face it, if you like Ray

Bolger, with a towel around his neck, consults with the cast and crew of *The Ray Bolger Show* on set prior to filming before a live studio audience in the 1953–54 season. Photo courtesy of Sylvia Lewis.

Bolger, you don't care about his doing anything else. This time around he's doing it with some attractive and talented people.

Another review said he possessed "old time grace." Old men with old time grace, Dorothy Gray soon realized, did not sell cosmetics very well.

The show was also struggling through its second season. Bolger had to contend with a major problem: his show's budget often did not permit him to buy rights to the songs that had made him most famous. Rather than perform his "Once in Love with Amy" dance to Frank Loesser's tune, he instead performed it to "Louise," a song made popular in 1929 by Maurice Chevalier. Bolger's scriptwriters desperately wanted to work a scarecrow routine into the show. Again, instead of performing "If I Only Had a Brain," Bolger had to settle for "I Whistle a Happy Tune." This number, however, represented the only time outside of *The Wizard of Oz* film that Bolger performed in his original Scarecrow costume. Bolger was able to perform a version of his Sad Sack Routine to Irving Berlin's "This Is the Army," but this did not garner him the ratings that performing, say, his original "Once in Love with Amy" dance to the proper song would have. His television series had not added any lasting new material to his repertoire, and television audiences had already seen the best of what he had to offer.

With talk of canceling his show swirling, Bolger flew to New York in February 1955. Decca wanted him to narrate L. Frank Baum's *The Wonderful Wizard of Oz* for a children's record. At the same time, NBC invited him to appear on its *Big Time* series. He made his color television debut when he appeared on the program with Milton Berle and Martha Raye. In his first attempt to leverage his star power for the common good via television, Bolger filmed a public service announcement for the United Community Campaigns, the beginning of a long association with the United Way Foundation. He also led the Red Cross Christmas Blood Drive with television spots.

While Bolger explored public service, Lehn & Fink, owners of Dorothy Gray, did in fact drop their sponsorship of *The Ray Bolger Show*. They received an opportunity to sponsor reruns of *I Love Lucy*, a program they realized would help them sell cosmetics more effectively. ABC would not carry a third season of a Ray Bolger program; the pendulum of advertiser demands was swinging back in favor of one-hour programs, and comedies were on the wane; the sitcoms that repackaged and sold old vaudevillians could not find their audience. Ray Bolger, George Jessel, and Walter Winchell (the noted journalist had started in vaudeville) all had ABC shows that were cancelled. Audiences wanted to use the medium to explore new formats. The president of ABC had collaborated with Warner Brothers to bring viewers *Cheyenne,* the first western to hit the airwaves and the first one-hour weekly drama with recurring cast members across seasonal plots.

ABC was even leading the charge for quality news and information broadcasts. The network had aired live all of the trials of the US Army against Senator Joseph McCarthy, which unfolded between April and June of 1954. The young network was now considered the equal of CBS and NBC, with more available programming than ever before. But it no longer had a place for Bolger.

Exhausted, he decamped to the desert. Although he made only half as much money in Las Vegas as he had made from television, it was for about a quarter of the amount of work. He got to rehash all his old favorites to adulation. No one expected anything new from Bolger any longer. In fact, in nightclubs and theaters around the country, dancers like Lou Wills Jr. and Budd Robinson were impersonating Bolger's old-time grace and made a career out of it, although they achieved no enduring fame. But the benefit of being old was that he could be introduced to another generation of fans. Resurging interest in *The Wizard of Oz* helped to accomplish this.

Bolger visits with Sylvia Lewis and her daughter, Catherine, at the Tropicana in 1957. The Bolgers remained lifelong friends with Lewis after *The Ray Bolger Show* ended. Photo courtesy of Sylvia Lewis.

In 1954, television networks wanted to acquire high-quality motion pictures to broadcast on television. This would help them to fill up their expanding broadcast schedules and to earn ever more advertising dollars with the lowest possible outlay. Most of the large movie studios, like Warner Brothers and MGM, balked at first. They worried that surrendering their highest-quality films would be taking money out of their own pockets. But for the right sums, deals were reached.

Judy Garland, who had been struggling with the ups and downs of poor health and marital difficulties since she and Bolger filmed *The Harvey Girls*, also made a film comeback in 1954. Her third husband, Sid Luft, produced a musical adaptation of *A Star Is Born* for Warner Brothers, with Garland in the lead role of Esther Blodgett. The film was directed by George Cukor, one of the most influential directors involved with the filming of *The Wizard of Oz*. Garland played opposite James Mason as Norman Maine. The result was triumphant, earning Garland an Oscar nomination, and to capitalize on her resurging fame, MGM decided to reissue *The Wizard of Oz* in movie theaters in the summer of 1955. The studio was also willing to release the film for television broadcast. CBS won the privilege of airing *The Wizard of Oz* after negotiating a tough deal of $225,000 for a one-time showing right. One of CBS's largest sponsors, Ford, paid an undisclosed amount to air the film as part of the network's *Ford Star Jubilee* series, which otherwise produced original, live variety episodes. The broadcast took place on Saturday, November 3, at 9:00 P.M., and was a two-hour event hosted by Bert Lahr and Judy Garland's ten-year-old daughter, Liza Minnelli. It far exceeded the ratings of the programs competing on the other networks.

For the first time, the pop culture felt the enduring quality of the film. And many viewers and reviewers were shocked to realize how well the music, the special effects, and the performances of the supporting cast held up after sixteen years. They were reminded of how much affection the Scarecrow character inspired and reinforced the emerging public perception of Ray Bolger as America's uncle. People might not respect him as a great film actor, but they began to give him a lot of credit for being a happy, charming, and respectable personality.

Bolger returned as star of a network television program just once more, with sixteen episodes of a series called *Washington Square* for NBC beginning in the fall of 1956. This opportunity gave him almost triple the production budget of his ABC series, as well as a more flexible format for him to introduce guests and specialty numbers. The reduced number of episodes in the season also made the television production process less strenuous for him. However, even with these plush circumstances, Bolger

Ray and Gwen celebrate their twenty-eighth wedding anniversary at the Sahara on July 9, 1957, while Ray is performing there. From the Everett Collection.

could not find success. In its review of *Washington Square*, *Variety* asked, "How much reliance can be put on the singular and—let's face it—single talents of a performer, no matter how gifted, who show after show, is obliged to fall back on variations of a Bolger choreographic theme?"[21] Bolger never again attempted to star in a television series of his own. Instead, he found greater success appearing as a guest star on other peoples' programs. Bolger found a new arena where his popularity could be useful: politics.

CHAPTER 10

All American

For the Bolgers, establishing Hollywood as the new center of their lives had unintended consequences. They were of course happy to be living closer to Gwen's family. Ray kept occupied with his film and occasional television appearances. Nightclubs were lucrative, and putting greens were plentiful. Golf became an increasingly important outlet for him. He strengthened his few Hollywood friendships—with Danny Thomas, Bing Crosby, and Bob Hope—by golfing with them and appearing frequently at the Pro-Am Classics held by Crosby and Hope. When he or Gwen was interested in investing in a new company, Bolger would play a round of golf with some of the company's executives. He also met many new people this way, including military and government officials. Admiral Red Yeager, Commandant of the 9th Naval District, became a close friend, as did many southern California Republicans.

Surrounded by wealthy and powerful men, Bolger realized that he had arrived at a point far removed from the way of life he had been born into. He also thought he knew how to fix the many problems the world was facing. Like many around him, he believed in the power of free enterprise to make the world more just and fair. He opposed communism in all forms and was a proponent of the burgeoning Vietnam conflict, which would deeply divide the United States.

Bolger found avenues for promoting his ideas of prosperity and democracy that stretched beyond the golf course. He began participating in activities that furthered the cause of the young Israeli nation. Although he had not spent time in Europe during World War II, he felt deeply the plight of those who had been displaced by the war, particularly Jews. Many of Bolger's closest associates in the entertainment world supported the formation of Israel as a safe haven for those affected by the Holocaust and a means to promote democracy, free press, and free speech in the Middle East. From the time of Israel's founding in 1948, American entertainment moguls pumped millions of dollars as well as influence into the new nation, with the aim of providing Israelis with an advanced entertainment industry. Abe Lastfogel in particular was heavily involved with the United Jewish Welfare Fund in Los Angeles, and when Bolger expressed interest in supporting the cause, as did many sympathetic non-Jewish talents, Lastfogel was able to provide him with those opportunities.

Bolger received an invitation to appear on the program for the Ambassador's Ball in Washington, DC. The black tie event, chaired by Supreme Court Justice Felix Frankfurter, sought to raise $500,000 in bonds for Israel. Thanks in part to the drawing power of the entertainment that evening—Bolger, the Meyer Davis Orchestra, Sophie Tucker, and Adolph Green and Betty Comden—the goal was reached. After the event, Attorney J. M. Arvey, one of the program's organizers, wrote to Bolger, "you are a great man—and behind your satire, pantomime, song and dance, is a heart dedicated to humanity." This was the sort of adulation Bolger wanted in his life. He wanted a Broadway show, too. He believed he could be received on Broadway with the same sort of reverence that private citizens were expressing.

Throughout the late 1950s, Bolger searched for another vehicle. In 1956, he engaged a team of little-known talents—a book writer, a lyricist, and a composer—to create a musical comedy called *The Congressman*, but the project never got off the ground. In 1957, he was floated as a possible star for Jose Ferrer's *Oh Captain!* The role went instead to Tony Randall. In 1958, Bolger accepted an offer to appear on an episode of the *London Palladium* variety show, just so he would have a reason to scour England for a show he could bring back to the United States. His last hit had been an adaptation of a British farce; perhaps his next hit would be, too. He returned to Hollywood empty-handed and discouraged. He suspended his search for a show and focused on his political pursuits and social causes. The Republican Party encouraged his participation in its activities. He performed for President Dwight Eisenhower and Richard Nixon at the 1957 inauguration. He would go on to work on three presidential campaigns for Nixon.

On November 8, 1960, the country was about to elect either Republican Richard Nixon, the incumbent vice president, or a Democrat, John F. Kennedy, junior senator from Massachusetts, to the White House. In the week before the election, the Congress of Industrial Organizations (CIO), a federation of trade unions in the United States and Canada, printed a four-page pamphlet, titled "Liberty or Bigotry?" It featured on its cover a photo of the Statue of Liberty and another of a hooded Ku Klux Klan member with a torch and a club. The literature suggested that union members who did not vote for John F. Kennedy were bigots, slighting a capable presidential candidate because of the country's anti-Catholic sentiment.

Bolger was livid. He contacted his friends at the Richard Nixon–Henry Cabot Lodge campaign. He wanted to speak out against this offense. The campaign assigned Bolger to travel to the swing state of Ohio. In the town of Portsmouth, Bolger would host his first campaign rally in support of the Republican ticket.

Advertisements went out in the local paper, declaring that the film and television star would be at the McKinley Junior High School auditorium for a free meet-and-greet. Bolger also delivered a speech upon arrival, explaining his visit. "Up until now, I have followed a very simple rule and that is in politics, actors should be seen and not heard," he said. He continued:

> As an Irish Roman Catholic Republican Bostonian, I often found it safer.... [H]owever, as an actor, I am a member of five unions, several of them affiliated with one of the huge unions (the CIO). Now this great union publicly announced in effect, that unless we vote for Mr. Kennedy, we are bigots. Well, my friends, this is where I must rise and express myself in violent disagreement with such a bigoted pronouncement.

Bolger continued, reminding the audience that they should be worried about Kennedy's youth and relative inexperience compared with Nixon:

> We are choosing a man to do a job and we want the man best equipped to do this job. It is not a no experience necessary, learn while you earn job. Whom would you like to see representing you across a table at some summit type meeting? A Boy Scout, who is just learning to tie the knots, or a scout master, who already knows the ropes? It is the biggest, toughest job in the world. There was a time when the finger pointing, fist thumping Khruschev oratory was considered proper politicking... but that sort of thing no longer can exist. The times are too troublesome.[1]

The address lasted about twenty minutes. The auditorium was enamored of Bolger, and the Nixon campaign declared the event a success. In the days before the 1960 election, he headlined rallies in Jefferson, Ohio; New York City; Pittsburgh and Wilkes-Barre, Pennsylvania, on behalf of the Nixon-Lodge campaign. While he was campaigning, Bolger learned he had received the New England Freedom Award from the State of Israel. The region founded by Puritans wanted to acknowledge those who had contributed to the betterment of the young nation of Israel. His political activities were certainly paying dividends.

The election of 1960 was the closest contest the country had seen since 1916. Kennedy won, thanks in part to his more efficient campaigning, which included extensive use of the new medium: television. In January 1961, before Nixon vacated the office of the vice president, he sent Bolger a letter, saying:

> I realize how much easier it would be for someone in your position to avoid taking sides on controversial questions which might adversely affect the popularity which is so essential for continued success in your chosen profession. For that reason, I am particularly grateful for the support which you gave so generously and unselfishly.... I hope it will not be to[o] long before we meet again so that I can express my appreciation personally.[2]

With the election over, Bolger focused on his Broadway pursuits. His reputation, in New York at least, was blemished. In early 1961, Bolger had two Broadway roles in the offing, and either of them seemed likely to provide a hit. He was being courted to play Fagan once *Oliver!* transferred from the West End to Broadway, and he had also been offered a role in Eugène Ionesco's *The Rhinoceros*, a bizarre idea until one remembers that Bert Lahr, the Cowardly Lion, became a very effective Estragon in *Waiting for Godot*. But *Oliver!*'s migration to America got delayed. That left only *Rhinoceros*, but difficulty set in again. Producer Leo Kerz originally approached Eli Wallach to play the lead, Berrenger, the last Frenchman in his village who does not succumb to the strange metamorphosis whereby humans are becoming rhinoceroses. Wallach had said he was unable to meet the production's start date due to a prior television commitment, so Kerz approached Bolger. Once the Wallach camp got wind of this, however, his agent threatened Kerz with a breach of promise suit and stated his client was in fact available to take the part.

To avoid the controversy, Bolger withdrew himself from consideration. In the spring of 1961, he decided instead to make a film appearance. Bolger's Republican activities had brought him close to leaders in Walt Disney's organization and to the head man himself. To buy time until he found a Broadway vehicle, Bolger accepted an offer to co-star in the Disney Studio's first live-action musical, *Babes in Toyland*, with the teen idols Tommy Sands and Annette Funicello in the juvenile lead roles. Bolger played the evil villain, Barnaby. All but twirling his handlebar mustache, he tried to convince young Mary Contrary (played by Funicello) to marry him instead of her beloved Tom Piper (Sands). Bolger was completely miscast, and the film has been remembered largely as a misfire.

Bolger was at last contacted about a Broadway show in November 1961. Joshua Logan, who had directed Bolger in the past, had attached himself to a show being produced by New York's newest up-and-comers, Edward Padula and L. Slade Brown. He recommended Bolger for the lead in a musical comedy called *All American*. The show hearkened back to the era that had shaped Bolger's core values. But, like so much of the art reflecting the culture of the 1960s, *All American* was actually out to lampoon them. A man who continued to rouse audiences with renditions of "Once in Love with Amy," Bolger was about to learn how much the times and tastes had changed back on Broadway.

During the making of *Where's Charley?*, Cy Feuer and Ernie Martin had been, in Gwen's estimation at least, the bullish young kids who lacked real taste. Broadway totally rejected this assessment. *Where's Charley?* may have been Bolger's pinnacle, but it was just the first in an unprecedented string of successes for the producing team. Feuer and Martin continued to launch shows, many of which became some of the biggest hits on Broadway in the 1950s. Between the original Broadway run of *Where's Charley?* and the return engagement, Feuer and Martin had produced *Guys and Dolls*. In 1953, they created *Can-Can*, starring Gwen Verdon. Michael Kidd staged the musical numbers. Their work on the show earned both of them Tonys. In 1954, Feuer and Martin introduced Julie Andrews to America with *The Boy Friend*, the show out of which she would be recruited to originate the role of Eliza Doolittle in *My Fair Lady*. Then in 1955, they brought *Silk Stockings* to the stage. All of these shows ran for at least a year on Broadway. They each spawned touring companies and, eventually, film adaptations. With five confirmed hits to their credit, they had truly graduated from their novitiates to become the tastemakers of the 1950s. Bolger, the seasoned pro from a previous era, would have to prove that his brand of entertainment still had a place on Broadway or, more intimidating still, he would have to innovate. By comparison, Bolger had spent the decade away from Broadway. It was he who had lost touch with the times.

Just as rock and roll was shifting the American music landscape for good, producers Padula and Brown came up with a show that caught the culture on the cusp of change, *Bye Bye Birdie*. The show wedded classic Broadway production values with the story of a teen rock idol. An emerging music-and-lyrics team, Charles Strouse and Lee Adams, provided the youthful score, introducing such songs as "Put on a Happy Face" and "A Lot of Livin' to Do."

By the time the houselights went up for intermission on opening night in New York, *Bye Bye Birdie* was already a hit. The tone for the new decade in American musical theater was set by a G flat on an electric guitar. Stalwarts of Broadway's old orders filled the mezzanine at the Martin Beck to see what sort of sensation had been born. This crowd included veteran director Joshua Logan, who ran into producer Ed Padula in the lobby. The show, Logan admitted, had entranced him. "Please find a show like that for me someday," he said.

Strouse *did* have another show in mind, even while *Birdie* was still selling out. He wanted to create another musical-turned-social-commentary and this time his source material was Vladimir Nabokov's lesser-known novel *Pnin*. The protagonist, an eponymous Russian professor, arrives in the United States to teach at a prestigious university. After a series of tragicomic events that lampoon academic bureaucracy, Pnin achieves contentment as a part-time, untenured professor, only to lose his position for unspecified administrative reasons. Strouse took his idea to the eminent author, but Nabokov refused to allow him to adapt the novel. Strouse was miffed. Then, Padula discovered another novel, *Professor Fodorski* by Robert Taylor, which had approximately the same plot and themes as *Pnin* but not, as Strouse said, "Nabokov's literary polish."[3] He and his partner, Lee Adams, were interested in the vehicle. Padula secured the rights. When it came time for someone to adapt the novel, Strouse and Adams turned to a young writer for a television show that had cracked them up: Mel Brooks, who was then writing comedy for *Your Show of Shows*. Brooks signed on and came up with the script for *All American*.

Strouse believed the role of Fodorski belonged to Victor Borge. Borge was interested, but scheduling conflicts kept him away. Strouse's second choice was Zero Mostel, who had not yet appeared in *A Funny Thing Happened on the Way to the Forum* or *Fiddler on the Roof*. Logan could not conceptualize Mostel as a romantic lead, and besides that, he wanted a "name" for the marquee. Then Logan approached Strouse with the person he thought was the perfect choice: Ray Bolger.

The decision baffled Strouse and Brooks, who could not imagine him playing the part of Fodorski, a Jewish immigrant. Despite their doubts, they relented, hoping that their choice of a leading lady, the dean of the college whom Fodorski falls in love with, could carry the show. Once again, Strouse made an apt choice—Barbra Streisand—but she declined. Instead Logan brought in Eileen Herlie, a well-respected British straight actress who could not sing. Strouse and Adams began to fret. They stayed sane by remembering that it was Logan who had directed *South Pacific's* unusual romantic leads—Mary Martin and Ezio Pinza—and had made history. They changed their minds when they heard Bolger read the part of Fodorski for the first time, trying to affect a Hungarian accent. Brooks turned to Strouse and asked, "Why is Ray speaking Japanese?" Even so, Padula boasted, "Bolger's part demands greater range than he has ever had to give before—dancing, singing, acting—and he'll be wonderful." Bolger would not be allowed even to soft shoe in the production until deep into the second act.

By the time the show opened in New York, it was apparent that Bolger did not have the versatility needed to carry off this role full of innuendo, pathos, singing, and satire. Professor Stanislaus Fodorski arrives at the fictional Southern Baptist Institute of Technology to live out his dream of teaching in America. He finds a campus that has been drained of intelligent students in favor of beefcakes who are only there to play football. Eager to be liked, Fodorski links work and play by conducting his physics lessons as a part of football practice. The professor succeeds in energizing the student body, and he is made the football coach. The dean of the college, Elizabeth Hawkes-Bullock, takes issue with this. She is fond of the quaint Fodorski, not the superstar version, and worries that his sincerity will be corrupted by fame.

In the meantime, Dr. Snopes, the conservative president of the college, spends most of his time breaking up the love-ins of quarterback and star student Edwin Bricker and his girlfriend, Susan. As Dean Elizabeth foresaw, Fodorski gets eaten by the publicity machine when advertising mogul H. H. Henderson tries to seduce him into a lucrative branding campaign, which will spread his "immigrant makes good" story throughout the country with a line of beverage coasters and lucky rabbits' feet. Dean Elizabeth helps to rescue Fodorski from Henderson. The older couple's affections for each other blossom and they, as well as their young counterparts Edwin and Susan, learn that true happiness comes from love, not fame.

The story was laced with zingers, both verbal and visual. Veteran scenic designer Jo Mielziner created a huge unit set, which operated with turntables and sliding panels. This allowed for quick changes of scene from the dormitories to the football field and back. The set pieces were filled with sight gags, like nude mannequins and live rabbits. Fritz Weaver, who played H. H. Henderson, believed the funniest material in *All American* is not remembered because it existed outside of the music, lyrics, and book. He advised those who read the script, "Remind yourself that a lot of the visual stuff isn't there. Mel Brooks . . . had the whole stage leaping with visual comedy."[4]

The most accessible vestige of *All American* is its cast album, one of the few Bolger productions to record one, and Columbia Records, a major investor in the $440,000 musical, eagerly exploited it. From the recording, it is clear that the show has a problem with addressing the generation gap between the older romantic leads, played by Bolger and Herlie, and the young lovers played by Ron Husmann and Anita Gillette. The latter display great vocal talent but received few songs compared with the older stars, neither of whom has talent for singing. Gillette's song, "Night Life," captures the essence of a college nymphomaniac and is well balanced by Husmann's "I've Just Seen Her," which he sings as Bricker steals a glimpse of Susan in her negligee. The college students get fun, rousing novelty numbers like "The Fight Song" and "Physical Fitness," which was sung by the well-oiled male chorus on Broadway. Bolger and Herlie's best song is "Once upon a Time," a beautiful love duet marred by their inability to sing. From the score, it's easy to see the show is in conflict with itself. Does it want to be a sexy, funny critique of individualism and Madison Avenue's exploitation thereof, or is it trying to be a conservative, traditional, boy-gets-girl romance?

The cast and the creative team had differing answers to these questions as the show went into production. From the time the actors arrived at the Erlanger Theatre in Philadelphia for the out-of-town tryout in February 1962, tensions flared. A very real generation gap emerged. Weaver recalled,

Bolger, as Professor Fodorski, takes center stage in front of his youthful chorus. The show business veteran irked many of the young cast members during the short run of the production. Photo by Friedman-Abeles © New York Public Library for the Performing Arts.

This is a moment in Mel Brooks' life, when he was at his peak, I would say, at his creative peak. He had ideas flowing out of him at every minute of the day and they were all good and fascinating ideas. Almost always, they were encountered with a kind of resistance, like, oh well, that's very funny, but I don't think so, and [this came] from Joshua Logan and from Ray Bolger. They were of the old school and Mel was the wave of the future. They didn't know it at the time.

The young members of the company hailed Brooks as an anarchist and a genius. He earned their love and loyalty from the first, even as Logan and Bolger dismissed many of his ideas. As Gillette recalled, "Everything he did was even funnier than what came before it. He didn't have a bad idea in those days, but few paid attention to him." She suggested that the reason Brooks bore the treatment with such good grace was because he was madly in love with Anne Bancroft, who came to Philadelphia for the out-of-town tryout. The anger he may have felt for Bolger and Logan was tempered by the great happiness he was experiencing for having found the love of his life.

Brooks also brought a crackling script with him to Philadelphia, which was quickly whittled. In the first act, Gillette had an additional number called "Animal Attraction," in which she explained her character Susan's infatuation with Edwin Bricker. The number stopped the show the first night it was performed. When the cast assembled the next day, Gillette learned "Animal Attraction" had been cut. She recalled the difficulties of rehearsing the show—first in New York, where Gwen was often sitting in a corner of the room, and later in Philadelphia:

We would have a lovely rehearsal, and feel we got pretty far ahead. And the next day [Bolger] would come in with a list of problems and nobody quite knew why that was, until it was identified as Gwen telling him, "This doesn't work, that doesn't work, you need to be represented better here."[5]

A social incident that occurred in Philadelphia, at an *All American* cast party, also illustrates the great divide between Bolger and the younger members of the company. Gillette recalled having her one-and-a-half-year-old daughter, and her nanny, in tow for the tryouts. Mel Brooks knew she was a young mother and teased her about this because she herself appeared so youthful. Gillette recalled that Brooks used to pinch her cheeks affectionately when he saw her. At the party, Brooks approached and launched into his usual business. She recalled him saying,

"Oh you're so cute. What a beautiful girl you are. You look like a baby yourself. How could you have a baby?" And it was a big party going on and for some reason the party got quiet, and in answer to his [Brooks's] question—"How did you get a baby?"—I said, "I fucked!" And the whole room heard what I said. Ray was appalled.[6]

That was the end of Bolger's attempts to socialize with his cast.

By the time the show reached New York, the script had been completely overhauled. The story was now disjointed and focused heavily on the romance of Fodorski and Dean Elizabeth. Its youthful punch was gone. The funniest scene that remained for Weaver was a ballet he performed with Bolger, as Henderson beguiled Fodorski into accepting an exploitation contract with Henderson's public relations agency. In rehearsals choreographer Danny Daniels had asked Weaver what his favorite type of music was. Bolger would go along with just about any kind of dance, and so they could create the number based on Weaver's preference. Weaver expressed interest in a Latin number, and Daniels came up with a Flamenco-inspired ballet. Weaver recalled, "I was not a dancer at all and in fact, the reverse of a dancer. So, learning this ballet was hard for me, but I mean all night long, going over and over the rhythms until they get so automatic that I couldn't fail in it and I counted [each step]."

Then, on opening night, as Bolger and Weaver stood in the wings preparing to go on, Bolger turned to him and said:

"Hey kid, you know in that ballet, that thing we do, you know when the trombones suddenly come out, and we both turn around and do this kind of clapping hands?"

I said, "Yeah, yeah." He said, "What do I do then?"

I said, "Ray for God's sake, you're asking me what you do?" And the reason for this is that he was such a brilliant improviser that he almost never stuck to the form and he couldn't remember what the original form was, which was the only thing I knew. That's all I had, nothing, no improvisational skill at all.

So I said, "Well, Ray, I think this is where you did this and you turned around and did that."

He said, "Oh, yeah, okay. Thanks kid, thanks a lot." Bolger couldn't stick to anything that was choreographed. He couldn't stick to it. He would climb walls and be funny, and then he was lost. He didn't know where he was.

They made it through their ballet and the first performance. And then the reviews came in.

Variety declared, "It's anything but a complete triumph.... Bolger isn't sheer perfection, or even the old Bolger approximation."[7] The notice pointed out that after eleven years away from Broadway, the star relied

Fritz Weaver as H. H. Henderson (*above*) manipulates Bolger as Professor Fodorski, the dancing puppet. Weaver said, "Bolger couldn't stick to anything that was choreographed." Photo by Friedman-Abeles © New York Public Library

almost totally on showmanship and his old tricks in his return to the stage. He had not innovated at all, aside from inserting a few token steps of the Twist into his routine. His voice and stamina were gone. The review continued, "But while...his acting, especially his ill-at-ease romantic scenes, are embarrassingly bad, he still has an old pro's savvy, with the personality and authority to wrap up an audience when the occasion requires. So *All American* is Bolger's show, after all."

The show eked by for several months on Bolger's personal appeal to the audience, if not to his co-stars. Weaver recalled the performances at the Winter Garden Theatre: "He would stand in the wings sometimes and look balefully out during other people's scenes and you kind of knew there would be notes afterwards about it. So, he was not loved by the company." Even his relationship with co-star Eileen Herlie, who was at least of his generation, grew frosty, and viewers noticed that during Bolger's love ballads with Herlie he would not even look at her. Then at Bolger's request, Logan approached Herlie one night with an order that she tape down her breasts: they were too large and unsightly on stage. She was devastated.

Bolger ultimately succeeded in isolating himself from his entire cast when he insisted on providing a long, maudlin curtain speech each night after the bows. Weaver and Gillette both recalled his reinforcing his conservatism in a cast full of liberals by making heavy use of the flag over on stage right. With tears in his eyes, Weaver said, he would wax on about the beauty of that flag and how the protestors in the streets desecrated it. He would then give a rendition of "Once in Love with Amy." It was a blatant sign of insecurity for the star to be rehashing his other shows. Gillette said, "We signed a petition so they would let us off the stage if he wanted to continue to do his nightclub act after the bows." When the show stumbled financially, Bolger began using his curtain speeches as a forum to plead with the audience. He asked them to return, to tell friends and relatives about the show. He admitted they were struggling to survive.

At the same time, though, Bolger was willing to snub a very lucrative offer that came to the attention of Joshua Logan and could have ensured their show's success. Logan was a member of the "old school" who sided with his star, but he also had experience promoting difficult musicals, particularly 1960's *Camelot*. Reviews for that loquacious musical had been mixed. However, shortly after *Camelot*'s opening, Ed Sullivan approached Alan Jay Lerner about doing a special program to celebrate the fifth anniversary of his earlier breakthrough musical, *My Fair Lady*. Lerner instead opted to adapt four of *Camelot*'s numbers for a program on *The Ed Sullivan Show*. Overnight, the struggling show transformed into a bestseller.

Logan, who was responsible for staging the *Camelot* episode, approached Ed Sullivan to see if he would accept *All American* on to the program. Sullivan welcomed the cast and crew, but Bolger crushed the entire idea. He was "hesitant for unspecific reasons" about appearing on the show, but he was likely fearful of how stilted he would come across on television.[8] To Bolger, begging his audience members to buy more tickets was more dignified than succumbing to the march of time.

Even as the show struggled, Bolger was requesting a larger salary. In May of 1962, John Shubert, who was providing the use of the Winter Garden Theatre via the Select Theatres Corporation, wrote to him, "If anyone is on the spot reputation wise, I feel it is you. I would work for one-half salary or less until they can hit a break-even figure between $42,000 and $43,000 per week. I feel that you are being badly advised by someone and if anyone takes the rap for a show closing, it is usually the star."[9]

Though the show would earn Bolger a nomination for Best Actor in a Musical for the 1962 Tony Awards, it closed on May 18, 1962, after just eighty performances.

Bolger tried to return to Broadway just one more time, in 1969. Broadway producers Albert W. Selden and Hal James, who had been responsible for the smash hit *Man of La Mancha*, approached Bolger to star in *Come Summer,* a whimsical, nostalgic story about New England peddlers on the cusp of the Industrial Revolution. They raised $450,000 to stage the production. *Come Summer* united two dancing greats: in addition to Bolger, Agnes de Mille was attached to the production, to stage dances and to direct. She had not been involved in a Broadway production since she choreographed *110 in the* Shade in 1963, and she had never directed a Broadway show before.

Bolger's experience with *Come Summer* was far different from that of all his other Broadway shows. The cast would be small, the music soft, and the scenery simple. The show's expansiveness would come from its themes and its symbolism, or so book writer Will Holt hoped. Holt adapted the script from the novel *Rainbow on the Road* by Esther Forbes, who was better known for writing *Johnny Tremain*. The story interested Bolger because it touched on New England nostalgia. Set in 1840, *Come Summer* starred Bolger as Phineas Sharp, an itinerant peddler-on-the-hoof who wanders the back roads of the Connecticut River Valley, plying broadsides full of scandals. Sharp has an assistant wanderer, the young and dashing Jude Scribner. The two are looking to enjoy, symbolically, the one "summer" of success and contentment every man gets in his life, as well as the last quiet summer in New England before the Industrial Revolution arrives. David Cryer was cast as the romantic lead, Jude. And Bolger's former colleague Margaret Hamilton, who had played the Wicked Witch of the West in *The Wizard of Oz*, played Dorinda Pratt, the hardnosed New England matron who tried to keep her niece safe from the devil-may-care Jude. Hamilton said of the experience, "People said, 'Oh, how nice, such a lovely reunion.' Well, there was no reunion about it. The only real scene that I had [in the *Wizard of* Oz] with any of them other than Judy [Garland] was the last scene where I set fire to the poor Scarecrow."[10]

The story's propulsion wasn't coming from the plot, or the folk-music score by David Baker, so de Mille tried to compensate by creating intricate ballets. The show's greatest asset, the cast knew from the first, was its dancing. She brought in dancers of the highest caliber and choreographed them in her well-known movements: flowing, bending, rushing forward. The clever scenery by Oliver Smith captured the whimsy of a children's book, and it moved with the assistance of treadmills, allowing farmers in the hills and river men in boats to roll along. De Mille played off the New England setting to great effect. She showed off her strong male chorus

Ray Bolger and Margaret Hamilton worked together thirty years after *The Wizard of Oz*, in the short-lived Broadway show *Come Summer*. It would be Bolger's last Broadway appearance. Photofest.

with a logging dance. A Bacchanalian square dance and a ballet in a haunted cemetery also added depth to the nostalgic feel of the show.

De Mille successfully integrated the Bolger style into her more traditional creations, while still ensuring he had a soft-shoe routine to please the crowd. While they rehearsed in New York City, she said, "During Ray's solos, I edit, sit around, encourage and discourage or whatever and beg him to save his goodies for the end. But I'm not going to change anything. What the public wants is his kind of dancing. This is a great stylist, a great individualist."[11]

Following rehearsals in New York, two out-of-town tryouts were planned: the first in Toronto, at the O'Keefe Centre, followed by three weeks in Boston at the Colonial Theatre. Then the show would open on Broadway at the Lunt-Fontanne Theatre. *Come Summer's* audiences in Toronto picked up on the show's problems from the first.

"What it hasn't got is coherence, excitement and...pace," wrote the reviewer for the *Globe and Mail*. Great praise was lavished on David Cryer, who seemed certain to "emerge as a star from all this," and on Margaret Hamilton.

A tremendous blizzard in the northeast United States delayed *Come Summer's* debut at the Colonial, and de Mille wanted to rehearse the show an extra day before opening the doors to audiences. When the show at last went on, the *Boston Globe* unequivocally panned it. Reviewer Kevin Kelly wrote, "Near the end of *Come Summer*...someone calls for a public humiliation ceremony. Well, there's no need. The show will be quite enough, thanks." Kelly did not go so far as to insult Boston's native dancer, but he wrote that Mr. Bolger "was in serious trouble." He seemed to be making up most of the show as he "softshoes his way" from "pause to pause." He did not hold back his criticism of de Mille's direction, which he called "dreadful." In his opinion, she left far too many people on the stage doing nothing at all. During one of Jude's ballads to his love interest, she stood "stone-eyed, expressionless, uncertain."[12] The show seemed doomed.

Even Bolger knew the show was in danger. During the tryout period, he made a nightly curtain speech, all but begging for leniency. Inveterate showman that he was, he disguised the appeal with humor, saying, "You are wonderful. We have read the notices.... I understand now that one of the critics is in the hospital suffering from bursitis. As a fellow Bostonian, I have a favor to ask of you, if you find the plot, please let me know."[13] With this vote of confidence in his show, Bolger and the cast headed to New York City.

The show had proven to be a massively expensive undertaking, and it accrued even more costs in its tryouts. For *Come Summer* to stay afloat, it would need to make at least $52,000 per week. In Boston, it averaged less than $30,000 per week. Not even Bolger's personal magnetism filled the house for its opening, and the New York press found just as much wrong with the show as the Boston critics had.

"*Come Summer* is so awful that I suspect it will not last until the spring—and already it is getting suspiciously warm for the time of year," the *New York Times* declared after the show opened. Bolger was acknowledged, however, as a star dancer returned to his rightful home:

> Bolger dances with a deftness no words can really do justice to. I have no idea how old he is—probably just slightly older than is polite to question—but he

dances with an ageless artistry. No one—except Paul Draper—can give such a sweetly nifty nuance to a tap dance phrase. He has style and an agile wit. And Miss De Mille's choreography gave him amiably homespun charm at every opportunity. [14]

Bolger's show closed after just seven performances, at a loss of $600,000. The 1968–69 season had witnessed a record number of "instant failures"—shows that closed after one to ten performances. Their downfalls could not be attributed to a lack of talent; many of these shows were stocked with veterans in their cast and creative teams. Certainly the fault lay in quality: the productions were not good enough, and the exorbitant costs of Broadway shows demanded that both audiences and reviewers be won over from the very start of a show's run.

Come Summer's greatest flaw was its dependence on nostalgia. Though few people understood what the show was even trying to get at, the message at its heart was the need for submission: submitting to marriage, to commitment, and to practicality. This moralizing fell flat with the Broadway audiences of the day. The leading show of the time, *Hair*, was filled with nudity, rock and roll, and mocking worship of the American flag. As *Variety* said of *Come Summer*, "Every inch of this musical is square and out of whack with the 1960's."[15]

Before returning home to Beverly Hills, Bolger sent a quick telegram to Abe Lastfogel, asking him to stop entertaining offers of Broadway shows going forward. "They just don't want me anymore," Bolger admitted.

A few months later, in June 1969, Bolger got his surest indication that an era had passed. While rehearsing in New York for a summer stock performance of *The Happy Time*, he received word that Judy Garland had died. He burst into tears. Bert Lahr had passed away two years before, and now only he and Jack Haley were left among the principal *Wizard of Oz* cast. Garland, to Bolger's mind, had been just a child when they filmed it, but her sudden death did not surprise him.

He had last seen her alive the spring before. He was appearing at the Waldorf-Astoria's Empire Room, and she had been in the audience. She came over to say hello after the show. She was frail and worn. Bolger had the sense then that she did not have long to live. Some audience member saw the two united in conversation and laughter, and they began demanding that Garland perform "Over the Rainbow."

Bolger intervened, announcing that Judy Garland had sung the song into their hearts, and that she didn't need to sing it again. Now, she never would.

Epilogue

No Sad Songs

After Bolger left Broadway, he took up permanent residence in his Beverly Hills home. New York became just a place to visit. He began touring the country's social clubs with a dance-lecture he called "Ray Bolger's World." This allowed him to share his philosophy, nostalgia, and dancing talent in small, intimate settings. He realized he didn't need the fuss of a big production, the grueling work, the personalities at odds. As Richard Rodgers, in his later years, had said of creating a musical, "I now realize that the whole business, from start to finish, is the most intense collaborative effort in the world, with the possible exception of running a war."[1] Bolger wanted to sit out the battles with young co-stars and avoid having the weight of a full-scale production on his shoulders.

He still appeared on television and on film, content to be a guest star on programs like *Battlestar Galactica*, *Little House on the Prairie*, *The Love Boat*, and *The Partridge Family*. He also performed at industry and trade shows, such as the Milliken Breakfast Show, which kept him in touch with business executives. These gigs provided socialization and income and kept him in the American consciousness. With Gwen's guidance, he also dabbled in real estate, investing in a retirement community in Palm Springs that provided him easy access to the golf courses. His dream was to create a dual retirement village and theme park, called The Wizardland of Oz, to rival the Disney parks in Orlando and Los Angeles. Despite several years of research and development, it never came to be.

Bolger remained physically active, even if his career in entertainment began to draw to a close. He played more golf and served as host for the annual Bob Hope and Bing Crosby Classics. He could be seen on the televised annual competitions doing splits in between taking strokes. He made countless charity appearances on behalf of the United Way, the Red Cross, and the Knights of Malta. His interest in religion intensified, and he and fellow Irish Catholic Jack Haley could often be found taking up the collection for Sunday Mass at their parish, the Church of the Good Shepherd in Beverly Hills.

After his experiences with the Nixon-Lodge campaign, Bolger's strong conservative values led him to a second career as a Republican stump speaker. He was also a strong supporter of the Vietnam War and grew disappointed with the youth culture of the late 1960s and 1970s. During a 1972 speech in Chicago he expounded on his background as a staunch Irish Catholic Republican from Boston: "There was one thing the New Englanders could not condone—a lack of patriotism—there was no indecisive America. I love you—right or wrong—you can do no wrong—the internal mechanisms may not work properly but the body is beautiful. I can see now revolving in their graves our New England forefathers. The beatniks and the beards. The long hairs and the LSDs. The various versions of their American foreign policy would surely shatter their senses."[2] He found refuge in annual visits to Bohemian Grove, the woodland outpost of the exclusive men's only Bohemian Club, which had been established in 1878. While Bohemians regarded the place as one where "men might come together in a finer fellowship, enlivened by an appreciation of music, drama, literature, and the performing arts, both serious and satirical," by the 1970s the annual Grove meetings were opened as media events and received a fair amount of press attention, which resulted in "stylized stories of corporate and governmental bigwigs cavorting as woodnymphs or peeing on trees appearing in newspapers across the world."[3] There Bolger danced and joked and sat at the feet of people like Richard Nixon, who gave speeches.

But he did more than condemn what he disliked in these two decades. He performed at supper clubs and hotels across the country as well as for a wide range of charity groups and causes. Now an old man, he radiated endearing, avuncular charm that kept him a fixture in pop culture. At this stage of his life, he found his relationships with his fans especially fulfilling. He dutifully responded to hundreds of letters each year from admirers of all ages. He took the time to respond to everyday people; he was genuinely interested in them and eager to show his appreciation.

In the late 1970s, Bolger completed two final film roles of significance. In 1975, composer Marvin Hamlisch was watching Laurence Olivier's *The Entertainer* when the idea struck him to make an American version of the story, which traced the demise of a third-rate music hall player who could not escape his performer-father's shadow. Hamlisch decided to set the adaptation in vaudeville. He got his first choices—Ray Bolger and Jack Lemmon—to play father-and-son duo Billy and Archie Rice for an ABC made-for-TV movie. The performance earned Bolger a Primetime Emmy nomination in 1976 for Outstanding Single Performance by a Supporting Actor in Comedy or Drama Special.

While promoting *The Entertainer*, Bolger went out of his way to get to know a film student named Michael Bergstein, whom he encountered while doing publicity for the film in Washington, DC. Bolger gave Bergstein his telephone number and told him to call if he was ever in Los Angeles. Two years later, Bergstein did call Bolger. Bolger instructed Bergstein to drive to his home in Beverly Hills, and from there the two proceeded to lunch at the Bel Air Country Club, Bolger in his big black Mercury station wagon, and Bergstein in his Pinto. Bergstein recalled:

> Bolger and I walked into the club and as we went down the long corridor people greeted him warmly, calling him either Mr. Bolger or Ray. He was, I could tell, a popular and well-liked man.
>
> The club room was downstairs, and since it was nearly two o'clock and past the lunch hour the room was fairly empty. We were shown to a large round table that seated eight, and ordered club sandwiches and bloody marys. Bolger was charming and relaxed, which helped me relax, and we chatted about various matters, including the movies—his and mine. About halfway through our lunch an elderly-looking man ambled over and sat down across the table from us. I didn't recognize him. He and Bolger started trading friendly remarks, and then my host said, "Come over here so I can introduce you to my friend from Pennsylvania."

Bolger's friend was Edgar Bergen. Bergstein sat between them for the rest of the luncheon, amazed that two bona fide stars would pay such attention to an unknown film student. Bergstein remembered that he was not the only one of the party who was starstruck: "As we went outside a white Audi Fox drove in and a very elderly man dressed in a brown suit and tie got out and shuffled past us. Bolger noticed him and grew quiet. He leaned toward me and murmured reverentially, 'That's Hal Roach.' In Hollywood, everyone is in thrall of somebody."[4]

In 1979, Stanley Kramer adapted Milan Stitt's Broadway play *The Runner Stumbles* for the large screen. The play had run for a thousand performances in the United States. Kramer had been intrigued by the themes of the show, in which a priest and a nun fall in love. He had a burgeoning reputation for making "thought pictures"—movies that displayed deep conflicts of human nature but ultimately left the audience to judge what about them was right or wrong.

Kramer was also developing a reputation for casting famous film dancers in straight dramatic roles, to good effect. Gene Kelly appeared in *Inherit the Wind*, and Fred Astaire was nominated for a Best Supporting Actor Academy Award for his role in *The Towering Inferno*. In *The Runner Stumbles*, Kramer cast Dick Van Dyke to play Father Rivard, a priest in a poor coal town who is ready to abandon his faith in God and his parish until Sister Rita, played by Kathleen Quinlan, arrives to teach at the parochial school. Sister Rita shows him the way Catholicism can create and nourish a positive worldview through her own love of life. Until this point, he has used the religion to fixate on life's shortcomings. In the span of a couple of months, however, admiration turns to passion. Bolger plays the monsignor whom the townspeople summon because of the controversy. He counsels Rivard to abandon the parish. On the night Father Rivard leaves town, Sister Rita is found murdered. The priest is accused and brought to trial.

Quinlan remembered being thrilled at the lavish premiere party in Seattle for the film in 1982. She recalled that Kramer loved to throw premiere parties in the grand Hollywood tradition and that he had hired a full orchestra to play at the Hilton in Seattle. Quinlan, who sat at a table close to the dance floor, had not brought a date. Bolger approached her table and asked her to dance. She said,

> My reaction was "Ahhh!" Every part of the school girl in me went, "Oh my God, . . . the best guy in the whole prom just asked me to dance." Thank God I knew something about dancing . . . because he threw me all over that dance floor. And you know, I was on the young side of the 60s and people weren't doing that kind of dancing, but I had been taught so I could follow him, and people just moved away and let us dance. It was amazing. I will never forget it.

The memory of how Bolger made her feel during that short dance stayed with Quinlan, who went on to become a celebrated actor, nominated for an Academy Award for *Apollo 13* in 1995. She said, "People always ask, 'What were some of the most memorable moments for you in your career?' And Bolger dancing with me is absolutely one of them."

David Hartman, then the anchor for *Good Morning America*, wrote to Bolger following his promotional appearance for *The Runner Stumbles*: "It is easy to tell why you have thrilled millions and millions of people for so many years with your craft and art. You bring the joy and excitement of your own life with you wherever you go and that stimulates us.... What a treat for all of us to have had an opportunity to meet you, either in person or on television."[5]

In June 1979, Bolger's friend Jack Haley, who had played the Tin Man in *The Wizard of Oz*, died of a heart attack. Bolger gave the eulogy at the Church of the Good Shepherd. With tears in his eyes, he recounted the days they had both orbited through vaudeville, not working directly together but knowing of each other in that frenetic, electric world that had once seemed without end. He admitted that it was not until they were both old men that they had become good friends, long after they had shot their most memorable movie. He concluded with the line, "It's going to be awfully lonely on that Yellow Brick Road now, Jack." Bolger was the last surviving principal cast member. He became the standard-bearer for the film's legacy.

Throughout the late 1970s and 1980s, Bolger received at least ten pieces of fan mail a day. These often included drawings, paintings, and poems from children. Retired servicemen also wrote in, thanking him for performances on Guadalcanal several decades before. For many fans, he remained a source of happiness and fond memories. In the end, it was for these feelings he inspired, almost more than his dancing skill, that he was remembered, and revered.

In 1984, at the age of eighty, he was still performing his one-man show. He stepped down from the stage one night after his set was over, and his hip gave out. At the hospital, X-rays reveal that all of the cartilage in his right hip had been worn away; he would need to have a hip replacement. After recovering from the surgery, he attempted to perform. Finding he was not up to his old standards, he decided never to dance again.

Not long into his new life without dance, his doctors diagnosed him with bladder cancer. Gwen began the final stage in her management career, keeping him as happy and content as possible in their remaining days together. Bolger wanted to die in Beverly Hills. He and his wife hired a nurse to help care for him, but Gwen preferred to care for him herself. At the age of seventy-five, she took over all aspects of Bolger's care: changing his sheets while he lay in bed, giving him sponge baths, cleaning his room, and preparing all of his meals. Bolger adored her, and he could no longer stand to see her strain herself on his account. In November 1986, he was admitted to St. John's Hospital, where the doctors told him he had entered the final phase of his illness. Bolger decided not to return home. He transferred from the hospital to an exclusive Catholic nursing home, Nazareth House. While there, he confided in a friend that without his wife, I'd have been gone a long time ago. We have lived out our love affair to the very last moment. And for that we're extremely grateful."

Gwen still visited every day. Bolger celebrated his eighty-seventh birthday in the nursing home. Among the visitors was Katherine Reeve, the chorus girl from *Where's Charley?* who had married Gwen's brother, Jim, thirty years before. A telegram from Ronald Reagan arrived from the White House, extending the president's sincerest wishes for health and happiness to his friend and supporter. Five days later, it was just Gwen and Ray together in his bedroom. "He just looked at me, and I knew the time had come," she said of the last day they spent together, January 15, 1987. "I took him in my arms and in seconds he was gone."

She proceeded stoically through Bolger's funeral at the Church of the Good Shepherd, on January 19, 1987, where she insisted no eulogy would be given, and where James Stewart and Bob Hope served as pallbearers. Back at home, alone, she faced the stacks of fan mail that had accumulated that month. She had carried many envelopes filled with birthday wishes and gifts to Nazareth House for Ray to enjoy before he passed away. After his death some belated greetings arrived that had been sent before word of his passing reached the public. One young girl had written a birthday poem for Bolger, on stationery featuring Judy Garland as Dorothy. Gwen wrote in response to an autograph request that went unfulfilled:

My husband was too ill to autograph.... He is gone now and all we have are memories of his remarkable career.

Sadly Yours,

Gwen Bolger

(Mrs. Ray Bolger)

Gwen lived a decade beyond her husband, during which time she developed and managed coronary artery disease. She lived a private and quiet life but stayed close to Flo Haley, Jack Haley's widow, her husband's friends, and her charitable interests. At home, she preserved her husband's vaudeville contracts, scripts, correspondence, and investment documents, with an eye to the day that someone might tell their story. She also carried out a final wish of Ray's: in the summer of 1987, Gwen relinquished her husband's Scarecrow costume to the Smithsonian Institution in the nation's capital, where the public would be able to enjoy the symbol of his best-remembered character. Tom D. Crouch, the museum's chairman of the social and cultural history department, responded with a letter. "Dear Mrs. Bolger," he began,

> On behalf of the National Museum of American History, I thank you for the generous donation of your husband's Scarecrow costume from "The Wizard of Oz."...It is a...wonderful, tangible reminder to the American people of Ray Bolger's remarkable career.[6]

Early in the morning of May 13, 1997, after living without her lifelong collaborator for more than a decade, Gwen Bolger suffered a heart attack and died at the age of eighty-seven. With no children to succeed them, it seemed as though the Bolger legacy would be lost, but this did not prove to be the case.

Bolger had gone on the nighttime talk show circuit in the 1960s. He popped up from time to time as a guest of Johnny Carson or Tom Snyder throughout that decade and the next, offering reminiscences of *The Wizard of Oz* and the American entertainment scene as he knew it. Frequently he was asked about how much money he made in residuals from his most famous film. His standard response was, "I receive no residuals from *The Wizard of Oz*. Just immortality. I'll settle for that." With the way that *The Wizard of Oz* is revered and remembered even now, well into the twenty-first century, Bolger's insight remains true.

Toward the end of his life, he reflected with amazement on the many sweeping changes he had lived to see. He wrote, "So many new and fantastic changes happened that it would take a tome as big as the Gutenberg Bible to even record the electronic and technological miracles of this century." Despite his deep affection for the people and places lost to time, he did not lament over the loss of the "good old days." He said, "No sad songs for me! I've seen and been a part of every exciting phase of it."[7]

Although he remained proud throughout his life to be part of such an enduring classic film, which captured on celluloid so many vestiges of vaudeville, Bolger also knew that, as a dancer, his essence would be lost to time. When he gave himself over to reflection in his old age, whether in telling stories over drinks or sitting down at home with a notepad and pencil, he reflected neither on the specifics of his difficult childhood nor on the richest or the most beautiful people he had encountered in his orbits. He chose always to tell the stories of the old vaudevillians he had seen and idolized at the Palace, or the obscure dancers who had shown him a few steps and got him into amateur nights in Boston. These are the people who spoke to his soul. It's not a stretch to say that many of them were folks that only he remembered, or esteemed: this was the nature of life on the stage. He wasn't afraid to join their ranks. In fact, it was his deepest wish. For his one-man show, he wrote his own lyrics for the signature song. In "Left a Little on the Floor," he summoned back the progenitors of his dance style, and replicated their routines in homage to them while singing:

> The author leaves the written word behind him
> The composer leaves his notes upon the score
> The dancer's fluid grace
> Has found the perfect place
> To commemorate his greatness evermore.
>
> . . .
>
> First of all came the great George Primrose
> With his effortless grace
> He put more in the book
> Of terpsichorical lore
> Because he left a little on the floor.
>
> . . .
>
> And next in line came a fine
> Comic man to entertain ya.
> Of eccentric legmania
> And with pride I say
> The time has come to honor you
> Mr. Jack Donahue . . .
>
> Now I come to my fav'rite dancer
> Wonder who that could be
> A combination of all of the others you see
> I'm referring to me
>
> And I'd like to say in conclusion
> Dancin's never a bore
> I'll be hoofin' around
> Like I hoofed it before
> And for many years more

But when I hang up my shoes
And I find I must close up the store
I hope and pray that they will say
Uncle Ray left a little on the floor.[8]

Bolger, at sixty-five years of age, performs a high kick in the rehearsal hall for *Come Summer*. Getty Images for Toronto Star.

NOTES

ABBREVIATIONS

UCLA/RB   Ray Bolger Papers at the University of California, Los Angeles, Special
Collections Division

USC/WB   Warner Brothers' Archive at University of Southern California

SFA   Shubert Foundation Archive, New York City

INTRODUCTION
The Timeless Wanderer

1. Maurice Zolotow, "Muscles with a Sense of Humor," *Saturday Evening Post*, July 30, 1949.
2. James Rickard, letter to Katherine Reeve Rickard, 1953. Private collection of Christianna Rickard.
3. Brooks Atkinson, "At the Theatre," *New York Times*, Oct. 12, 1948.

CHAPTER 1: "WHAT WILL YOU BE? IT'S UP TO YOU!"

1. UCLA/RB, Norman A. MacLeod, letter to Ray Bolger, March 11, 1976.
2. Barbara St. Lawrence Combs (Ray Bolger's second cousin), e-mail message to author, May 23, 2012.
3. UCLA/RB, holographic writing by Ray Bolger, Box 40, Folder 5.
4. Seymour Fisher and Rhoda L. Fisher, *Pretend the World Is Funny and Forever: A Psychological Analysis of Comedians Clowns, and Actors* (Hillsdale, NJ: Erlbaum, 1981), 49–50. The Fishers offer a fascinating portrait of the psychiatric traits of several kinds of performers of Bolger's era.
5. UCLA/RB, holographic writing by Ray Bolger, Box 40, Folder 5.
6. Ray Bolger, interview by Ronald L. Davis, Southern Methodist University Oral History Project, Number 97, Aug. 5, 1976.
7. UCLA/RB, holographic writing by Ray Bolger, Box 40, Folder 5.
8. Constance Valis Hill, *Tap Dancing America* (New York: Oxford University Press, 2010), 5.
9. Ibid., 6.
10. Ibid., 61.
11. UCLA/RB, Rickard family letters, Box 42, Folder 8.
12. UCLA/RB, holographic writing by Ray Bolger, Box 32, Folder 3.
13. Paul Kneeland, "Ray Bolger Was a Timid Male Wallflower at Dorchester High Senior Prom," *Boston Sunday Globe*, July 24, 1949.

14. Ray Bolger, interview by Ronald L. Davis, Aug. 5, 1976.
15. Richard Holden (one of Rusakoff's last surviving students), e-mail message to author, July 19, 2012.
16. Ray Bolger, interview by Ronald L. Davis, Aug. 5, 1976.
17. UCLA/RB, Ernest A. Hoffman, letter to Ray Bolger, August 1, 1949.
18. Kneeland, "Ray Bolger Was a Timid Male Wallflower."
19. Ibid.
20. Ibid.
21. Marge Champion, interview with the author by phone, September 18, 2012.
22. UCLA/RB, holographic writing by Ray Bolger, Box 32, Folder 3.
23. UCLA/RB, Contracts, Box 57, Folder 11.
24. UCLA/RB, Ray Bolger, holographic writing, Box 32, Folder 3.
25. Roland Gammon, "Mr. Rubberlegs," *Pageant*, October 1949.
26. UCLA/RB, Ray Bolger, holographic writing, Box 32, Folder 3.
27. Ibid.
28. Ibid.
29. Ibid.

CHAPTER 2: ENTERING SHOW BUSINESS

1. UCLA/RB, holographic writing by Ray Bolger, Box 32, Folder 3.
2. Ibid.
3. Arthur Frank Wertheim, *Vaudeville Wars: How the Keith-Albee and Orpheum Circuits Controlled the Big-Time and Its Performers* (New York: Palgrave Macmillan, 2009), 98.
4. Fred Allen, *Much Ado about Me* (Boston: Little, Brown, 1956), 332.
5. David Naylor, *American Picture Palaces: The Architecture of Fantasy* (New York: Van Nostrand Reinhold, 1981), 31.
6. Ross Melnick, *American Showman: Samuel "Roxy" Rothafel and the Birth of the Entertainment Industry, 1908–1935* (New York: Columbia University Press, 2012), 102.
7. Ibid.
8. James Bolger had relocated to Irvington-on-Hudson, New York, to be nearer his son and the excitement of Manhattan; Ray paid for the move.
9. Lee DeForest, creator of the Lee DeForest Phonofilm sound-on-film process, and Edwin Miles Fadiman.
10. It is unknown if the Fleischers did this to poke fun at Bolger's failed banking career.
11. UCLA/RB, professional biography written for Bolger by the William Morris Agency, 1946, Box 48, Folder 5.
12. J. J. and Lee Shubert's brother, Sam, was also involved in the family theatrical business until he died of injuries sustained in a train wreck in 1905, when he was twenty-six years old.
13. John Anderson, "The Shuberts Install 'The Merry World' at the Imperial," *New York Post*, June 6, 1926.
14. Ray Bolger, interview by Ronald L. Davis, Southern Methodist University Oral History Project, Number 97, Aug. 5, 1976.
15. Ibid.
16. Anderson, "The Shuberts Install 'The Merry World' at the Imperial."
17. Ray Bolger, interview by Ronald L. Davis, Aug. 5, 1976.

18. Gus Edwards shows traditionally debuted in Atlantic City, in the summertime. Due to Bolger's summer Shubert obligations, and supported by a lack of mentions in press coverage, it is likely Bolger joined the cast after it had gone out on the road in the fall of 1926.

19. UCLA/RB, Review from Washington, DC, publication and author unknown, in James Bolger's scrapbook, Box 73, Folder 2.

20. UCLA/RB, Review from New Haven, CT, publication and author unknown, in James Bolger's scrapbook, Box 73, Folder 2.

21. "Year in Vaudeville," *Variety*, Dec. 29, 1926.

22. Ibid.

23. UCLA/RB, holographic writing by Ray Bolger, Box 32, Folder 3.

24. Ibid.

25. "Palace (St. Vaude)," *Variety*, Dec. 7, 1927.

26. Ibid.

27. Ibid.

28. Wertheim, *Vaudeville Wars*, 242.

29. UCLA/RB, holographic writing by Ray Bolger, Box 32, Folder 3.

30. UCLA/RB, Rickard family letters, Box 42, Folder 8.

31. UCLA/RB, holographic writing by Gwen Rickard, Box 32, Folder 3.

32. Ibid.

33. J. D. Spiro, "Here's Raymond! Light Footed Ray Bolger Adds TV to His Triumphs," *Milwaukee Journal*, June 11, 1954.

34. Draft letter from Gwen Rickard to Leonard Lyons, private collection of Christianna Rickard. It is worth noting that Charles M. Schwab, to whom Gwen was most likely referring, also lost his wealth in the Crash of 1929.

35. Ibid.

CHAPTER 3: STEPPIN' IN SOCIETY

1. Maurice Zolotow, "Muscles with a Sense of Humor," *Saturday Evening Post*, July 30, 1949.

2. USC/WB, *Look for the Silver Lining* publicity material, July 9, 1949.

3. Richard Rodgers, *Musical Stages: An Autobiography* (Cambridge, MA: Da Capo Press, 2006), 126–27.

4. "Paramount, N.Y.," *Variety*, Jan. 14, 1931.

5. Rodgers, *Musical Stages*, 126.

6. Ibid.

7. "Wall St. Lays an Egg," *Variety*, Oct. 30, 1929.

8. Ibid.

9. Ibid.

10. Draft letter from Gwen Rickard to Leonard Lyons, private collection of Christianna Rickard.

11. "Legitimate: Plays on Broadway—Heads Up," *Variety*, Nov. 13, 1929.

12. Ibid.

13. "Heads Up!' Proves Lively Diversion," *New York Times*, Nov. 12, 1929.

14. "New Plays on Broadway," *Billboard*, Nov. 23, 1929.

15. "News and Gossip of the Street Called Broadway," *New York Times*, Nov. 17, 1929.

16. UCLA/RB, holographic writing by Gwen Bolger, Box 32, Folder 4.

17. Arthur Frank Wertheim, *Vaudeville Wars: How the Keith-Albee and Orpheum Circuits Controlled the Big-Time and Its Performers* (New York: Palgrave Macmillan, 2009), 253.
18. John Lahr, *Notes on a Cowardly Lion: The Biography of Bert Lahr* (New York: Knopf, 1969), 109–10.
19. UCLA/RB, *The Blue Mill* materials, jokes written in Gwen's hand, Box 41, Folder 11.
20. P. D. Spiro, "Here's Raymond! Light Footed Ray Bolger Adds TV to His Triumphs," *Milwaukee Journal*, June 11, 1954.
21. Ray Bolger, interview by Ronald L. Davis, Southern Methodist University Oral History Project, Number 97, Aug. 5, 1976.
22. "Song Writing Trio Dissolve Partnership," *New York Times*, March 5, 1931.
23. Ray Bolger, interview by Ronald L. Davis, Aug. 5, 1976.
24. "'Scandals' Has Exciting First Night," *Hartford Courant*, Sept. 20, 1931.
25. Brooks Atkinson, "The Play," *New York Times*, Sept. 15, 1931.
26. "'Scandals' Is Grand Show; Marshall, Howard, Vallee, Merman, Ray Bolger Score," *New York Daily News*, Sept. 15, 1931.
27. UCLA/RB, "Mirth Ray Bolger's Goal in His Dancing Devices," Ben Washer, in Gwen Bolger scrapbook, Box 51, Folder 7.
28. "Seen on the Stage," *Vogue*, Nov. 15, 1931.
29. "White Loser in Radio Tilt," *Billboard*, Oct. 24, 1931.
30. UCLA/RB, "Newest Scandals Hailed as the Best," Julius Cohen, in Gwen Bolger scrapbook, Box 51, Folder 7.
31. "Ray Bolger, Vanities Comedian, Claims College Education Is Very Important in Show Business," *Pennsylvanian*, Jan. 22, 1934.
32. UCLA/RB, "A Swank Dancer's Duds," *Vanity Fair*, in Gwen Bolger scrapbook, Box 51, Folder 7.
33. UCLA/RB, Louis Sobol, "The Voice of Broadway," in Gwen Bolger scrapbook, Box 51, Folder 7.

CHAPTER 4: DEPRESSION DAYS

1. Arthur Frank Wertheim, *Vaudeville Wars: How the Keith-Albee and Orpheum Circuits Controlled the Big-Time and Its Performers* (New York: Palgrave Macmillan, 2009), 276.
2. Ibid., 348.
3. Daniel Okrent, *Great Fortune: The Epic of Rockefeller Center* (New York: Viking, 2003), 16.
4. Ibid., 56.
5. Ibid.
6. Ibid., 57.
7. RKO Productions was a subsidiary of the Radio-Keith-Albee Corporation.
8. Ross Melnick, *American Showman: Samuel "Roxy" Rothafel and the Birth of the Entertainment Industry, 1908–1935* (New York: Columbia University Press, 2012), 346.
9. Okrent, *Great Fortune*, 216.
10. UCLA/RB, John Chapman, "Mainly about Manhattan," in Gwen Bolger scrapbook, Box 51, Folder 7.
11. UCLA/RB, Ed Sullivan, "The Voice of Broadway," in Gwen Bolger scrapbook, Box 51, Folder 7.

12. UCLA/RB, Robert Garland, "Cast and Miscast," in Gwen Bolger scrapbook, Box 51, Folder 7.
13. UCLA/RB, letter from Gwen to Ray, Box 47, Folder 8.
14. UCLA/RB, letter from Gwen to Ray, July 21, 1932, Box 47, Folder 8.
15. UCLA/RB, holographic writing by Gwen Bolger, Box 32, Folder 4.
16. "Vaudeville: Development of Future Stars Is Started by Morris Agency," *Billboard*, June 23, 1934.
17. Ibid.
18. "Events on the Stage," *Chicago Tribune*, April 6, 1934.
19. Harold Meyerson and Ernie Harburg, *Who Put the Rainbow in the Wizard of Oz?* (Ann Arbor: University of Michigan Press, 1993), 76.
20. SFA, *On Your Toes*, publicity materials.
21. Ray Bolger, interview by Ronald L. Davis, Southern Methodist University Oral History Project, Number 97, Aug. 5, 1976.
22. "News about the Players," *Boston Globe*, June 17, 1934.
23. "Twentieth Century Plans to Employ Legitimate Theater as Screen Laboratory," *Washington Post*, June 28, 1934.
24. UCLA/RB, holographic writing by Gwen Bolger, Box 49, Folder 7.
25. Meyerson and Harburg, *Who Put the Rainbow in the Wizard of Oz?*, 78–79.
26. Ibid., 83.
27. Ibid., 85.
28. Robert Kimball, *The Complete Lyrics of Ira Gershwin* (New York: Alfred A. Knopf, 1994), 227. The silly lyrics of "Things" sung in Lahr's pseudo-serious style was a precursor to "If I Were King of the Forest" in *The Wizard of Oz*, which Harburg and Arlen would write for Lahr as the Cowardly Lion.
29. Brooks Atkinson, "The Play," *New York Times*, Aug. 28, 1934.
30. "Plays on Broadway," *Variety*, Sept. 4, 1934.
31. UCLA/RB, holographic writing by Ray Bolger, eulogy for Harburg, Box 32, Folder 3.
32. Letter from Dr. M. S. Sacks, Jan. 19, 1935, Rickard Family Papers, Hilo, Hawaii.
33. Ray Bolger, interview by Ronald L. Davis, Aug. 5, 1976.

CHAPTER 5: BROADWAY GOES WEST

1. Steven Bingen, Stephen X. Sylvester, and Michael Troyan, *M-G-M: Hollywood's Greatest Backlot* (Solana Beach, CA: Santa Monica Press, 2011), Location 528. Kindle e-book.
2. Ray Bolger, interview by Ronald L. Davis, Southern Methodist University Oral History Project, Number 97, Aug. 5, 1976.
3. Ibid.
4. Roland Flamini, *Thalberg: The Last Tycoon and the World of M-G-M* (New York: Crown, 1994), 5.
5. Ibid., 6.
6. Ibid, 184.
7. Mark Vieira, *Irving Thalberg: Boy Wonder to Producer Prince* (Berkeley: University of California Press, 2010), 385.
8. "M-G's $1,500,000 for Takeover of 'Ziegfeld' from U," *Variety*, Feb. 27, 1935.
9. "Keep Me Out of It, Burke Edict to MG 'Ziegfeld,'" *Variety*, Feb. 19, 1936.
10. Richard Rodgers, *Musical Stages: An Autobiography* (Cambridge, MA: Da Capo Press, 2006), 175.

11. Ray Bolger, interview by Ronald L. Davis, Aug. 5, 1976.

12. Ibid.

13. "Interrhyming" as Hart defined it is exemplified by these lines from "Nobody's Heart Belongs
    to Me": "Only my book in bed / knows how I look in bed."

14. Ray Bolger, interview by Ronald L. Davis, Aug. 5, 1976.

15. Balanchine married four times in his life, to four of his dancers, and he
    continued to work with them after they divorced.

16. Ray Bolger, interview by Ronald L. Davis, Aug. 5, 1976.

17. Ibid.

18. Maurice Zolotow, "Muscles with a Sense of Humor," *Saturday Evening Post*,
    July 30, 1949.

19. Ray Bolger, interview by Ronald L. Davis, Aug. 5, 1976.

20. Fred Stone, *Rolling Stone* (New York: McGraw-Hill, 1945), 196.

21. Ray Bolger, interview by Ronald L. Davis, Aug. 5, 1976.

22. Maurice Zolotow, "Muscles with a Sense of Humor," *Saturday Evening Post*,
    July 30, 1949.

23. UCLA/RB, Contracts, Box 57, Folder 11.

24. Ray Bolger, interview by Ronald L. Davis, Aug. 5, 1976.

25. "'On Your Toes,' Being a Musical Show with a Book and Tunes and a Sense of
    Humor," *New York Times*, April 13, 1936.

26. Percy Hammond, "The Theaters: On Your Toes," *New York Herald Tribune*,
    April 13, 1936.

27. Ray Bolger, interview by Ronald L. Davis, Aug. 5, 1976.

28. Ibid.

29. Zolotow, "Muscles with a Sense of Humor."

30. Ray Bolger, interview by Ronald L. Davis, Aug. 5, 1976.

31. Ibid.

32. Ibid.

33. In fact, over a dozen different writers would tinker with the script, including
    Herman Mankiewicz, co-author of *Citizen Kane*, and the poet Ogden Nash.

34. Vieira, *Irving Thalberg*, 397.

35. Aljean Harmetz, *The Making of the Wizard of Oz* (New York: Knopf,
    1977), 118–19.

36. William Stillman and Jay Scarfone, *The Wizardry of Oz: The Artistry and Magic of
    the 1939 M-G-M Classic* (New York: Applause Theatre & Cinema Books), 86.

37. Jack Haley Jr., interview with Bolger from *The Wonderful Wizard of Oz: 50 Years
    of Magic* (1990). Documentary film.

38. "Came the (Jack) Dawn," *New York Times*, Aug. 6, 1939.

39. Ibid.

40. Harmetz, *The Making of the Wizard of Oz*, 168.

41. William Stillman, comments to the author, December 20, 2017.

42. Harmetz, *The Making of the Wizard of Oz*, 169.

43. Between Ebsen's departure and Haley's arrival, the Tin Man makeup was
    changed from the dangerous aluminum powder to paste.

44. Harmetz, *The Making of the Wizard of Oz*, 142.

45. Ibid., 143.

46. John Lahr, *Notes on a Cowardly Lion* (Berkeley: University of California Press,
    2000), 196.

47. UCLA/RB, holographic writing by Gwen Bolger, Box 32, Folder 3.

48. Harmetz, *The Making of the Wizard of Oz*, 168.
49. Haley, interview with Bolger from *The Wonderful Wizard of Oz*.
50. Lahr, *Notes on a Cowardly Lion*, 196.
51. Lupton A. Wilkinson, "Fame Is Fun: For Judy," *Los Angeles Times*, Oct. 8, 1939.
52. Michael Sragow, *Victor Fleming* (New York: Pantheon Books, 2013), 302.
53. UCLA/RB, holographic writing by Ray, Box 32, Folder 3.
54. Ibid.
55. "Film Reviews: The Wizard of Oz," *Variety*, Aug. 16, 1939.

CHAPTER 6: JUPITER FORBID

1. Thomas Baker, Gary W. Potter, and Jenna Meglen, *Wicked Newport: Kentucky's Sin City* (Charleston, SC: History Press, 2008), 43.
2. "Variety House Reviews: Chicago, Chi," *Variety*, Jan. 24, 1940.
3. Amanda Vaill, *Somewhere: The Life of Jerome Robbins* (New York: Broadway Books, 2006), 58–59.
4. "Out-Of-Town Opening: 'Keep Off the Grass,'" *Billboard*, May 18, 1940.
5. Dixie Tighe, "Cash and Celebrities Jam Huge Allied Relief Ball," *New York Post*, May 11, 1940.
6. John Barber, "Now Noël Coward Takes His Bitter-Sweet Revenge on Hollywood," *Daily Express*, Nov. 29, 1951.
7. UCLA/RB, holographic writing by Gwen Bolger, Box 32, Folder 3.
8. Lynn O'Neal Heberling, "Soldiers in Greasepaint: USO—Camp Shows Inc. during World War II." Thesis, Kent State University, 1989; accessed via ProQuest Dissertations and Theses.
9. Ray Bolger, interview by Ronald L. Davis, Southern Methodist University Oral History Project, Number 97, Aug. 5, 1976.
10. Ibid.
11. UCLA/RB, telegram from Ray to Gwen, Nov. 10, 1941.
12. Jane Pickens, "'V' for Variety Entertainment, As Important as 'V' for Victory," *Variety*, Jan. 7, 1942.
13. UCLA/RB, telegram from Ray to Gwen, Nov. 10, 1941.
14. "War Conditions Due to Change Set-Up of Entire Industry; Aid to Nabe Biz; Central Spots Hit," *Billboard*, April 4, 1942.
15. Perhaps as a nod to the Cullmans' participation in their show, Rodgers and Hart wrote the comic song "Life with Father" for the Sapiens character.
16. Ray Bolger, interview by Ronald L. Davis, Aug. 5, 1976.
17. Ibid.
18. "Play on Broadway: *By Jupiter*," *Variety*, June 10, 1942.
19. Eugene Burr, "New Play on Broadway," *Billboard*, June 13, 1942.
20. Brooks Atkinson, "One for the Book," *New York Times*, Aug. 30, 1942.
21. On the West Coast, scenes were being shot at RKO studios.
22. Ed Sullivan, "Little Old New York," *Daily News*, June 16, 1943.
23. UCLA/RB, letter from Gwen Bolger to Meyer Davis, Aug. 8, 1943, Box 43, Folder 2.

CHAPTER 7: SOLDIERS IN GREASEPAINT

1. UCLA/RB, letter from Gwen Bolger to to Louis Sobol, June 1943, Box 43, Folder 2.

2. In fact, Unit #89 received a baggage waiver, allowing them to bring an extra forty pounds of luggage with them, so that Little could bring his accordion along.

3. UCLA/RB, Ray Bolger's story as told to Gerald Lyons, Dec. 23, 1943

4. Even this huge number represented only about 20 percent of the country's military activity in the world.

5. UCLA/RB, Ray Bolger's story, as told to Gerald Lyons, Dec. 23, 1943.

6. Ibid.

7. Ibid.

8. "Letters Back Home to B'way," *Variety*, Sept. 29, 1943.

9. UCLA/RB, letter from Gwen to Ray, Sept. 22, 1943, Box 47, Folder 8.

10. UCLA/RB, letter from Gwen to Ray, Oct. 1, 1943, Box 47, Folder 8.

11. UCLA/RB, letter from Gwen to Ray, Oct. 8, 1943, Box 47, Folder 8.

12. "General News," *Billboard*, Dec. 18, 1943.

CHAPTER 8: *WHERE'S CHARLEY?*

1. UCLA/RB, Margaret Lloyd, "He Who Doesn't Get Hit," Aug. 21, 1943, unpublished article, Box 48, Folder 10.

2. UCLA/RB, holographic writing by Gwen Bolger, Box 32, Folder 4.

3. Lewis Nichols, "The Play," *New York Times*, March 3, 1946.

4. Lewis Nichols, "The Revue Returns," *New York Times*, March 17, 1946.

5. George Jean Nathan, *The Theatre Book of the Year, 1945–1946* (New York: Knopf, 1946), 359.

6. Cy Feuer, *I Got the Show Right Here* (New York: Simon & Schuster, 2003), 81.

7. UCLA/RB, holographic writing by Gwen Bolger, Box 32, Folder 4.

8. UCLA/RB, letter from Ray Bolger to Edna Nelson Rickard, Box 42, Folder 8.

9. Ibid.

10. Ibid.

11. Sam Zolotow, "2 Directing Chores for Miss Webster," *New York Times*, Aug. 3, 1948.

12. Katherine Reeve Rickard, interview with the author by phone, June 15, 2012.

13. Ibid.

14. UCLA/RB, holographic writing by Gwen Bolger, Box 32, Folder 4.

15. UCLA/RB, letter from Gwen Bolger to Edna Nelson Rickard, Nov. 16, 1948, Box 43, Folder 2.

16. Lewis Funke, "News and Gossip Gathered on the Rialto," *New York Times*, Jan. 16, 1949.

17. "Plays Out of Town: *Where's Charley?*" *Variety*, Sept. 15, 1948.

18. Maurie Orodenker, "Out-of-Town Opening: *Where's Charley?*" *Billboard*, Sept. 25, 1948.

19. Ibid.

20. Katherine Reeve Rickard, interview with the author by phone, June 15, 2012.

21. Brooks Atkinson, "At the Theatre," *New York Times*, Oct. 12, 1948.

22. John Martin, "The Dance: Bolger," *New York Times*, April 4, 1949.

23. Brooks Atkinson, "The Comic Step," *New York Times*, Oct. 24, 1948.

24. Irene Selznick, letter to Gwen Bolger on personal stationery, undated. Private collection of Christianna Rickard.

25. UCLA/RB, holographic writing by Ray Bolger, Box 32, Folder 3.

26. "The American Theatre Wing of the Allied War Relief," shortened to "The American Theatre Wing" along the way, was a service organization through

which theatrical professionals helped the war effort. One of the organization's major contributions was the Stage Door Canteen project. After the war ended, the organization created "The American Theatre Wing's Antoinette Perry Award for Excellence in the Theatre." The awards are known colloquially as the Tony Awards, and remain the most important accolade given to Broadway shows and performers.

27. "'Salesman,' 'Kate' Win Perry Awards: Rex Harrison and Martita Hunt Also Get 'Tonys' for Roles in Broadway Shows," *New York Times*, April 25, 1949.

28. UCLA/RB, letter from Gwen Bolger to Edna Nelson Rickard, Jan. 11, 1951, Box 42, Folder 7.

29. UCLA/RB, Gwen Bolger, letter to Flora and Clara Nelson, May 20, 1949, Box 43, Folder 2.

30. William J. Lederer, *All the Ships at Sea* (New York: Sloane, 1950), 16.

31. USC/WB, Frank Cahill, letter to Nathan Levenson, March 7, 1951, *Where's Charley?* collection.

CHAPTER 9: THE NEW TRIPLE THREAT MAN

1. USC/WB, letter from Frank Cahill to Nathan Levenson, March 7, 1951, *Where's Charley?* collection.

2. Michael Kidd, interview with Betsy Baytos, March 28, 1997, Los Angeles.

3. USC/WB, Gerry Blattner, letter to Steve Trilling, Aug. 24, 1951, *Where's Charley?* collection.

4. Howard Thompson, "'Charley' Abroad," *New York Times*, Feb. 3, 1952.

5. USC/WB, Gerry Blattner, letter to Steve Trilling, Aug. 24, 1951, *Where's Charley?* collection.

6. UCLA/RB, Letter from Gwen Bolger to Edna Nelson Rickard, Rickard Family Letters, Box 42, Folder 8.

7. Doris Day, as told to A. E. Hotchner, *Doris Day: Her Own Story* (London: W. H. Allen, 1985), 117.

8. David Butler, interview by Irene Kahn Atkins, *A Directors Guild of America Oral History* (Metuchen, NJ: Directors Guild of America & Scarecrow Press, 1993), 227.

9. Bosley Crowther, "Inanity Strikes Back: 'Where's Charley?' Shows That Film Musicals May Still Be Illogical," *New York Times*, June 29, 1952.

10. "Film Reviews: *Where's Charley?*" *Variety*, July 2, 1952.

11. Frank Rose, *The Agency: William Morris and the Hidden History of Show Business* (New York: HarperBusiness, 1995), 3.

12. Bill Willard, "Sahara, Vegas' $5,500,000 Desert Song, Now Officially No. 6 on Rue de La Pay," *Variety*, Oct. 15, 1952.

13. Jack Gould, "Ray Bolger Rings the Bell on N.B.C. Video Show—Small Revue Has Wit, Grace and Style," *New York Times*, Dec. 24, 1952.

14. Ray Bolger, "Bolger Relives a TV Show & Quotes a Lastfogel Proverb," *Variety*, Oct. 7, 1953.

15. Rita Moreno, interview by Marla Miller, June 22, 2000, http://emmytvlegends. org/interviews/people/rita-moreno#.

16. "TV Film Reviews: *Where's Raymond?*" *Billboard*, Oct. 17, 1953.

17. Sylvia Lewis in discussion with the author, July 11, 2012.

18. Sylvia Lewis, interview with the author by phone, September 1, 2012.

19. Ibid.

20. "Film: Eastman Tri-X Film Designed to Cut Costs," *Broadcasting, Telecasting*, Jan. 10, 1955.
21. Earle Ludgin, "Television Reviews: Washington Square," *Variety*, Oct. 24, 1956.

CHAPTER 10: ALL AMERICAN

1. UCLA/RB, holographic writing by Ray Bolger, Box 32, Folder 2.
2. UCLAB/RB, letter from Richard Nixon to Ray Bolger, Jan. 19, 1961.
3. Charles Strouse, *Put on a Happy Face: A Broadway Memoir* (New York: Union Square Press, 2008), 106.
4. Fritz Weaver, phone interview with the author, Aug. 9, 2012.
5. Anita Gillette, phone interview with the author, Dec. 4, 2015.
6. Ibid.
7. "Legitimate: Shows on Broadway—*All American*," *Variety*, March 21, 1962.
8. UCLA/RB, letter from Joshua Logan to Ray Bolger, May 2, 1962, Box 13, Folder 3.
9. UCLA/RB, letter from John Shubert to Ray Bolger, May 2, 1962, Box 13, Folder 3.
10. Aljean Harmetz, *The Making of the Wizard of Oz* (New York: Knopf, 1977), 304.
11. Anna Kisselgoff, "Bolger and Agnes de Mille Team Up," *New York Times*, Dec. 25, 1968.
12. Kevin Kelly, "'Come Summer' Should Go Away," *Boston Globe*, Feb. 17, 1969.
13. "Despite Cool Reviews, Bolger Warms Theater," *Boston Globe*, Feb. 21, 1969.
14. Clive Barnes, "'Summer' Won't Last Until Spring," *Chicago Tribune*, March 19, 1969.
15. "Legitimate: Show Out of Town—*Come Summer*," *Variety*, Jan. 29, 1969.

EPILOGUE
No Sad Songs

1. Richard Rodgers, "The Kings and I," *Music Journal*, October 1961, 23.
2. UCLA/RB, holographic writing by Ray Bolger, Box 32, Folder 1.
3. Kevin Starr, "Is There a Future for Men's Clubs?" *Bohemian Club Library Notes*, July 18, 1982, 1–2.
4. Michael Bergstein, "My Year in Pictures" (unpublished essay provided by Bergstein to the author via e-mail, Milan, 2016), 20.
5. UCLA/RB, letter from David Hartman to Ray Bolger, Nov. 19, 1979, Box 10, Folder 1.
6. Tom D. Crouch, letter to Gwen Rickard Bolger, 1987, Smithsonian Institution Department of Social and Cultural History records.
7. Ray Bolger, "Ray Bolger Writes 'Variety,'" *Variety*, Jan. 14, 1981, 16.
8. UCLA/RB, "The Wonderful World of Ray Bolger" Program Materials, Box 28, Folder 1.

SELECTED BIBLIOGRAPHY

BOOKS

Abbott, George. *Mister Abbott*. New York: Random House, 1963.

Allen, Fred. *Much Ado about Me*. Boston: Little, Brown, 1956.

Andrews, Maxene, and Bill Gilbert. *Over Here, Over There: The Andrews Sisters and the USO Stars in World War II*. New York: Kensington, 1993.

Atkinson, Brooks. *Broadway*. New York: Macmillan, 1970.

Barker, Thomas, Gary W. Potter, and Jenna Meglen. *Wicked Newport: Kentucky's Sin City*. Charleston, SC: History Press, 2008.

Bingen, Steven, Stephen X. Sylvester, and Michael Troyan. *MGM: Hollywood's Greatest Backlot*. Santa Monica, CA: Santa Monica Press, 2010.

Critchlow, Donald T. *When Hollywood Was Right: How Movie Stars, Studio Moguls, and Big Business Remade American Politics*. New York: Cambridge University Press, 2013.

Cullman, Marguerite. *Occupation: Angel*. New York: Norton, 1963.

Ebsen, Buddy. *The Other Side of Oz: An Autobiography*. Newport Beach, CA: Donovan, 1993.

Feuer, Cy, and Ken Gross. *I Got the Show Right Here: The Amazing, True Story of How an Obscure Brooklyn Horn Player Became the Last Great Broadway Showman*. New York: Simon & Schuster, 2003.

Fields, Armond, and Marc L. Fields. *From the Bowery to Broadway: Lew Fields and the Roots of Popular American Theatre*. New York: Oxford University Press, 1993.

Fisher, Seymour, and Rhoda L. Fisher. *Pretend the World Is Funny and Forever: A Psychological Analysis of Comedians, Clowns, and Actors*. Hillsdale, NJ: Erlbaum, 1981.

Flamini, Roland. *Thalberg: The Last Tycoon and the World of M-G-M*. New York: Crown, 1994.

Frommer, Myrna, and Harvey Frommer. *It Happened on Broadway: An Oral History of the Great White Way*. New York: Harcourt Brace, 1998.

Harmetz, Aljean. *The Making of The Wizard of Oz: Movie Magic and Studio Power in the Prime of MGM, and the Miracle of Production #1060*. New York: Knopf, 1977.

Hart, Dorothy. *Thou Swell, Thou Witty: The Life and Lyrics of Lorenz Hart*. New York: Harper & Row, 1976.

Hill, Constance Valis. *Tap Dancing America: A Cultural History*. New York: Oxford University Press, 2010.

Kiel, Richard, and Hugh Abercrombie Anderson. *Out without My Rubbers: The Memoirs of John Murray Anderson*. New York: Library Publishers, 1954.

Lahr, John. *Notes on a Cowardly Lion: The Biography of Bert Lahr*. Berkeley: University of California Press, 2000.

Laurie, Joe Jr. *Vaudeville: From the Honky Tonks to the Palace*. New York: Henry Holt, 1953.

LeRoy, Mervyn, and Richard Kleiner. *Mervyn Le Roy: Take One*. New York: Hawthorn Books, 1974.

Logan, Joshua. *Josh, My Up and Down, In and Out Life*. New York: Delacorte Press, 1976.

Marmorstein, Gary. *A Ship without a Sail: The Life of Lorenz Hart*. New York: Simon & Schuster, 2012.

Melnick, Ross. *American Showman: Samuel "Roxy" Rothafel and the Birth of the Entertainment Industry, 1908–1935*. New York: Columbia University Press, 2012.

Meyerson, Harold, and Ernest Harburg. *Who Put the Rainbow in the Wizard of Oz? Yip Harburg, Lyricist*. Ann Arbor: University of Michigan Press, 1993.

Mordden, Ethan. *Sing for Your Supper: The Broadway Musical in the 1930s*. New York: Palgrave Macmillan, 2005.

Okrent, Daniel. *Great Fortune: The Epic of Rockefeller Center*. New York: Viking, 2003.

Raabe, Meinhardt, and Daniel Kinske. *Memories of a Munchkin: An Illustrated Walk Down the Yellow Brick Road*. New York: Back Stage Books, 2005.

Rickard, Christianna. *Remembering Oz: My Journey with the Scarecrow*. Mustang, OK: Tate, 2010.

Rodgers, Richard. *Musical Stages: An Autobiography*. 2nd ed. (Richard Rodgers Centennial ed.). Cambridge, MA: Da Capo Press, 2002.

Rose, Frank. *The Agency: William Morris and the Hidden History of Show Business*. New York: HarperBusiness, 1995.

Scarfone, Jay, and William Stillman. *The Wizard of Oz: The Official 75th Anniversary Companion*. New York: Harper Design, 2013.

Scarfone, Jay, and William Stillman. *The Wizardry of Oz: The Artistry and Magic of the 1939 M-G-M Classic*. New York: Applause Theatre & Cinema Books, 2004.

Schechter, Scott. *Judy Garland: The Day-by-Day Chronicle of a Legend*. Lanham, MD: Taylor Trade, 2006.

Stagg, Jerry. *The Brothers Shubert*. New York: Random House, 1968.

Stone, Fred. *Rolling Stone*. New York: Whittlesey House, McGraw-Hill, 1945.

Strouse, Charles. *Put on a Happy Face: A Broadway Memoir*. New York: Union Square Press, 2008.

Taper, Bernard. *Balanchine: A Biography*. Rev. and updated ed. New York: Macmillan, 1974.

Vaill, Amanda. *Somewhere: The Life of Jerome Robbins*. New York: Broadway Books, 2006.

Vieira, Mark A. *Irving Thalberg: Boy Wonder to Producer Prince*. Berkeley: University of California Press, 2010.

Wertheim, Arthur Frank. *Vaudeville Wars: How the Keith-Albee and Orpheum Circuits Controlled the Big-time and Its Performers*. New York: Palgrave Macmillan, 2006.

PUBLIC DOCUMENTS AND UNPUBLISHED MATERIALS

California death records; Connecticut birth and death records; Massachusetts birth, death, and marriage records; city directories of Boston and Fall River, Massachusetts; New York marriage records; US census documents.

Heberling, Lynn O'Neal. "Soldiers in Greasepaint: USO—Camp Shows, Inc., During World War II." PhD diss., Kent State University, 1989.

ARCHIVAL COLLECTIONS

Library of Congress: Recorded Sound Research Center, Ruth Gordon and Garson Kanin papers

Margaret Herrick Library: Edit Angold papers; Hedda Hopper papers; SMU Collection of Ronald L. Davis oral histories on the performing arts; Bill Thomas scrapbooks; Victor Fleming scrapbooks; Metro-Goldwyn-Mayer miscellaneous material

New York Public Library for the Performing Arts: Billy Rose Theatre Division; Theatre on Film and Tape Division

The Shubert Archive, New York

UCLA Special Collections: Ray Bolger papers; Jimmy Durante papers; Metro-Goldwyn-Mayer Research Department Files, 1930s–1940s; RKO Studio Records, ca. 1928–1958

USC Cinematic Arts Library: Warner Brothers Archives

INDEX

Page numbers in **bold** refer to illustrations.